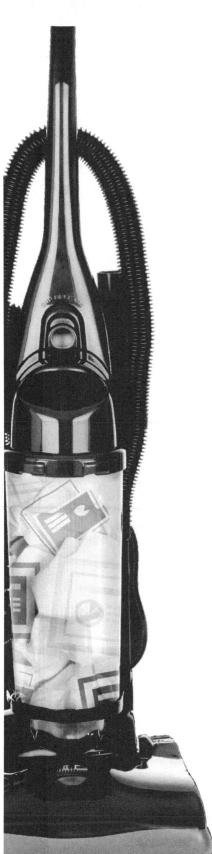

WHY MOST
POWERPOINT
PRESENTATIONS
SUCK

And how you can make them better

RICK ALTMAN

Why Most PowerPoint Presentations Suck

And how you can make them better

by Rick Altman

June 2007: First Edition
May 2009: Second Edition
May 2012: Third Edition

Published by:
Harvest Books
1423 Harvest Rd.
Pleasanton CA 94566
925.398.6210
www.betterpresenting.com

Library of Congress Control Number
2007924582

ISBN
978-1-477-68543-3

Printed in the United States of America

To my four girls—beloved wife Becky, darling daughters Erica and Jamie, and loyal canine Coco. Once in a while, my household rank improves to fourth...

Contents

Part One   **The Pain**

Part Two   **The Solution**

Foreword

My morning routine starts with a 7:00a trip to my favorite local drive-thru latte stand and I've found that in just 10 minutes, I can be back in my office checking emails with a hot beverage in hand. Recently my favorite spot went belly up so I drove a block further to another stand. "Double tall 20 oz. mocha - light on the chocolate," I requested. As far as lattes go, this order is pretty much a no-brainer so I was frustrated to find that it didn't taste at all like my usual drink.

At lunch I tried another stand and was frustrated with yet another version of a light chocolate mocha. The whole experience left me scratching my head. Everyone used pretty much the same ingredients but the results were dramatically different. The real magic is in the hands of the craftsperson, not their tools.

For the most part, presenters today have access to all the same tools as well. They have a version of PowerPoint that isn't more than a few years old, an image editing program and maybe even a vector drawing application. But much like my latte experience, given the same basic ingredients, presenters and presentation designers manage somehow to produce dramatically different outcomes. One person using an older version of PowerPoint produces a masterful work of personal communication art, while another using the latest software packages only manages to build a mind-numbing, convoluted, self-indulgent presentation that does little to accelerate information and ideas.

If audiences really are asking for more and we have a higher level of sensitivity to what doesn't work, why do so many still fail to deliver on those higher expectations? The answer is easy. Presenters and presentation designers still believe their presentations are all about them.

Audiences don't care about how much fun presenters are having with PowerPoint. Their brains go numb every time a presenter fills their screens with sub-sub-sub level bullets. Use of animation is often gratuitous and the pervasive stock flavor of everything is a constant reminder that their presentations are courtesy of Microsoft wizards, not a single original thought.

All this said, take heart. There are those helping us better navigate the presentation design process and within these pages, Rick Altman helps shed some much needed light on this important business communication process. He challenges what's all too easy but also provides some much needed insight into what does work and how to do it. If you're like most presenters or presentation designers, you're looking for resources to help take your presentation visuals to the next essential level. Read on and begin to fill up your personal toolkit with the kinds of fresh insights and creative skills you can put to use in your next presentation.

Your audiences want more. It's time to finally deliver for them.

Thanks To...

It might take a village to raise a child, and there are times when I feel a book cannot adequately be written without an entire community. I am fortunate to be part of a phenomenal one. The professional presentation community has many gathering points today, not the least of which is the Presentation Summit, the annual end-user conference which I have hosted since 2003.

Each year, I have been privileged to have met some of the most passionate, enthusiastic, and dedicated presenters, designers, and content creators anywhere in the world. Their group energy is an almost intoxicating call to action for anyone who thinks out loud in public and I am so very grateful for having them in my head throughout this process.

And surprise, surprise, I don't have to venture past this group to assemble an excellent team of editors:

Chantal Bossé is a gifted trainer and presentations specialist from Quebec Canada. She is not only an eagle-eye through the text, but with English as her second language, she is a great reality check against some of my runaway jargon. She now knows what *bass-ackwards* means, so the relationship has been of mutual benefit. **www.chabos.ca**

Geetesh Bajaj is one of the legions of the Microsoft Most Valued Professional team of dedicated volunteers who help PowerPoint users with issues and questions. A trainer and consultant based in India, Geetesh creates custom PowerPoint presentations and templates and is a featured speaker on presentation technologies. **www.indezine.com**

Sandra Johnson blends impeccable design sense, practical slide-making expertise, and fastidious attention to detail. In other words, she dings me on bad-looking slides as well as misplaced modifiers...nothing that a few sessions of therapy won't solve... (Oh, and she doesn't like when I use ellipses.) **www.presentationwiz.biz**

Finally, three cheers for a wonderful group of readers of previous editions who offered to give the third edition an early read:

Valerie Carnett, Talahasse FL
Kjell Brataas, Oslo Norway
Cindy Parman, Powder Springs GA
Lynette Johnson, Irvine CA
Jen Card, Fairview OR

Introduction   The word he used was *meshuga*, known by both Jews and non-Jews alike to mean "crazy." And my father was looking right at me when he said it.

"You're going to say *that* in the book?"

"Actually, Dad, I'm going to say it in the title."

"You must be meshuga!"

And there you have either the most compelling reason to, or not to, author a book without the assist of a large publishing house. I've written for Sybex Books, Peachpit Press, Que Publishing, and several others, and I have the distinct impression that, were I to have followed that path this time, you would now be holding a book in your hands of a different name. Pretty good chance, also, that a vacuum cleaner would not grace its cover.

My reason for choosing a private-label publisher was not because I sought an edgy title, although I do admit to enjoying the shock value that comes along for the ride. I did so because of a seven-year-long frustration with being asked (make that required) by traditional publishers to include in any book proposal a clump of PowerPoint-centric topics that few in my intended audience find interesting.

Let's take a poll of one: Do you need to be taught how to create a slide? Did you buy this book because you don't understand how to make a string of text bold or how to make the bullet square instead of round?

If you bought this book for its intended purpose, it's because you have bigger issues.

- Your weekly load has now exceeded 200 slides and you are beginning to feel like a slide factory.

- Your presentations are not being received the way you were hoping they would and you're not sure why.

- You have good instincts but they need to be honed.

- Your co-worker messes up your templates and you're about to scream.

- Your boss creates the most dismally-ugly slides and you don't know what to do about it.

- Or maybe...just maybe, it is you who needs a refresher in the principles of good presentation design.

Really, the potential market for this book is plenty vast without catering to the brand new user. How many horrible presentations did you sit through last month? In the face of how many colleagues or potential vendors would you like to shove this book and say "Here, please read this"?

I remember the first time I experienced it. I refer, of course, to the phenomenon we all know as Death by PowerPoint. The year was 1990, and three representatives from a well-known public relations firm wanted my partner and me to pay them $10,000 to help us market a series of seminars.

They were smartly dressed, meticulously coiffed, and perfectly eloquent, as they proceeded to bore us out of our minds with drivel about value-added propositions, proactive initiatives, and positively-reinforced task-based personalization.

Every slide was read word for word, and each of us had a spiral-bound booklet that duplicated the slides.

Technically, this wasn't Death by PowerPoint; the software had not yet been invented. It was Death by Overhead Slide. Just as bad...

Who should read this book?

As lead author, I would like to think that any presenter, presentation designer, or content creator in the world would enjoy the pages of this book. The fact that I won't try to convince you of that is a sure sign that I have no future as a marketing consultant. From my annual conference and my on-going work as a presentations consultant and coach, I have a pretty good sense of the typical PowerPoint user. If I'm right, you fall into at least one of the following categories:

- You are thought of as the Slide King or Queen of your department and are called upon to crank out untold volumes of them. Getting the job done on time becomes your sole focus.

- You are a presentation designer, where you have a bit more opportunity than the Slide King/Queen to consider the aesthetic side of content creation, but every project given to you is due yesterday.

- You are on the road a lot, giving sales presentations to audiences of various sizes. You have a well-worn template that fits you like an old shoe, never mind that it was designed from a wizard back in the 1990s. You have gotten pretty good at swapping in new content for old, but have begun to wonder what you are missing by not learning more about the application.

- You are an outside consultant brought in to work with people in the marketing department who have absolutely no idea how to refine a concept, crystallize an idea, or shape words into a message.

- You are hired to help terrified public speakers learn not to throw up all over themselves when in front of an audience.

- You work with the executives of your firm, and no matter how great the work is that you give to them before they board their plane, by the time they touch down at their destination, they've mauled your slide deck.

- You have worked your way into a position, created just for you, in which your expertise as a presentation professional is genuinely appreciated. You are given creative freedom and latitude, and are encouraged to cultivate your skills.

That last example is not fantasy; it only sounds too good to be true. There are just enough forward-thinking organizations and skilled presentation professionals to create optimism for the community at large. In fact, since our first edition, we have seen this trend quickening its pace. Even through the economic downturn that began in 2009, many of us who act as presentation consultants have seen an uptick in our businesses. Companies are indeed finally starting to get it.

In order for that community to grow and thrive, we need a universe of PowerPoint users who have moved past, as we describe in the first chapter, their first 30 minutes of training.

That is the thrust of this work. You don't need help with the basics of PowerPoint. You know your way around the program. You need someone to speak frankly to you about the issues, the challenges, the joys, and yes the perils associated with modern-day presentation creation and delivery. With this book, I accept that challenge.

How to use this book

There's an insulting headline for you. (*To use this book, start at the top of the page, read from left to right, and turn pages with your right hand...*) Proud authors like to insist that good books aren't used; they're read. But we in fields of technology know better. We know how people use computer books—lots of dog-eared pages, notes in the margin, table of contents brutalized—and I'm fine with that.

My hope, however, is that you do find it to be a good read. By design, it is written very unevenly. Some chapters are just a few pages long, others close to 40. Some topics we hammer and others we ignore. And I do not pretend that these 27 chapters are some sort of sterile, objective listing of "advanced tips," whatever that even means. This book is one person's view of the presentation community and the functions and nuances of PowerPoint that seem particularly relevant. It is full of bias and subjectivity and you are invited to disagree with it at any point. In fact, if you agree with everything that I say here, this book's value is probably diminished.

In choosing my editors, it was practically a prerequisite that they disagree with me on occasion. As a result, these pages alternate between first-person singular and plural enough to drive a grammarian nuts. And that is my prerogative—there are times when I speak for the team...there are times when I speak on behalf of a community of thousands. And there are times when I feel as if I'm on Survivor's Exile Island. It's all good.

To download a file, go to www.whypptsucks.com and find the file named after the figure that represents it.

But no book should be an island—it's challenging enough to ask static pages to cover a medium of motion. And that is why we consider the book's web site, **www.whypptsucks.com**, to be a full partner in this endeavor. You'll see our constant references in the margins to files that you can download, view, and dissect, and most of the time, the filename mirrors the name of the particular figure or illustration. New to this edition is a slew of QR codes sprinkled throughout the margins to enable smartphone and iPad owners to more easily access supplemental content.

◆

There are no appendices to know about and there is no particular order in which you need to read this. **Part One** is where we bring the big hurt. We share our research and our conclusions about all that is wrong with the presentations industry and the software that is at its helm. Hopefully before the onset of depression, **Part Two** offers solutions to all of the pain we uncover in the chapters that precede it. **Part Three** channels the inner designer in all of us, providing strategies and advice for those who did not come to presentation from an art academy. **Part Four** is devoted to skills and techniques that you can adopt to help you become a better public speaker, whether you are a natural at it or not. And **Part Five** steps up the volume considerably and covers several truly advanced topics and ideas in which you can indulge.

What version do you need?

In many cases, it matters little what version of PowerPoint you use, and we encounter hundreds of presentation designers every year still using Versions 2003 and XP. A good designer needs only a blank slide; a good presenter could use a 1993 copy of Harvard Graphics.

That said, we make the assumption that you are using what we refer to as "modern versions" of PowerPoint—defined as versions 2007 and 2010 on the PC and 2008 and 2011 on the Mac. All of our screen images are of the Windows version, but Mac users will find mostly seamless relevance to their experiences. And when there are significant changes to discuss, we bring the conversation to version 2003 for context. With Office 15 on the horizon, we wonder if the Fourth Edition will be right around the corner!

If I have written this book correctly, it will prove to be bad for my business as a presentations consultant. A good chunk of my time as a hired gun is spent retraining, or untraining, to be precise. Many of the people with whom I work have read the reference guide and have taken some sort of introductory course, but never really learned any rules or guidelines for using the software.

By the time they bring me in, their slides often have dozens of unused placeholders, text boxes with bullets stuffed into them, random applications of animation, and multiple backgrounds.

Before I can teach them anything new, I have to strip off all of the old. I intend to provide you with the strategies, the techniques, and the tools for becoming completely proficient with the projects that you need to produce. I intend to leave you with a more complete understanding of how the program operates. And I intend for you to not have to rely upon consultants like me as often. I guess you could say that this book attempts to reduce by half my billable hours.

♦

Finally, the wonders of print on demand are numerous, chief among them the agility with which we can print new versions...perhaps starring you. If you: a) have created a presentation that illustrates a technique discussed herein; b) disagree with an assertion that we make; c) have an alternative technique to propose; d) want to suggest a topic for us to cover or expand upon; or e) just want to comment on a passage, please write to me at ricka@betterpresenting.com. We will not hesitate to include noteworthy commentary in an upcoming version, which, if sales go well, could be as early as next month...

Part One

The Pain

This book is not about pessimism despite the somewhat bawdy title. In fact, I would argue that this book explores the opposite: the ultimate message contained in these 321 pages is enabling and optimistic.

Nonetheless, first there are dues to pay. As countless experts on messaging will attest, good storytelling is often about first identifying the pain. And as tennis great Martina Navratilova once said to me personally, "No pain...no gain." She was talking about physical fitness, not creating slides, but I couldn't pass up a chance to name drop...

Chapter 1

The 30-Minute Syndrome

If only I could earn the proverbial nickel for every time I have heard the following. It could be any setting in which the conversation might turn to PowerPoint, which in my case is frequently.

"Oh," the person says, in response to almost any remark made about the software. "PowerPoint is easy. I learned it in about a half hour."

Let's start by acknowledging that the statement is generally true: PowerPoint is not difficult to pick up and begin using. Both of my daughters created slides for school projects before the age of 10, and indeed, a reasonably astute grownup can begin making slides within 30 minutes.

Microsoft might have you believe that this is a virtue of the software. In fact, it is bad. It is very, very bad.

1

Who Are These People?

Creating a presentation can be an extraordinarily creative experience, but it rarely starts out that way. And that is because PowerPoint's default settings are not very creative and because most PowerPoint users do not come to the software from a creative field. They start out elsewhere in the Office suite. They are Excel crunchers, Outlook gurus, Access junkies. They are used to software with a steeper learning curve and a point of entry that requires much more effort before they can do much of anything. When they encounter PowerPoint and discover that they can begin using the program with effect in less than an hour, they are like kids with new toys.

But again, this is not a good thing; it's a bad thing. These people declare themselves proficient after their requisite 30 minutes of training. These same people who get really good at their 30-minute skill set call themselves advanced users. And those who teach it to others are considered gods.

But they don't get beyond those first 30 minutes of skills. And then they go forth and commit high crimes against innocent businesspeople everywhere. Death by PowerPoint.

▶ We point our finger of accusation at both of the two main camps that we speak to in this book: those who create presentation content and those who deliver presentations. Often, one person wears both hats, but there is plenty of blame to go around. Inexperienced content creators and ill-equipped presenters both contribute to the poor reputation endured by the software and the presentation industry in general.

The creative disconnect

Missing from the equation, of course, is the creative component. And you can't fault the typical number-crunching, word-processing Office user for not grasping that. These software programs are tools, wielded to perform tasks. You learn the tool well enough to perform the task, you go home for the day, and what happens in the cubicle stays in the cubicle.

But PowerPoint is different. With PowerPoint, you practice your craft in public, and this craft is forever linked with death and taxes as the three things humans fear most.

This is much more than the converted Excel user bargained for. It's possible, make that likely, that she had no experience at all speaking before a group; she simply taught herself how to make bullet slides.

And herein lies the biggest disconnect of all. The company that this innocent Excel-cum-PowerPoint user works for might spend millions of dollars on its brand: expensive design firms to create glossy brochures...P.R. firms with lots of names on their door, hired to spin messages...high-powered marketing firms to ensure maximum exposure.

And this same company then sends someone out with 30 minutes of training to make what will likely be a company's first impression: the sales call in the boardroom.

Why Is This Happening?

In the 1990s, Canada's Corel Corporation was flying high in the graphics world, owning the most heralded and most popular graphics program around, CorelDRAW. Back in 1993, Version 4.0 added two programs to the suite: Chart and Show, to facilitate the creation and animation of charts and graphs.

Figure 1.1
Corel's charting program was ahead of its time and not ready for prime time, but the graphic artists and illustrators who dabbled with it back in 1993 produced some very nice work.

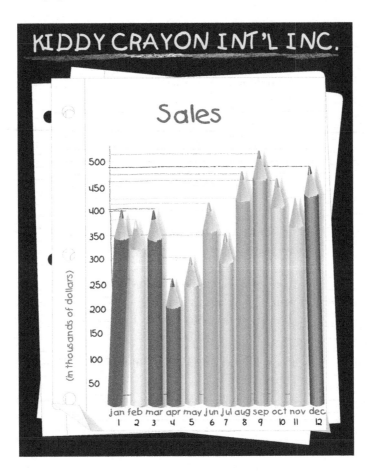

They went nowhere, they were full of bugs, and most Draw users ignored them. Two years later, they were out of the suite, banished to small footnotes in the history of a smallish software maker. But a few users did dabble with them and their creations were quite impressive, as you can see in Figure 1.1. They were like nothing that any PowerPoint slide or Harvard Graphics chart (remember that?) ever produced.

This was perhaps the first time that a presentation tool was placed into the hands of a creative professional, and this little story from the past speaks volumes about the dilemma that the presentation community faces today. The issue is two-pronged:

- People are thrust into a position of being the company's creative force even though they do not have a background in the arts or come from a creative field.

- Those who do have a creative background and are capable of producing excellent work with PowerPoint don't have a place in their company's org chart.

I would also like a nickel for every time that I have met a PowerPoint user with an obscure and obtuse title, or simply the "admin." Not to impugn in any way the workforce of administrative professionals; the title does not and should not imply that a graphically talented person is holding the position.

Companies have simply not made enough of an effort to identify, define, and cultivate the role of the presentation professional. Therefore, it usually is assigned in haphazard fashion to anyone willing to step up to the plate, including the person who is simply good with Microsoft Office.

◆

Have I described you yet? Odds are, I'm in trouble one way or the other. If I have identified you as the person thrust into the role of PowerPoint jockey, I've either offended you or made you defensive. If you are the creative professional honing your craft with presentations, I've reminded you of your biggest frustration and now you're mad at me for that. There's pain in this part of the book for me, too.

There's hope for all of us...but we're not yet done with the pain. In other words, if I didn't offend you in this chapter, I have several more opportunities upcoming.

Chapter 2

The Cram-Everything-In Obsession

Did you watch *Super Size Me*, the 2004 documentary on overeating at McDonald's? ("A film of epic portions.") Both of my daughters vowed that they would never eat another Big Mac again, and one of them actually kept that vow across several years (she's in college now, so all bets are off). It espouses one of America's most robust sentiments: bigger is better, and more is more better.

I remember watching an episode of *The Apprentice*, where a handsome, well-dressed twenty-something young professional pleaded his case to Donald Trump by reciting every business slogan he could possibly think of, as fast as he possibly could, interspersed with the robotic "I'll be great for your organization, Mr. Trump" at every breath. And it worked: Trump fired the other guy.

This is a very real phenomenon in today's culture—the sense that it's better to say everything than risk forgetting to say the one thing that you really need to say. And nowhere is this more evident than in the typical slides that project onto the whiteboards and white screens of companies everywhere.

This plays out in a fairly predictable way by those who prepare their own slides for a presentation:

- They sit down at their desk.

- They open PowerPoint.

- They start thinking of every point that they need to make.

- Soon they start thinking of how they are going to make each point.

End result: they have written a speech.

I want to be fair here: If you have little or no experience speaking before a group of people, you have no idea that this is the wrong approach to take. This might seem like a perfectly logical way to prepare: write down what you want to say and then say it. And hey, there's this software program that will show you everything that you've written down, so your audience can see it, too. How cool is that?

This might not be such a bad proposition for the uninitiated public speaker; as we all know, it's a horrible proposition for her audience. The woman from Arizona probably thought she was on the right track when she perpetrated the slide shown in Figure 2.1. It said everything she wanted to say.

No question about it: one of today's most acute pain points is when speakers use their slides as notes. In many cases, it is because they have no idea that the Notes view exists, and even if they do, they simply don't know any better. Message crafting is not part of their resume.

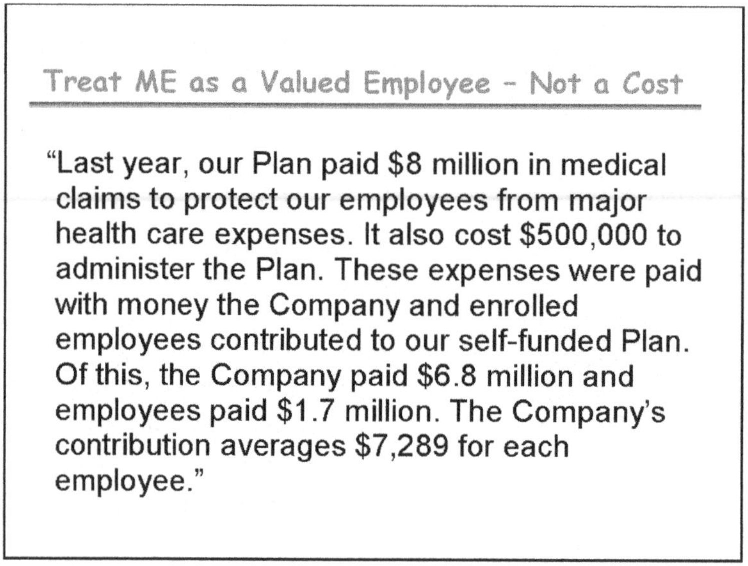

Figure 2.1
This slide says everything the speaker wants to say, so what's the problem?

Treat ME as a Valued Employee – Not a Cost

"Last year, our Plan paid $8 million in medical claims to protect our employees from major health care expenses. It also cost $500,000 to administer the Plan. These expenses were paid with money the Company and enrolled employees contributed to our self-funded Plan. Of this, the Company paid $6.8 million and employees paid $1.7 million. The Company's contribution averages $7,289 for each employee."

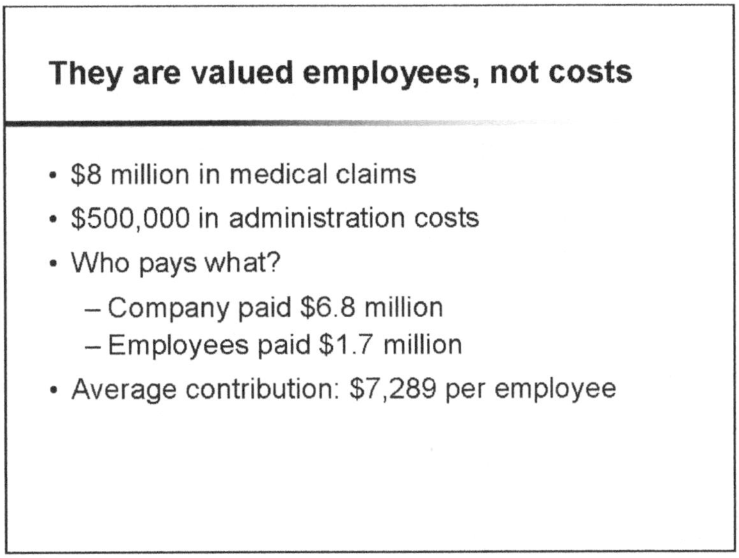

Figure 2.2
What a difference five minutes can make. You might actually stop and read this slide now.

They are valued employees, not costs

- $8 million in medical claims
- $500,000 in administration costs
- Who pays what?
  - Company paid $6.8 million
  - Employees paid $1.7 million
- Average contribution: $7,289 per employee

This leads to the first of several universal axioms that we will put forth across these pages. It is Universal Axiom No. 2 and it goes like this:

> **If a slide contains complete sentences, it is practically impossible for even the most accomplished presenters to avoid reading them word for word.**

Watch for it the next time you attend a presentation: the more verbiage a slide contains, the more likely is the speaker to read all of it. Talk about your double-whammy. We discuss strategies to work around this in Chapter 20, and they are important, because Universal Axiom No. 2 leads directly into Universal Axiom No. 3:

> **When you read your slides word for word, you sound like an idiot.**

Figure 2.2 is the result of a five-minute makeover. We did nothing more than parse out the main ideas and add a rule. If you take 10 seconds, you'll get the gist of what this presentation is about, but you probably would not have invested even one second trying to sift through the original slide.

More important, we might stand a chance of hearing the real person come out if she speaks to the second slide, as opposed to the drone who would have read the first slide. Gone is the compulsion to recite the slide verbatim; now she'll have to actually collect her thoughts. Scary? Perhaps at first. But this five-minute slide makeover will also turn her into a better presenter.

But we're getting ahead of ourselves. First, more pain...

Chapter 3

Look at Me!!

It was the fall of 2003 and life as I knew it was about to change forever. We were in Tucson AZ for the debut of the Presentation Summit, the annual conference that I have hosted for over a decade, and PowerPoint expert Glen Millar had traveled from Australia to lead a session on animation. Glen is a brilliant crafter of presentations who has dreamed up and forgotten more techniques than you or I will learn in our lifetimes.

Glen was upfront about what he was about to show his audience. "You're about to see some really gratuitous stuff here," he said in his Down Under drawl, to which the audience laughed. "In order to discover the potential of what the software can do, sometimes you just have to experiment."

3

With similar irreverence, the slide was entitled "Absolute Nonsense," and it looked like Figure 3.1. You'll want to take a trip to the whypptsucks.com web site and download 03-01.pptx to see what Glen showed his audience that day. Gears turning, pistons pumping, paddles flapping, balls bouncing...all controlled by PowerPoint animation.

▶ To download any of the files referenced in this book, point your browser to www.whypptsucks.com and find the file by its figure number. Depending upon your browser, you might be prompted to choose between opening the file in your browser window or downloading it. In most cases, we recommend downloading the file to your computer and opening it in PowerPoint.

Each of the elements on this slide are carefully timed to become part of a working, almost organic, system of motion. Most in the audience had never seen anything like this and had never considered the use of animation in this way. If you look up *epiphany* in the dictionary, it really should reference Glen's October 18, 2003 workshop on animation.

The buzz lasted all day; I knew, however, the impact of this presentation would be more lasting. And I was a bundle of conflict. After all, what better advertisement for a conference in its rookie season than 200 disciples returning to their colleagues and saying, "I can't wait to show you what I learned at the Presentation Summit!"

Figure 3.1
When the audience saw Glen's animation contraption in 2003, their lives changed. They saw an entirely new dimension to the potential of attracting the attention of their audience.

But the specter loomed of those same disciples returning to their places of work and wasting not a moment finding an occasion to use their new skills. This tendency is remarkably human and cuts across all disciplines and all ages. My wife Becky and I can remember as if it happened yesterday the moment that our six-month-old daughter Erica discovered that she could flex a muscle in her throat and emit a sound. The cause and effect relationship was captivating to her and nothing short of a tranquilizer would stop her from demonstrating her new skill that night. And I'll show you the very essay in which our other daughter Jamie, then in third grade, discovered adjectives.

In software parlance, I refer to this as use of a feature based on recency of discovery, not appropriateness to the task. You use it because you just learned it. Rounded corners on rectangles back in the desktop publishing boom of 1986…dressing up your C:\> prompt in 1988…drop shadows in 1993…related database fields in 1997…Excel pivot tables in 2000…and "Absolute Nonsense" in 2003.

The urge to place into operation that which you have just learned might be one of the finest human traits ever. Imagine the innovation that has come from this tendency and the advances across all disciplines and pursuits. Intellectual curiosity is a wonderful thing; watching it play out in human achievement is even more wonderful.

Unless, of course, you practice your craft in public. Then it has potentially lasting implications of a different sort. You can usually tell when a person has just learned, say, how to make bullets go dim after appearing, or how to make a title fly in letter by letter, or how a motion path can turn static objects into ambulatory ones. When you see the effect in action, but it has no context or purpose whatsoever, there's a good chance that recency of discovery is the driving force behind its use.

I should note that we who considered ourselves Glen's colleagues that day were not left out of the epiphany. When he showed a little-known trick of hiding the background and showing pieces of it through other objects (see Figure 3.2), he sent us all scurrying to our notepads or notebooks.

To this day, many of us on that debut teaching team in 2003 still look for excuses to use this background trick, even if it is not suitable to the context of the presentation. We too cannot always resist saying "Look at me!" in public.

By its nature, PowerPoint is an extroverted activity. People turn to it for the purpose of communication—often in person, often to large audiences. You put your ego on the line when you do this, so it helps to have a sturdy and healthy one. In fact, showing off is almost part of the essential nature of the discipline and should not be viewed as a necessarily negative trait.

Figure 3.2
Even the experts at the Presentation Summit learned something new when Glen Millar showed how to place a photo on the background, cover it up with a full-sized rectangle, create an object on top of the rectangle (the ellipse), and fill it with the background image.

The insatiably curious among our readers can deconstruct this cool technique by downloading 03-02.pptx.

But there are right ways and wrong ways to get attention, and there must always be purpose behind it. This chapter's pain is brought to you by the compulsion to add gimmicks to PowerPoint-driven presentations when there is no legitimate reason to do so. *The fact that you just learned how to do it does not change anything.* If it doesn't contribute to the message, it has no place on your slides. Let's say that again:

**If it doesn't contribute to your message,
it has no place on your slides!**

Chapter 13 discusses some of the healthier ways to show off in public.

Chapter 4

Is Your Message Upside-Down?

When you enter a room to give a presentation, what are you thinking and feeling? Are you comfortable? How will audience members perceive you? Will they like you? What can you say about yourself to instill confidence in them? How can you credential yourself right from the start?

If you actually address these questions, it could mean that you are one of the millions of people speaking before groups who just doesn't get it. It could mean that you are guilty of sending a message to your audience that is completely upside-down.

That's pretty harsh, you might say—all you were doing is caring what your audience thinks about you. How did that turn into such an unpardonable sin?

Read on to learn about one of the most common misconceptions about presentations today and one of the least understood dynamics. It might compel you to take an entirely different approach to your presentation content and delivery. Or it might cause you to swear at me and throw this book in the trash. That's okay, too...

4

It's All About Whom?

"Hello, my name is Susan Sorenson, and today I'm going to talk to you about my five-step approach to home loans and how it has become the talk of the industry. First, let me tell you a bit about myself and my business..."

If you are like most, you have probably heard openings like that dozens of times, and perhaps you have employed something similar during your own presentations. It is as common as coffee; it has become the accepted backdrop for modern-day presentations.

And it is all wrong.

Let's imagine Susan's audience entering the room for this seminar. Do you suppose that a single one of them is looking forward to getting to know her? Are they hoping to become friends with her?

Not likely. They are probably wondering what they need to do to stay in their homes! They are expecting to learn something that can help them through these difficult financial times. They are seeking help with their own situation.

"Hello, my name is Susan Sorenson, and I know why you're here..."

Unless your mother is in your audience, you can't expect that anybody enters the room caring a lick about you. Forgive the candor, but it's simply not their job or their place to. They have their own issues and their own concerns, and your welfare is not likely to be one of them.

> **It's not their job to care about you;**
> **it's your job to care about them.**

It is your job to understand, recognize, appreciate, and connect with the issues and concerns that they have.

"Hello, my name is Susan Sorenson, and I know why you're here. You're afraid of losing your home, aren't you? I don't blame you—my sister just lost hers and I live with her pain nightly."

Notice how different the focus is between this intro and the one at the top of the page. In the first one, our fictional speaker tells her audience how (1) she is going to talk about (2) her approach to lending, but first (3) she is going to talk about (4) herself and (5) her business.

You have probably become so accustomed to the standard opening that you no longer notice, and you've probably witnessed a few hundred times the presentation that begins like the one in Figure 4.1.

Figure 4.1
If these three slides are batting leadoff in your slide deck, it tells your audience members that you care more about how great your organization is than you do about their welfare.

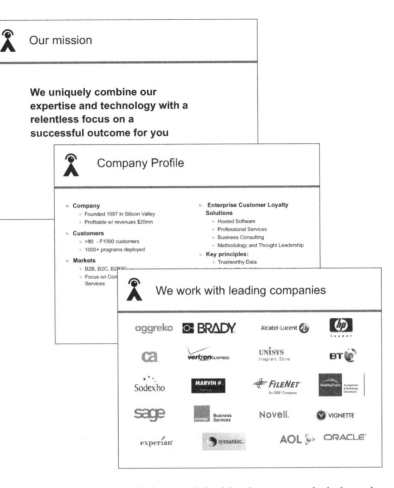

There is nothing wrong with having slides like this in your deck, but what does it say about you if these are the first three slides after the title slide? What does it say about your priorities and your ability to connect with your audience? At a minimum, it certainly does not convey to your audience members that you identify with their concerns or that you understand their pain.

And yet, few things in the world of presentation are more important than that. Apologies in advance if you read this more than once; I'll probably write it a dozen times:

> **Audience members rarely make decisions to act based on what they hear or see. They act on what they feel. The gut guides them more than the brain.**

In order to create an emotional connection with them, you have to show that you understand and care about them. You do that by talking about them, not about yourself.

"Hello, my name is Susan Sorenson, and I know why you're here. You're afraid of losing your home, aren't you? I don't blame you—my sister almost lost hers and I live with her pain nightly.

"I know this concerns you; it concerns me too. You're going to get answers today, this is certain. But you also will be comforted and encouraged to learn that you can do something to improve your situation. In addition to the tactics and strategies that we will discuss, you should leave here feeling that your future is within your control."

This opening creates a fundamentally different feeling among the audience—it is at the core of an audience-centric message, which is what you should aspire to deliver every single time you speak in public.

The promised land for you is this: instead of you offering up your credentials on Slide 2 and your customer list on Slide 3, your audience members become so compelled by your message that they want to know these things and they ask you about them during Q&A. At that point, seeing how they asked, you click a hyperlink on the slide (see Chapter 25 to learn how) and call up those credentialing slides.

◆

It does not take a Sally Field ("you really like me!") moment to understand that people want to be liked. If you are a living, breathing person, you would prefer for your audience members to like you, respect you, care about you, etc. You get there not by credentialing yourself, but by showing them those same emotions and feelings that you would like them to show you.

If you show that you care about them, they'll care about you. That is the order in which this must happen.

Chapter 5

Bitter Backgrounds

As we continue through the sources of pain, annoyance, and angst around presentation content, we note the cruel irony of the fate that all too often befalls the skilled presenter with engaging content. What could go wrong with that scenario, you ask? How about slide backgrounds that drown out the content on them? Indeed, little is more frustrating than slides that could have legitimate appeal but cannot be easily read.

If you know that a presentation is terrible, you can leave the room or start texting your friends ("lol, omg this sux ur lucky ur not here…l8r"). When the speaker is good and the content actually interesting, it could be even more frustrating when the visuals work against him or her.

Invariably, this happens when content creators louse up with their backgrounds, and this usually can be traced to a fundamental lack of understanding about what makes a good background.

5

Backgrounds Shouldn't Be in the Foreground

We can put this entire problem to rest with one sentence:

Put black type against a white background.

Done. Problem solved. Stop reading, go home. If you're already home, go out to a movie. In the history of presentations, no deal has ever been lost, no contract not awarded, no grant not granted because a presenter used black text on a white background. It's the ultimate chicken soup for PowerPoint: it could never hurt you.

At the same time, we pundits have been telling you that photos can make a world of difference for your presentations, so it's no surprise that many of you choose to integrate them into the backgrounds of your slides. And today, you all have digital cameras; you're all content creators. The problem is that sometimes you choose photos that are too good!

Witness Figure 5.1. This is a well-composed photo of a Silicon Valley building—nice angle, very cutting edge and modern. It would vibrate well with today's businessperson.

I would love to use it in a presentation...I could envision burning type into it for dramatic effect...I might pan across it...I could even set it to music.

But I wouldn't use it as my presentation's background, certainly not in its present form. It steals the show; it refuses to stay in the background. It does

Figure 5.1
Great photo, lousy background.

the one thing that you don't want your background to do: it takes attention away from your foreground—your text. Once you do that, you're done.

Now if the photo *is* the message, that's different. If the photo conveys your message without the need for lengthy text, that's the holy grail of presenting! But that doesn't happen very often, and most of us need to be content with integrating a photo with our text-based message.

Figure 5.2
This photo has too much contrast and too many points of interest. Bullets don't stand a chance and you cannot pick any one color of text that would have sufficient contrast against this photo.

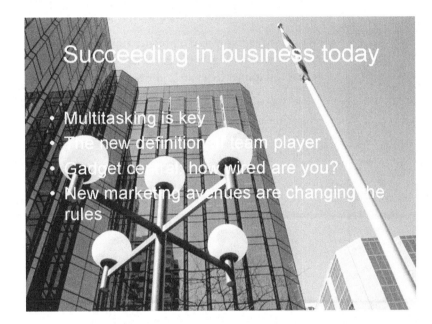

Looking for Contrast in All the Wrong Places

Integrating standard bullets into this photo would be exceedingly difficult. Where would you put them? Figure 5.2 shows the folly of trying to approach this design from a conventional perspective—there's no traditional layout that is going to give you readability.

The culprit here is contrast and it is the single most misunderstood concept among those just starting to get experience blending imagery with standard PowerPoint content. If you had to sit through 30 slides that looked like this one, you wouldn't care if the speaker was the incarnation of Albert Einstein. You'd tune out.

The most important interplay between foreground and background is contrast. In short, you want a lot of it! You want dark text against a light background or vice-versa. People who had this mantra hammered into their heads sometimes go on auto-pilot and hear the singular message "look for high contrast." They find photos with high contrast and then get frustrated when their designs don't work properly.

A photo that has high contrast is going to fight against your efforts to create appropriate contrast between foreground and background, and Figure 5.2 illustrates this problem perfectly. In order for you to rely on your background photo to provide good contrast with your foreground content, that photo itself must have low contrast.

As a commentator to the presentation community, I love that content creators are beginning to integrate visuals into their work. And as with any other discipline, there are right ways and wrong ways to do this.

See Chapter 12 for an in-depth exploration of integrating photos, mastering contrast, and understanding transparency.

Chapter 6

The Scourge of Custom Animation

There I sat, not three feet away, and I couldn't believe what I was hearing. I the consultant, he the client, trying to determine the best course of action with a slide whose content was not communicating the right message.

"It seems that we're not quite getting to the central point," I said to him. "It's not just that you save your customers time, they also benefit from a sales team that speaks a dozen different languages. I think we need to drive that point home with more strength."

I swear I'm not making this up, his response to me: "How about if we make those bullets fly in when I say it?"

"_____"

"Rick? Are you okay?"

Okay, so that last part of the exchange was made up. I didn't actually go comatose. No doubt, though, a camera focused on me would have captured a look of utter bewilderment at the notion that gratuitous animation applied to a clump of words was actually the answer. However poorly this reflected on my client's sensibilities, it was even more insulting to his theoretical audience whom he hoped would be persuaded to take action as a result of bullets flying onto the screen.

That, in one 30-second exchange, sums up an international obsession. We prefer television to radio, movies to books, and slides that move to ones that don't. We learned this at our first conference when the seminar on animation overflowed into the hotel foyer; now we offer that session in the general ballroom that can hold over 200 and we don't even consider offering any other seminars at the same time.

The irony of this situation is delicious. Earnest PowerPoint users are so completely taken with animation, they would gladly stand in the back of a hotel ballroom for 60 minutes in the hope of picking up a new trick or two. And at the same time, every single poll ever taken about PowerPoint's most annoying characteristics (Google "PowerPoint" and "annoying" to see how many polls have actually been conducted) lists bad animation in the top five, without fail.

This much is clear: whatever skills we learn in those first 30 minutes of training, restraint and good taste with animation do not seem to be among them.

Your Audience is at Your Mercy

There is a reason why this topic strikes such a raw nerve among those who suffer through poorly-crafted presentations, and to understand it, we will now introduce Universal Axiom No. 1:

> **When something moves on screen, your audience has no choice but to watch it.**

This is a response that occurs at a subconscious level. We are like moths drawn to a light; we cannot help ourselves.

In response to a skeptic at a recent seminar, I prepared the following experiment. I stood off to the side of the room, about 20 feet from the screen, and began to talk about this topic. In mid-sentence, careful not to take my eyes off of the audience, I sent a gear flying across the screen, just as you see in Figure 6.1.

Everyone looked.

Figure 6.1
For better or for worse, you have no choice but to watch objects as they move on screen.

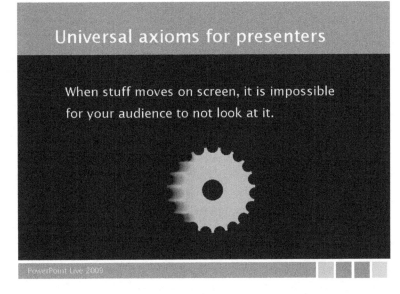

"Hey, I'm over here," I said playfully, as the audience returned their gaze to me. Five seconds later, a photo that was on screen suddenly drifted off.

Everyone looked.

"You see what I mean? You can't help it!"

At that point, I had a smiley face appear and disappear in a blink. There wasn't enough time for anyone to take their eyes off of me, but they all still saw the flashing ellipse in their peripheral vision and responded by looking over. Everyone laughed and I knew that I had made my point.

Your Covenant with the Audience

This implies a tremendous obligation on our part as presenters and content creators. Our industry needs its own variation of the Hippocratic Oath: Above all, we shall practice no excess.

If we know that our audience is compelled to track movement on the slide, it is incumbent on us to make sure that we use that power wisely and responsibly. We must treat it like a sacred covenant.

That rarely happens.

More likely, inexperienced PowerPoint users apply animation in knee-jerk fashion. If they haven't applied animation to something on the slide, they feel as if they haven't done their jobs. Our creative editor, Sandra Johnson, was told this quite succinctly by the CEO of a large corporation: "The slide is incomplete without animation."

I don't have to go further than a nearby bedroom, the one occupied by my 16-year-old daughter, to witness this dynamic first-hand. We live in an environment in which multimedia distractions are part of the background noise. I truly believe that today's teenagers feel somehow dysfunctional without them. It seems that we have created that same environment for our presentations. If a slide consists solely of bullets, we are compelled to animate them. An otherwise ordinary ruling line below a title is inflated in importance by a Fly In From Left. Slide transitions can't just fade; they must dissolve. We have created the implication that if an object just sits there, it must not be very important. It must move; it must exude some level of energy. And every time we do it, the members of our audience are compelled to watch, whether they want to or not.

How Much is Too Much?

Some animations are worse than others, and now you know the barometer by which it should be measured: are audience members forced to track motion across the slide? The ones that move the most are the most potentially intrusive.

We have prepared the Official Rick Altman Pain Scale for you, to be consulted whenever you feel the urge to make something move:

Animation	From / To	Pain Quotient (5 is the worst)
Boomerang, Spiral, Swivel	Anywhere	6
Fly	From side to side	5
Fly	From bottom to top	4
Zoom Out	Anywhere	4
Fly	From left edge to one inch onto the slide	3
Zoom In	Anywhere	3
Wipe Slowly	n/a	2
Wipe Quickly	n/a	0
Fade	n/a	0

Chapter 7

Can PowerPoint Make You Stupid?

One of the most inflammatory ideas circulating among PowerPoint skeptics has received quite a bit of credible press in the past decade. In a widely-circulated 2004 article, *New York Times* columnist Clive Thompson all but blamed the space shuttle Columbia accident on the use of PowerPoint. (www.whypptsucks.com/shuttle).

And the ever-bombastic Edward Tufte has essentially made a living out of attributing many of society's communication problems to Microsoft's venerable slide-making tool.

It's hard to imagine that a software program could be credited with something as profound as affecting one's intellect, but read on—there is a real dynamic at work here, making up the final chapter identifying PowerPoint pain.

Where Good Ideas Go to Die

Several years ago, my friend Lon came to me for assistance with a keynote address he was giving to a group of professional tennis teachers. These teachers were working with some of the most talented junior players in Northern California, so they were well beyond teaching the fundamentals of tennis. Their jobs were to turn these kids into seasoned athletes, help them land college scholarships, and maybe prepare them for professional tennis.

Lon had some innovative ideas to share with these teachers about how to turn kids with raw talent into strong competitors and winners. His concepts were novel and bold about helping exceptionally talented athletes reach beyond their potential.

I'm an avid tennis player and loved talking with him. When his ideas were flowing, he was a joy to listen to. Over a beer, he was amazing, fluent with such heady concepts as the ideal performance state, living in the present moment, and his most novel theory, having to do with calming the mind to maximize the body's energy.

Lon needed to distill all of his wonderful ideas into a 45-minute after-dinner talk, and he wanted to show me the PowerPoint slides that he had created so far. My first reaction surprised him.

"Why do you need to show slides?"

"I'm sure that they're expecting it."

"I'm expecting you to do the unexpected."

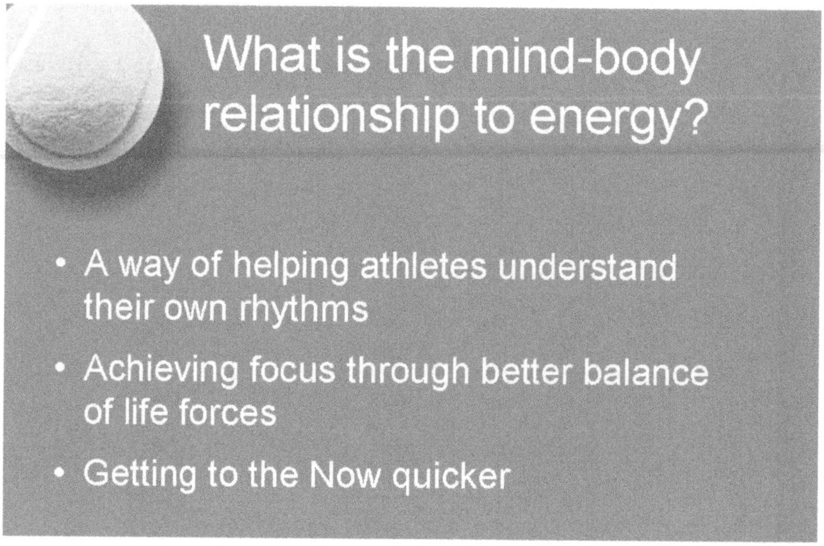

Figure 7.1
Can this slide help a coach talk to other coaches? Not likely...

What is the mind-body relationship to energy?

- A way of helping athletes understand their own rhythms
- Achieving focus through better balance of life forces
- Getting to the Now quicker

Figure 7.2
This slide did not inhibit Lon's ability to articulate his thoughts.

Once he untangled himself from my circular argument, he insisted that slides would make his talk go smoother.

He was wrong. Figure 7.1 showed his weak attempt to fit his thoughts onto a bullet slide. It sounded like mumbo-jumbo, something his ideas never did when he spoke about them informally. Worse, when he practiced his speech with his slides, he found himself trying to explain the meaning of the words on the slides, instead of just sharing the thoughts in his head. I call this "going on defense" and it is a sure sign that you are at risk for committing Death by PowerPoint.

Ultimately, I convinced Lon to go with Figure 7.2 instead. His ideas were more than enough to carry the hour; all he needed were a good image to evoke an emotional response and a few talking points. And when he realized that his original slides were doing him no good, he decided to forego slides altogether. Good call, Lon.

This was a classic example of good ideas getting torpedoed by PowerPoint. Lon's ideas were far too nuanced to be contained within one title and three bullet points. Most good ideas can't survive such a boiling down, yet that is the default medium for sharing ideas in public. When smart people try to represent their good ideas with such a limiting medium, they come off sounding less smart.

PowerPoint does indeed dumb them down.

One chapter from now, you will read about my prescribed "three-word challenge"—a call to distill long bullets down to short ones. This might sound like a contradiction to the point I am making here, and it certainly won't be the last time you feel that way. I will explain the difference more fully then; for now, I will specify that the danger here is trying to use bullets to *explain* an idea, instead of just *represent* it.

Talking Points Can Create Talking Heads

Unless presenters practice with their material and with the medium, even simple and succinct bullets can derail them. I witnessed a good example of this while watching a volleyball match on ESPN. (Two sports anecdotes in one chapter? Get used to it—ask anyone who knows me: sports is my metaphor for everything in life.)

Calling the action were Chris Marlowe, an experienced play-by-play professional, and Vince, a former Olympic player. Each of them was required, at various times during the broadcast, to comment on a statistic or a notable fact being displayed in a graphic.

One of Vince's assignments was to discuss the factors that he thought were significant during a particular match. The graphic displayed three items: return of serve, ability to set a double-block, and free-ball passing. With only a few months of experience as a television commentator and no formal training or background, Vince did nothing more than read, word for word, the three items in the graphic. He would have done far better if he were instructed to describe, in his own words, the three key elements of the match. The audience didn't need to see the graphic, but when ESPN showed it, it paralyzed Vince, reducing him to a cue-card reader.

Chris Marlowe is much more experienced in these matters. The graphic he was asked to elaborate on showed how many times UCLA, the top-ranked team in the nation at the time, had come back to win after the other team had reached game point. While the graphic showed the percentages and statistics, Marlowe said, "You don't win four championships in six years without playing the big points well, and here is why so many consider UCLA to be one of history's most successful teams."

Now that's the way to speak to bullet points! Marlowe didn't insult his audience's literacy by reading the graphic. Instead, he made the moment greater than the sum of its parts by telling us something more than just the raw facts.

Even though he is on live television and the stakes are high, Marlowe actually has an advantage over the person giving a speech. As a play-by-play announcer, Marlowe does not know what is about to happen, he does not work off of a script, and often he doesn't have any idea what he is going to say next. That promotes spontaneity and creativity, two of the most important ingredients of good public speaking.

While inexperienced with talking points, Vince proved to be an acute analyst of the game. When allowed to simply react to what he was watching, he was articulate, relaxed, and confident.

I suspect there are many executives and corporate speechmakers who are like Lon or Vince: astute, well-spoken, but ultimately hampered by the implicit (or explicit) requirement that all high-tech speeches be accompanied by a PowerPoint slide show. I had lunch recently with a Silicon Valley-based executive and he summed up the situation perfectly. First, he acknowledged that most of his colleagues are too busy to spend more than a half-hour working on their slides.

"Is it so important that they have slides?" I asked.

"Today," he replied, "you can't give a talk in this business without showing slides."

"But what can you do in 30 minutes?"

"Copy and paste your notes into the bullet holders."

"But if you just turn your notes into slides, your slides will be the same as what you say."

"That's right."

"That's sad."

"That's right."

You can't give a talk today without showing slides. Those are some of the most distressing words I have ever heard. *Too busy to spend more than 30 minutes on their slides.* Executives with good speaking skills don't necessarily need slides as they speak, and if they do, their slides should elaborate on their ideas, not repeat them. And executives who lack speaking skills make the situation worse with bad slides that compel them to read their speech instead of deliver it.

The Wrong Place to Start

Where do people go wrong? Often, their fatal errors are made in the first 10 seconds of a project: they put hand to mouse, after which it becomes exceedingly difficult to think creatively.

Even though it doesn't involve PowerPoint, a recent experience I had crystallized this issue for me. On a flight home a few years ago, I sat inbetween two businessmen, both using their notebook computers. I couldn't resist spying on them.

One of them was using CorelDraw, a graphic drawing program that I have been using since its inception in the late 1980s. The other was composing in Microsoft Word. The man using Draw was producing some sort of flier or publicity sheet, and he was struggling. He kept creating objects and text strings, fiddling with them, and then deleting them. He appeared to have no direction or objective.

I couldn't see what the other man was writing about, but what struck me was that he spent half his time making notes on a yellow legal pad. Funny, I thought, why doesn't he just use Word to keep his notes, and I asked him that very thing.

> **"This is the way I've always done it," he said, "and I can't break the habit. I always make my outlines longhand before writing."**

Well, the irony of this situation was delicious. The man who least needed to use pencil and paper before embarking on a computer-based project couldn't work without them, and the man who desperately needed to do a bit of sketching or scribbling was trying to create a drawing using an eraser head to move the cursor.

Why do we computer users do this to ourselves? I think I know the answer, but first, let's point out the obvious: when you embark on a task—any task—first you decide what it is you want to do, then you determine how you are going to do it, and then you do it. That's how people do things in real life. All too often, however, users of creative software, like CorelDraw or PowerPoint, go about everything bass-ackwards. They sit in front of the computer, place their hand on the mouse, and start creating objects, hoping that a finished piece will spontaneously occur. In no other aspect of their lives do they expect to achieve success in this manner, but they hold exempt from natural laws their relationship with their software applications.

People come to graphics and presentation software from so many different professions and pursuits, it's impossible to generalize about work habits. But one thing is clear: most users do not arrive at the software with a formal background in any creative field. They have not had significant experience with sketch pads, light tables, dark rooms, or any other traditional creative tool. Their software is likely the only tool for working on a creative project that they have been exposed to, so it's only natural that they would use it for the entirety of a project.

This was certainly the case with the man in 16C. He knew that he had to produce a flier on a particular topic, but I doubt that he started with much more direction than that. He kept drawing shapes, creating text, moving them around, stopping, thinking, stretching, rotating, filling, deleting, redrawing...and all the while growing visibly frustrated. He expected CorelDraw to act as his sketch pad, or better yet, to magically produce the flier for him.

We see this same dynamic among PowerPoint users, usually to the same detriment. The cold hard fact is that programs like CorelDraw, Photoshop, Dreamweaver, and PowerPoint are the wrong tools for the beginning phases of a project, totally wrong. This is not a criticism of PowerPoint and the others—let's please just acknowledge that these programs are finishing tools, not starting tools.

PowerPoint lets you do a lot of things quickly and easily, but sketching or roughing out a creative concept is not one of them. There's way too much temptation to make everything perfect, and that's exactly what you don't want to do at the initial stages of a project. When starting work on a presentation, experienced content creators look to get ideas out as quickly as they think of them. This is the time to open the creative canal as wide as possible—to scribble, cross out, throw away, start over, blab to colleagues,

Figure 7.3
Even the pros begin with pencil and paper, not with slides.

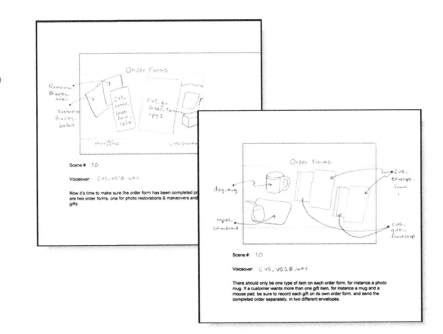

and do all of that all over again. It is not the time to be thinking of transitions, animation choices, backgrounds, or color schemes. In fact, it's not the time to be handling the mouse at all.

The man in 16A had the right idea. While only creating a word-processed document, he realized that he's better off mapping out his route on paper first. Even a simple program like Word offers too many temptations to make a first draft perfect, what with spell and grammar checkers, document controls, wizards, and paragraph formatting tools. He just wanted a brain dump, and the best dumping ground is the legal pad. He didn't have very good handwriting; I doubt that he got an A in third grade penmanship. But that is of no consequence during the idea stage.

Figure 7.3 shows a sketch of a presentation prepared by Julie Terberg, one of the most prominent and talented presentation designers in the world. She is a regular at the Presentation Summit, where she shares her vast knowledge of design theory and how it is best applied to the presentation medium. Many in the audience were surprised when she showed this sketch, but in her own words, "I always start with pencil and paper. I'm freer that way."

It is not the product of your sketching that is so important to the process, it is the *act* of sketching. Sketching...doodling...free-associating...these are the secret ingredients to brilliance!

Kind of funny when you think of it. One of the secrets to using PowerPoint effectively is knowing when not to use it.

♦

As we conclude our identification of everything wrong with modern-day PowerPoint usage, we have already produced for you one recipe for creating pleasing and potentially effective presentations:

- Organize your thoughts away from your computer

- Use black text

- Create white backgrounds

- Use only wipes or fades

If you confine yourself to those four practices, if you don't read past this point, if you *throw this book in the trash right now,* I'll be satisfied that we have reduced by one the number of people in the world who could potentially commit Death by PowerPoint with annoying and obnoxious presentations.

The Solution

If you're still with me after the first seven chapters, you're in need of a good catharsis, and the rest of this book seeks to provide just that. If you have reached the conclusion that yes, most PowerPoint presentations do indeed suck, rest assured that there are solutions at hand.

We won't shy away from the direct tone that we adopted in Part 1; each of us remains just one poor choice away from committing Death by PowerPoint. But from here on, our objective is to arm you with the tools, strategies, principles, and perhaps above all, the philosophy behind the creation of truly excellent presentations.

Chapter 8

Surviving Bullets

We have chosen the order of these first few chapters carefully. Exhaustive articles have been written on the evils of bullets. My colleague, Cliff Atkinson, wrote an entire book, *Beyond Bullet Points*, espousing alternative approaches to creating content slides.

I disagree with neither the sentiment nor the philosophy behind this argument. Presentation content creators who go on autopilot often crash and burn. The world does not need any more bullet slides in order to prosper.

But we have to be pragmatic here. Irrespective of your opinion about bullets, there is no escape from them. They are as inevitable as colds in the winter and mosquitoes in the summer. You read what the executive said on page 33 about slides being a virtual requirement for corporate presentations. While ridding the world of bullet slides is a noble pursuit, let's also give some merit to the effort to make them a bit better.

Three Words

What if a law were passed prohibiting bullets from exceeding three words in length? Could you abide by it? Perhaps not, but humor me on this one, because it stands as one of the best exercises you can do, whether you are the presenter, the content creator, or both.

▶ This section pertains to presentations delivered live via a presenter. Presentations designed to be sent electronically and read on screen by the recipient (without voiceover) are not subject to the same verbiage issues. In short, it's okay to be more wordy with a self-running presentation, because those are the only words available to the recipient.

Fresh off all that pain in Part 1, you probably don't need a reminder about Universal Axioms 2 and 3, but you're getting one anyway:

If a slide contains complete sentences, it is practically impossible for even the most accomplished presenters to avoid reading them word for word.

When you do that, you sound like an idiot.

Figure 8.1 is a classic culprit. Somebody simply did an idea dump right into his or her slides, and anyone who tries to speak to this slide is doomed to become a drone. Before you read on, I want you to clean this slide up by

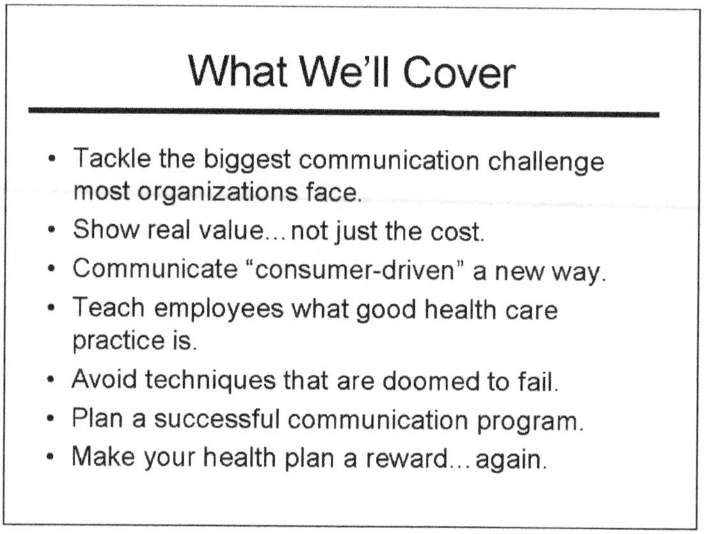

Figure 8.1
Pity the poor presenter who has to work with this slide.

What We'll Cover

- Tackle the biggest communication challenge most organizations face.
- Show real value…not just the cost.
- Communicate "consumer-driven" a new way.
- Teach employees what good health care practice is.
- Avoid techniques that are doomed to fail.
- Plan a successful communication program.
- Make your health plan a reward…again.

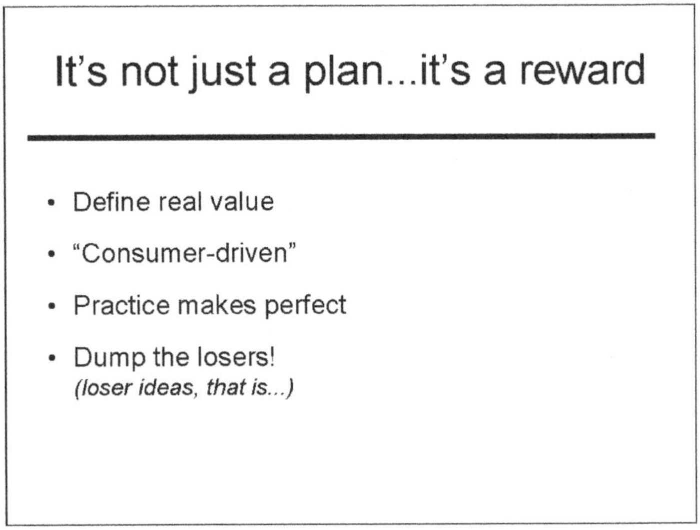

Figure 8.2
This slide no longer gets in the way. It frames the subjects and allows the presenter to find his or her natural speaking rhythm.

> # It's not just a plan...it's a reward
>
> ---
>
> - Define real value
> - "Consumer-driven"
> - Practice makes perfect
> - Dump the losers!
>   *(loser ideas, that is...)*

mentally reducing each bullet point down to three words. Ditch the adjectives, jettison the pronouns, eliminate the flotsam.

Even with your sharpest knife, you might not be able to cut all the way down to three words, but the reward is in the attempt.

Figure 8.2 shows our attempt with the three-word challenge. You can see that we failed with one of the bullets, but the sum of our effort and our failure was an unqualified victory. The slide is much stronger now, and even though I have no familiarity with the subject, having gone through this process, I feel as if I could almost present on it now.

Several important things take place when you make an earnest attempt to get within three words:

Your slides are friendlier

With just that one task, you create slides that are much easier on the eyes of your audience. Eye fatigue is the silent killer of presentations. When you ask your audience to sit in a dimly-lit room for 30 or 60 minutes, their eyes are going to be the first to go. The more words each slide contains, the quicker the onset of fatigue. Fewer words, less fatigue. Your bullets might not be as descriptive, but that's okay—it's your job to do the describing.

Your pace improves

Something almost magical happens when you reduce the amount of words on a slide. Everything seems snappier. The slide draws more quickly, audience members absorb the information more efficiently, and you most likely project more energy.

You create intrigue

In three words, you are not going to be able to fully explain your points. But that's not bad; it's good. In fact, it's terrific! Without even trying to, you create mystique and intrigue. You invite audience members to use their imaginations. Once you get good at the three-word rule, you will become a better writer of bullets. You will begin to write with color and humor. All of this will help you engage your audience on an emotional level. And that, dear reader, is the holy grail of presenting.

You learn your material better

Of the many bad things associated with dumping complete sentences onto slides, perhaps the worst is how lazy it makes the presenter, whether it is you or someone for whom you create slides. Excess verbiage sends a subtle but powerful message that you don't need to prepare as much, because everything you want to say is already there.

Parsing the words increases your burden as a presenter, but once again, this is a noble burden. Adhering to the three-word rule forces you to learn your content at a level you otherwise might not have reached.

One of my favorite quotes about presenting comes from Mark Twain:

> **"If you want me to speak for an hour, I am ready today. If you want me to speak for 10 minutes, it will take me two weeks to prepare."**

The three-word challenge is a microcosm of the wonderful dynamic that Twain articulated. In order to get down to three words, you really need to study the text. You need to truly understand what you intend to communicate and you need to pick three words that create the perfect backdrop for your ideas. Getting down to three words requires that you practically get intimate with your text.

Looking back on Figures 8.1 and 2, there are a few things to note:

- We eliminated altogether the two bullets about communications. This is purely subjective, but good communication is so fundamental to this topic, it doesn't need a bullet. As the theoretical presenter, I have made a mental note to discuss its importance in my opening remarks. Seven bullets on one slide is too many, anyway.

- The point of the "consumer driven" bullet is that the phrase is being redefined. The quote marks around the words imply that so no other words are needed. If I were the presenter, the quote marks would be all the reminder I would need about this topic.

- The final bullet has been promoted to title. If I were the content creator, I could see planning the entire presentation around that catchy phrase. In fact, if the company were looking for a marketing catch phrase, this could be it. At a minimum, it serves well as the title for this slide.

For more ranting about leave behinds and further discussion about reducing text on your slides, see Chapter 16.

- Finally, our revised slide will not function nearly as well as a leave-behind document. Good. Great! You should never try to create one deck for these two purposes.

In the case of bullets, less is so much more. Taking the three-word challenge is one of the best devices to get you to less. It took four passes and over 45 minutes to create the revision. Mark Twain would have been proud...

Brief bullets, stupid bullets...what's the difference?

In Chapter 7, we wrote how ill-conceived bullets could keep you from fleshing out your ideas. (Actually, we wrote that they could make you stupid.) How is the three-word challenge different? This is a legitimate question and detractors of this strategy would argue that coy or evasive bullets offer no guarantee that an important idea will be shared, while a verbose bullet at least ensures that the idea will be made public.

In the previous chapter, we also warned against verbose bullets taking over your responsibility of telling your story, and that is the central point, as far as I am concerned: bullets that try too hard to tell your story rob you of the chance to tell it yourself. That in turn robs audience members of what they came to hear.

The three-word challenge does not excuse you from fleshing out your ideas; it *demands* it. By distilling a slide down, you take ownership of the content—if you don't share your ideas, they don't get aired. This is as it should be. You are the presentation; your ideas are the main attraction.

From this perspective, it is obvious that slides that have been *three-worded* will support the presentation of ideas better than ones that drone on.

The War Against "On Click"

There is a battle of wills being fought in the boardrooms and in the trenches where America creates its presentation content. (Overseas as well—our technical editor, Geetesh Bajaj, from India notes the same battles there.) The controversy has raged on for over five years and numerous articles and scathing editorials have been written about the bitter battle. We refer, of course, to the issue of bullet advancement: do you display them all at once or click by click?

Part Two: The Solution

When the Words Must Display

We know of several organizations that require that bullets be fleshed out into complete thoughts and displayed for the audience. (One company actually suffered through litigation based on the charge that it did not divulge visually specific information to an audience of shareholders...oy vey.)

So how do we overcome Axiom Nos. 2 and 3? You might be required to show the text and recite the text, but must you do it in that order? Probably not, and when you avoid that, the experience is altogether different.

If you are the one tasked with presenting this fictitious report to your fictitious shareholders, start with this basic slide:

Now say everything that you are required to say about these five points. When you are done, then transition to this slide:

This slide could be word-for-word what you just told your audience, but when you say it first and display it afterward, it is an altogether different experience for your audience.

The axiom about being an idiot for reciting a slide only applies if the slide is present while you are reciting it. If the words appear afterward, you're not an idiot, you're omniscient.

Say it first, then display it. That's the solution for situations that require you to do both.

I come down on a particular side of this issue and I'm pleased to report that my side is winning: advancing one by one through bullets is losing favor. In this section, I will tell you why the all-at-once choice is the better approach to take and how to best incorporate it.

We understand the appeal for advancing bullets "On Click." It could make pacing easier and it assures that everyone in the room will be on point. More likely, you simply accepted the default choice of On Click when applying animation to the bullet placeholder. But there are three significant downsides to this approach that you must take into account:

Loss of context

When you reveal ideas one by one, you ask the audience to absorb each piece of information by itself, and this often results in less-than-total under-standing of the concept you are trying to share. As the presenter, you understand the connection between Bullets 1 and 3, but when you remove the forest and only show the trees, one by one, the audience doesn't get the same chance to connect the ideas.

Is it over?

When you advance bullets one by one, you might lose the forest yourself! You increase the chances that you will forget which bullet is the last one and then have to do the advance-oops-sorry-go-back shuffle. Not the end of the world, but a needless disruption of your flow.

How dare you!

Most important, when you spoon-feed simple information to your audience, you could actually insult them. Some of your audience members could infer that you don't think they are worthy of the context. They see it as commen-tary on their intelligence. In the polls that we have taken, about one in 15 have reacted this way. If you're speaking to a room of 100, you would be offending six people just by the way you have created your bullet slides.

Figure 8.3 represents the nadir of this design approach—dimming bullets after you're done with them. This is downright condescending and will be felt on a conscious or subconscious level by more than just one in 15. Not only do you imply to your audience that they are not worthy of seeing what you have to say next, but that they need to be told when to stop paying attention to the last point.

You didn't mean any of that. You were just trying to be helpful. Or perhaps you just learned how to do all that stuff with the dimming feature of the Custom Animation task pane and you wanted to try it out. How did this get so out of hand?

Life is Too Short

Bullets on slides are just not worth this kind of trouble. Everyone's life is made easier when you display your bullets all at once and then speak to them. You insult nobody and you eliminate the risk that you might lose your own place.

This is especially true if you have successfully three-worded your text. They're now short and sweet, so just get them out there! You make your life easier as the presenter, too—one click and you're there. No pretense, no false drama, no unncecessary commotion.

Nay-sayers will argue that audience members will run ahead and stop listening to you. Get real. How far ahead can they go? Do you have 22 bullets on the slide? I know presenters who refrain from distributing their handouts for this reason, and that is a legitimate point of view. But if your audience is having trouble paying attention to you, don't blame your bullets. It's your job to keep your audience on point.

When you liberate your bullets in this way, you also get the opportunity to practice one of my favorite animation techniques for text blocks: the "cascading fade," performed the same with any version of PowerPoint from 2002 (XP) forward:

1. Select the bullet placeholder and apply a Fade for an entrance. Set Start to With Previous and Duration to 1.00 second (version 2010) or Speed to Fast (version 2007, below).

2. Click the downward-pointing arrows to expand the animated elements into their individual bullets, and if necessary, right-click on one of them and choose Show Advanced Timeline.

Download 08-04.pptx from whypptsucks.com to see the effect.

Not seeing the downward arrows? Your text is probably in a text box instead of a placeholder. Right click the animation and select Effect Options. Click the Text Animation Tab. Use the drop-down arrow to change the Group Text option to By 1st Level Paragraph, then click OK. Now you should see the arrows and be able to proceed.

3. Click and drag the second bullet's duration (its orange bar) to the right by .2 seconds.

4. Drag each subsequent bullet to the right an additional .2 seconds.

5. Press Shift+F5 to play the current slide and witness your masterpiece.

This is one of the most elegant treatments of text animation that we know. It is softer than a standard fade and very pleasing to the eye. It has only one drawback: because it involves different animations to the same level of bullets, it

Asking for Directions Would be Wonderful

As the sayings go, men refuse to ask for directions and women don't realize they need to. Gender aside, we hope that Microsoft's development team learns how to. It would make the lives of advanced users oh-so-much more enjoyable.

Let's consider the technique that we just showed, the one we refer to as the "cascading fade." This name is made up; PowerPoint does not refer to it in any way. We don't think that the development team imagined anyone wanting to do it, and we do not fault them for this oversight—hundreds of thousands of users have developed techniques well outside the fundamental construct of the program.

Back to the cascading fade. (This is a sidebar; we're allowed to digress. See, I just did it again.) Those are semi-involved steps that you would have to undertake to create the effect, and after awhile, it becomes tedious. I willingly deal with the tedium because I like the effect so much. However, I'd love to not have the tedium.

I could get my wish, too, if the development team would add one modest setting to the Fade animation: direction.

Imagine if you could ask that a headline Fade In From Left? That would eliminate the weird and awkward workaround that many undertake using Zoom and Fade together. And if I could set my bullets to Fade In From Top, they would naturally cascade down the slide.

That would put my technique out of business, and I would happily mourn its passing. Two clicks for a set of bullets instead of multiple clicks for each bullet? That's a no-brainer.

Best of all, because that would be an action performed on an entire bullet level, it could be programmed into the slide master. No more going slide to slide.

I'm not sure this qualifies as my No. 1 wish-list item—animation styles would still get the nod over this—but it's close. Very little was done to the Animation engine in Version 2007 or 2010, and it is my hope that the next version will see notable new features with animation. In anticipation, I will start whining and kvetching for direction to be added to Fade in the next version of the software.

cannot be globally programmed from a layout; it can only be created on content slides. Therefore, I do not employ this technique when I am looking to automate a 300-slide presentation.

The Art of Compromise

There will be occasions when you are either compelled by specific circumstances or by certain people (who sign your paycheck) to either advance bullets one by one or do the dreaded dim thing. And to be fair, we can think of situations in which it is appropriate to advance bullet by bullet or to highlight the specific idea that is being discussed. Here are a couple of recommended strategies for those times.

Is this the last bullet on your slide??

If you are compelled to display bullets one by one, here is a trick that will insure against your inadvertently advancing beyond the last bullet and switching to the next slide before you wanted to. The steps are the same across all modern versions of the software.

1. Open the slide in question and make note of its background color. In our example, it is navy blue.

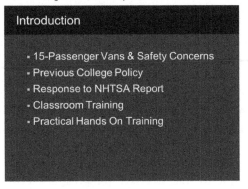

2. Create a thin rule in an out-of-the-way place, close to the color of the background. We placed ours along the bottom of the slide and filled it with a blue that is a bit lighter than the background.

3. Animate it, using the generic Appear for the type and After Previous for the Start. Make sure it is at the bottom of the animation sequence.

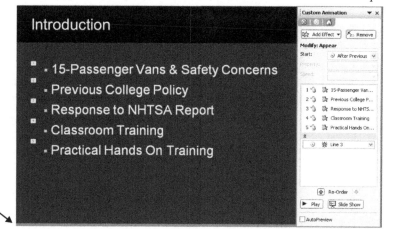

Download 08-05.pptx to see this tactic in action.

Now when you show this slide, that thin rule will inconspicuously appear immediately after the last bullet appears. You know that your bullets for that slide have all displayed and you can focus on your ideas, without having to wonder if you dare click your remote one more time. It's an opportunity to reduce by one the things a presenter has to think about while in front of an audience.

Your audience probably won't notice your end-of-slide cue, but who cares if they do? I know presenters who display a prominent "End of Slide" text box on their slide, in full view of everyone, after the last element appears. I don't think there is any problem at all allowing your audience to see the plumbing in your PowerPoint house. That just shows that you have given this some thought and are striving to create a smooth experience for everyone.

You are here

Should it become necessary to highlight the particular bullet you are speaking on, there are right ways and wrong ways to do it.

- Dimming everything except that bullet is the wrong way.

- Showing everything and then highlighting the current one is the right way.

Download 08-06.pptx to see this effect in action.

The following example assumes that you need to show a lengthy list and discuss many of the points on that list. Our slide has 20 items, so we used the side-by-side layout, requiring that the following steps be performed twice.

1. Animate your bullets however you normally do. We chose a fast fade on the slide master or layout, set After Previous.

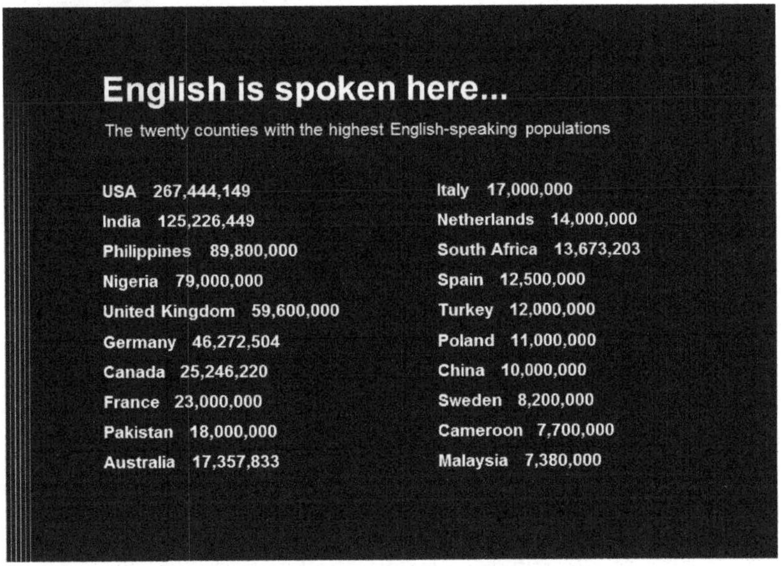

Figure 8.6
Lengthy lists like
this one are good
candidates for a
double animation
that highlights the
current point.

2. On the slide, select the bullet placeholder and add the Change Font
   Color emphasis. Pick a color close to the font color. With our white
   text on a dark background, we chose yellow.

3. From the Effects dialog box (right-click on the object in the Animation task pane to get there), set the After Animation to be the original
   color of the bullets.

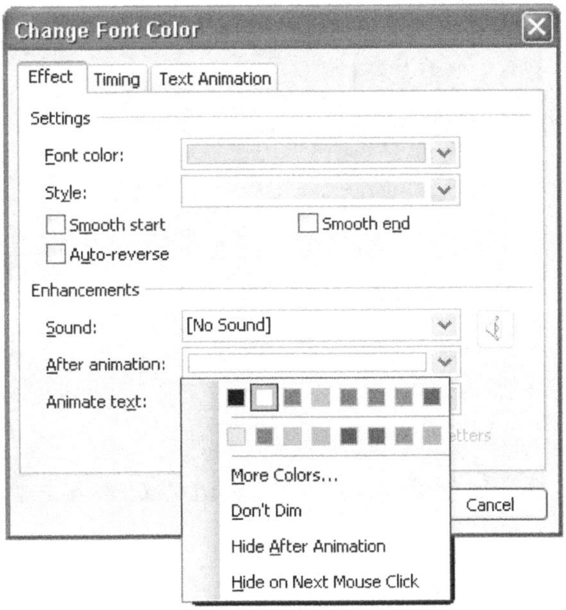

To summarize, there are two animations applied to the text. The first one is a conventional fade that brings all of the bullets in at once. The second animation, set On Click, changes the color of each bullet with each click of the mouse or remote. And while each click changes a bullet's color, it also sets the previous bullet's color back to its original.

I vastly prefer this to dimming or spoon-feeding the text. This double-animation technique gets all of the text out there at once and then allows you to highlight each one without being condescending.

We spent many minutes coming up with an example that we think justifies this type of treatment—the lengthy list of countries in Figure 8.6. Here it would be completely appropriate to highlight each country that you intended to speak about as you addressed it. Figure 8.7 is our best attempt to illustrate this using black toner and white paper—pretend that the gray text is white and the Canada line is yellow.

To reiterate, we don't think you should have to resort to these tricks very often, because we don't think that clicking bullets or highlighting text is a good habit. We might only employ a technique like this once a year. Please do not use it without good cause!

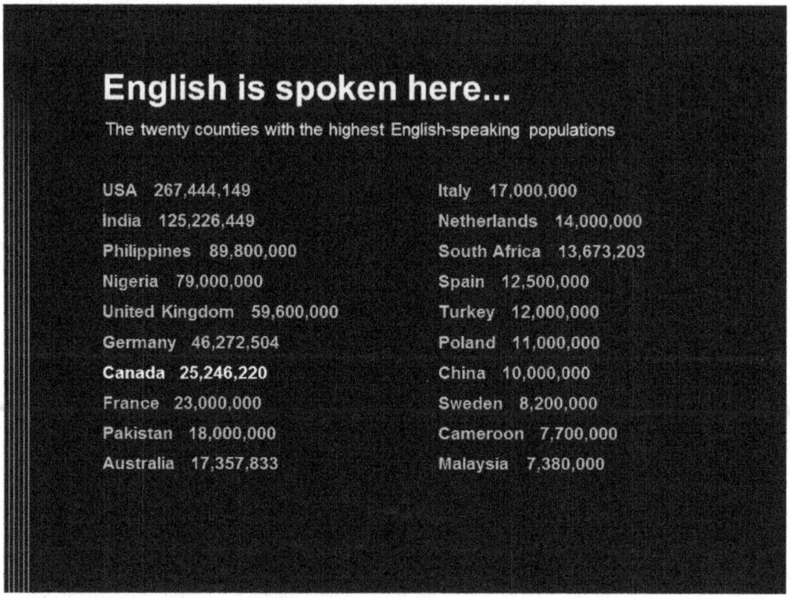

Figure 8.7
With each click of the mouse, the subsequent bullet highlights.

English is spoken here...

The twenty counties with the highest English-speaking populations

USA 267,444,149	Italy 17,000,000
India 125,226,449	Netherlands 14,000,000
Philippines 89,800,000	South Africa 13,673,203
Nigeria 79,000,000	Spain 12,500,000
United Kingdom 59,600,000	Turkey 12,000,000
Germany 46,272,504	Poland 11,000,000
Canada 25,246,220	China 10,000,000
France 23,000,000	Sweden 8,200,000
Pakistan 18,000,000	Cameroon 7,700,000
Australia 17,357,833	Malaysia 7,380,000

Chapter 9

Thriving with Masters and Layouts

There are myriad reasons why Office 2007 did not exactly take the world by storm, and we who interact with corporate America see the chief reason on a daily basis: corporate wheels turn oh-so-slowly and many large organizations were not ready for the migration path and the learning curve of a new office suite. We still have clients using Version 2003.

Office 2007 was, and Office 2010 is, a stroke from a completely different brush. Ribbons replace menus and groups stand in for toolbars. Office 2007 was perfectly fine software; most of the resistance to it was due to its *otherness.*

9

This is a quality that many did not appreciate in their basic computing tools, and we understand that sentiment. If, for the past 20 years, you have counted upon Word, Excel, a screwdriver, a can opener, your shoelaces, or the faucet at your sink to function a certain way, how excited would you be if everything about its appearance and function changed?

This is all notwithstanding the fact that PowerPoint 2007 and 2010 are sound software programs with few bugs plaguing them and several compelling new features. And the most compelling of all? In the eyes of many, it would be the paradigm for global formatting: slide masters and their corresponding layouts.

Are You Still in a 2003 Mindset?

Chances are that sometime over the past few years, you made the move to either Version 2007 or 2010 of PowerPoint, but the important question is this: Are you still thinking like a Version 2003 user? In many cases, the answer might be yes. In my travels among our corporate clients, I encounter hundreds of people each year who are still creating multiple slide masters to accommodate design variations and who are limiting their use of placeholders to titles and text.

If this is you, it's time to wake up!

▶ When necessary, we will make the distinction between versions. Otherwise, we will use the term "modern versions" to refer to both versions 2007 and 2010. And while we don't officially cover Mac versions 2008 and 2011, many of our discussions apply to them, as well.

Version 2007 made fundamental changes to the relationship between slide masters and layouts, offering better control and better access. In short:

You no longer apply a slide master to a slide
The slide master identifies a group of layouts, any one of which is applied to a slide.

The layout is now the primary formatting tool
While you have always had plenty of layouts to choose from in pre-2007 versions, you had little control over their appearances, and most went unused and even unnoticed. Now you have complete control over them. You decide what they are called, what elements are placed on them, and how many to keep within a given slide master.

You choose the placeholders

Previous versions offer various combinations of title, subtitle, and up to two text placeholders, forcing even moderately ambitious designers to place repeating elements on the slide itself. The classic example being the title slide designed to hold a speaker's name, her position, and maybe a photo. There has been no provision for those common elements on the masters, so you have had to build them on the slide itself, and then take care to maintain consistent formatting across those slides that are to be formatted that way.

In modern versions, you can create placeholders on the Title layout for those elements, ensuring their consistent placement, size, and format.

One-stop shopping for your designs

You no longer have to jockey between the Slide Design and Slide Layout task panes to format your slides. When you pull down the Layout gallery, every layout contained within any slide master is available for selection, and you no longer have to worry about inadvertently applying one of them to every slide in the deck. In my opinion, it is the single most important interface improvement offered by modern versions.

The Relationship Between Slide Masters and Layouts

Upon entering Slide Master view, the thumbnails on the left reveal a clear parent-child relationship, with the slide master appearing larger than the layouts underneath. Formatting applied to the slide master is reflected on the layouts:

- Set the title bold and all title placeholders in all layouts become bold.

- Increase the typesize of bullet text and most text placeholders adjust.

- Add animation to a level and you'll find it on all layouts that have that level of text.

- Add a logo to the lower-right corner and you'll instantly see it appear on every layout.

Any layout can be overridden with local formatting and some layouts do not follow the slide master. For instance, if you change the size of bullet text, the two-column layouts will not reflect that change—perhaps the developers felt that these layouts should have an identity all their own, and that makes sense to us.

Quick Access

The more you use modern versions of PowerPoint, the more you will come to appreciate the so-called Quick Access Toolbar (QAT), where you can add favorite and often-used commands.

The QAT lives either above the Ribbon or below it (above by default) and just about any command available across the program can be added to it. Commands cannot be shown by text, so you will need to memorize location or learn which icon represents which command.

You can customize the QAT from File | Options or by right-clicking any part of the Ribbon (it's part of the redesigned PowerPoint Options super dialog). Once there, you can search for any command and add it to the QAT.

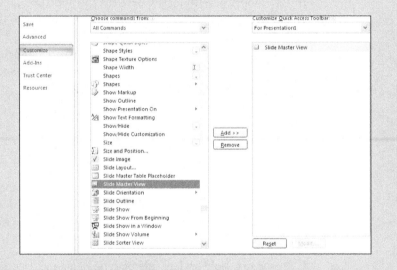

While you're at it, add Normal view to the QAT also, so you can easily return to normal slide work.

You can also add commands to the QAT by finding them on the interface, right-clicking, and choosing Add to Quick Access Toolbar.

Perhaps more important, press Alt and note that every item on your QAT is assigned a number. Remember those numbers and the Quick Access Toolbar truly lives up to its name.

Once you ask the most global of questions like typeface, style, size, basic alignment and the like (the ones that would be addressed on the slide master itself), you then dive into the layouts, where you will find more control than ever before. It is here where you make the decisions that have the most direct and basic affect on your slides.

There are layouts for a dizzying array of scenarios. And if any one of them is not quite right, change any aspect of it. Perhaps more important, create your own layouts, based entirely on the needs and demands of your slide design. This is light years from the blunt distinction between title master and slide master or the rigid layouts that could not be tailored.

The slide master is the king of the castle

From its perch, the slide master presides over all of its layouts, but it does so like a king over his country: with aloofness. While a slide is identified as belonging to a particular master, you do not overtly apply the master to a slide. It is not actually possible. Instead, you choose a layout, from any slide master that exists in the file. It doesn't matter how many slide masters there are or how many layouts each might contain—every layout that exists in a file is available for use, as you can see in Figure 9.1

The layouts are the royal guards

Reporting directly to the king, the layouts are the real power brokers in the royal court. They directly control how a slide looks, feels, and behaves. They are much more powerful than slide layouts of older versions; in fact, they are more like version 2003 slide masters.

The slides are the people

As with previous versions, the slides themselves are governed by those higher up in the power structure. As with any constituency, the masses have little authority but without them, nothing would be possible.

The mechanics of working with layouts involves skills that any capable PowerPoint user already possesses, regardless of version. Once in Slide Master view, you can select, rename, create new, and delete layouts all with right-clicks. You edit them by adding elements. There are plenty of nuances, and we'll get to them, but the core fundamentals of object creation and placement are no different than regular slide work.

▷ You can only delete a layout if no slide is using it. This is wise insurance for new users, and a source of irritation for advanced users.

Part Two: The Solution

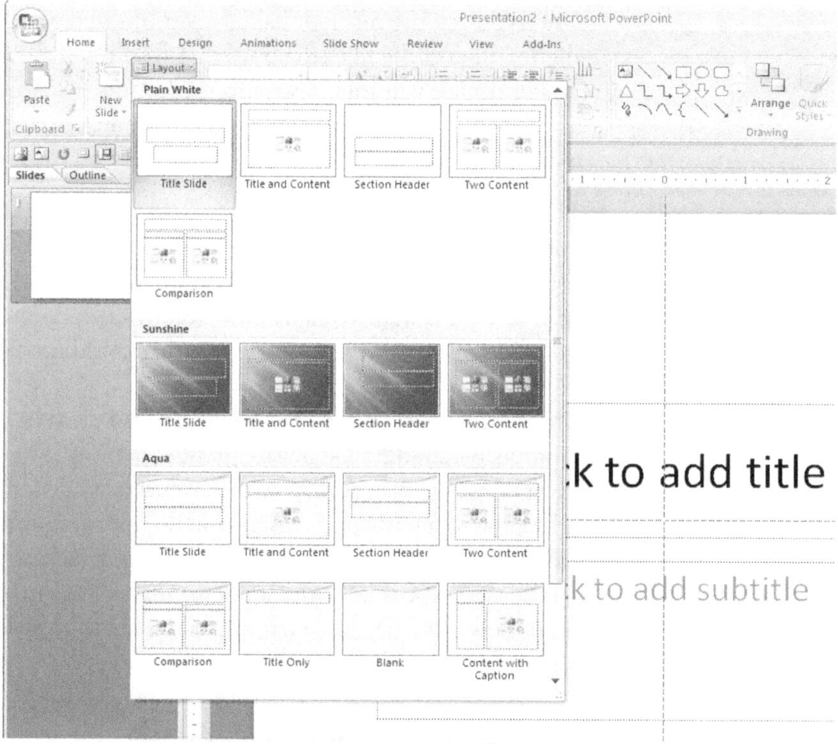

Figure 9.1
This slide deck contains three slide masters and 17 layouts. All 17 are available to be applied to the current slide.

Being Smart With Layouts

Layouts can take on any design motif imaginable—different typefaces, different colors, different animation schemes, different backgrounds. Elements can be moved anywhere on the slide and formatted with all of the robust controls available across the application. It is possible to make layouts of the same slide master look entirely different from one another.

Possible, yes. Wise…that's a deeper conversation. Smart designers resist making these types of wholesale changes to a layout, preferring instead to use the same basic design for all layouts of a given slide master. If a set of slides is to have a radically different look, they create a second master. (And if it really is a single slide that warrants unique treatment, you can just format the slide itself.) Mitigating this is the common practice of creating a layout that takes the theme's accent color and makes it the predominant color. This is typically used for transition slides that signal a shift in topic. And it is done with forethought and care and with regard for the established color scheme.

As with previous versions, there is a lot of flotsam in the layout choices. But unlike previous versions, you can jettison any unwanted layout, and more important, create new layouts. As we observe people using Slide Master view, we note two things:

- Some are hesitant about removing a layout for fear that they might decide later on that they want it after all.

- Others keep all the layouts in place and have difficulty wading through all of them.

Our advice is to make the interface as easy to work as possible and that argues for removing layouts you do not intend to use and making room for your own layouts. We think the more layouts you build from scratch (or clone from existing ones), the more deft you become with the process.

▶ If you remove a layout and later decide you want it back, you can retrieve it from a new presentation with a simple copy-and-paste maneuver. Layouts copy from one presentation to another just as slides do. A pasted layout takes on the attributes of the slide master that it is joining.

Flexibility vs. universality

One of the pleasant problems created by layouts is the question of just how specialized to become. For instance, what if you were creating a slide design that called for some slides to have standard left-aligned text under the title and other slides to have photos to the right of the text? Figure 9.2 shows these two different designs. But should they literally be different designs? Do they need two separate layouts?

- If you create two layouts for them, you might be able to create the slides faster (more flexible).

- If you use one layout for both of them, you can control formatting changes more easily by not having to repeat those changes across two layouts (more universal).

In the top slide, the placeholder's right margin is tighter to allow for the photo, while the bottom slide allows the text to stretch further to the right. With a dedicated layout for the slide with the photo, you would have less slide fiddling to do, no question about it. However, with a criterion as exacting as this, you are liable to create many layouts, making control over them more difficult.

You enjoy far more control than in previous versions, no matter which way you go—whether you group multiple designs around a common layout or make layouts for every design permutation.

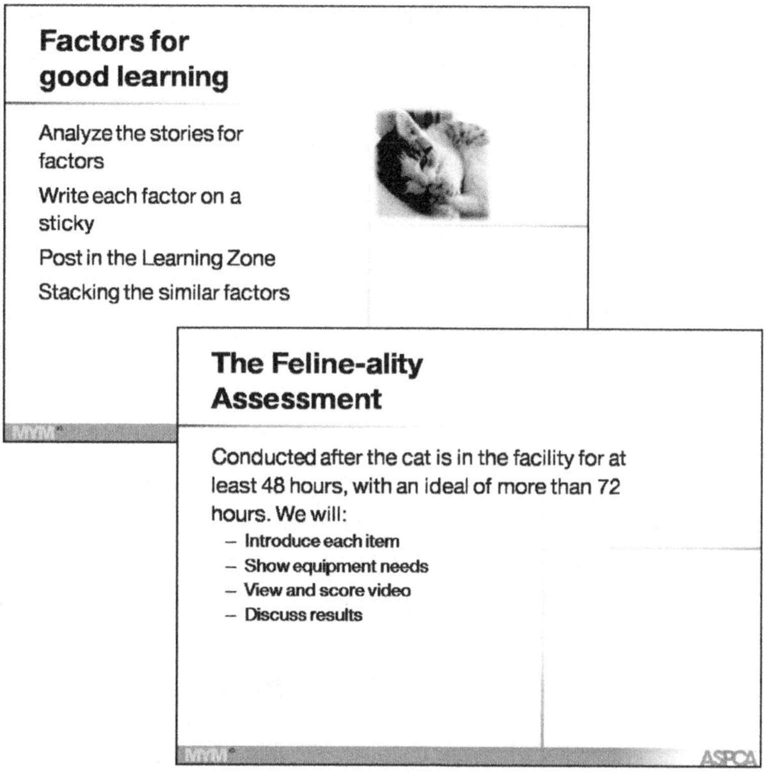

Figure 9.2
Does the presence of a photo warrant the use of a separate layout in Version 2007? Maybe...

We're not willing to offer definitive advice to this question; usage patterns and preferences are so personal and we don't believe there is one right answer. Instead, we suggest you ask two questions of yourself as the litmus test:

- Can I save time and/or effort by creating an extra layout?

- Will I create more work for myself if I have to manage two or more layouts when one layout might do the job?

We will be definitive with one piece of advice: If you regularly backsave to version 2003, think twice about creating many layouts. Layouts are converted to v03 slide masters and the usual result is a mess of redundant slide masters.

Ordering, naming, and identifying

In older versions of the software, slide layouts were displayed in a pre-ordained sequence, irrespective of your usage or preference. Modern versions allow you to determine the order of the layouts and we suggest you take full advantage of that. Furthermore, while you used to be stuck with the names that the developers devised, now you can create your own names and give them much more context than "Title, Content and 2 Content."

See the upcoming case study on the ASPCA for some strategies for layout creation and implementation.

The ASPCA case study also addresses the one aspect of layouts that we think was handled poorly: identifying them. While tool tips identify each layout in Slide Master view, there is nothing to tell you which layout is used when in Normal view. The Status Bar only identifies the name of the Slide Master used by that slide (and it incorrectly refers to it as a "theme"). This is not nearly as useful as knowing which layout is being used by a slide.

Adding Placeholders

We plead guilty to burying the lead: down here on the ninth page of this chapter is perhaps the most valuable aspect of modern layouts—the ability to add additional placeholders to slides.

Let's return to the classic example we alluded to earlier: the title slide that is to serve to introduce each seminar and person speaking at a multi-day conference. Figure 9.3 shows one of the slide designs we used at the 2011 Presentation Summit, created by Tany Nagy of Michigan, the winner of our Design-a-Template contest that year.

This title slide has several elements that should all be consistently formatted across three days and over 40 presentations. In older versions, all elements except title and subtitle would have to be placed on the slide and constantly

Figure 9.3
There are four elements on this slide whose content will change every time, but whose formatting should never change. This is a job for custom placeholders on layouts.

checked against accidental repositioning, reformatting, or other hazards that could befall them. Not so today. Here is how we built this layout:

1. On the slide master itself, we placed all of the background elements: the fence image, the Texas badge, and the red ribbon.

2. While still on the slide master, we assigned basic formatting to the title and text placeholder: 36pt Segoe UI for titles, 24pt Segoe for text. This is not required, just helpful to give layouts a headstart, as layouts inherit these attributes.

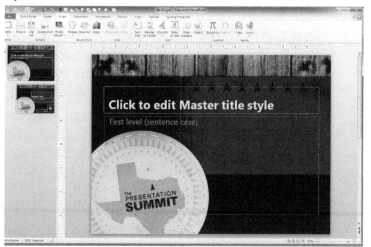

3. On the Title layout, we moved the title into the desired position and changed the placeholder text to read "Seminar Title." This too is not required but we're sick of seeing "Click to edit..." on all of our placeholders.

4. As we did not plan on having subtitles for the seminars, we deleted the subtitle placeholder.

5. From the Slide Master tab of the Ribbon, we clicked Insert Placeholder to get a drop-down menu of our choices.

6. We chose Text and then dragged a marquee in the general location we had laid out for the name of the presenter.
Good thing we can change the placeholder text—what a mess with all five levels of bullets being anticipated. We wish we could change the

Apply layouts via the QAT

The Layout gallery is located on the Home ribbon, which is designed as the location for the most popular commands across the program. Yet Murphy's Law usually demands that I am always on a different ribbon when I want to apply a layout to a slide.

So I have placed the entire Layout gallery on the Quick Access Toolbar. This is most easily done with a simple right-click on the menu. It takes up the sixth position on my QAT, so I have committed to memory that Alt+6 will open it. With my fingers already on the keyboard, I then navigate through my layouts with the arrow keys and then press Enter to apply the one I want.

Much faster and easier than finding it with the mouse.

Right-click your way to a layout

You can also reach the Layout gallery from the context, or right-click menu. You can right-click on an empty part of the slide or on the thumbnail.

Your own custom notes in the slide margin

On the opposite page, I share the trick of creating a text string just off the slide to identify the layout in use. Let's do that maneuver one better with a place to write notes. Just create a text placeholder off the slide, as I have done in Figure 9.5, close enough to the edge so that you can see it while editing the slide. Keep the placeholder narrow and the text small, like about 12pt, and pick a color with good contrast (white if the placeholder is near the bottom where the color is dark or black if you have parked it near the top).

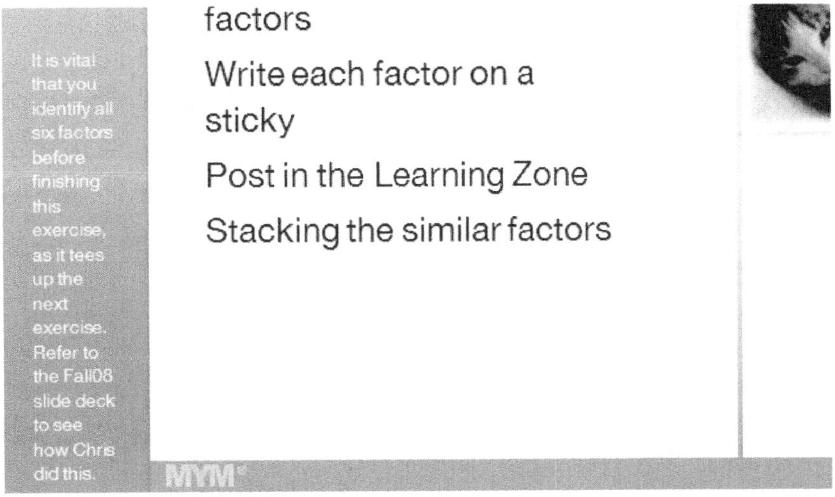

Figure 9.5
Placeholders off the slide can be useful too. This one is for notes to self or commentary to others.

It is vital that you identify all six factors before finishing this exercise, as it tees up the next exercise. Refer to the Fall08 slide deck to see how Chris did this.

factors

Write each factor on a sticky

Post in the Learning Zone

Stacking the similar factors

MYM®

Part Two: The Solution

The Best Templates are .pptx Files Loaded with Content

In observing the behavior of hundreds of clients over the years, we have concluded that template files are best left for the cookie-cutter templates that come with the product. When you create your own templates, make them .pptx files, not .potx files. It makes life easier for all.

When you start a project by applying a .potx file, PowerPoint loads the slide masters, but no content. The idea of a template is to provide a starting point.

But most people prefer a starting point that has content. Boilerplate text, slides that represent typical ideas, builds of specific graphs, skeleton org charts, etc.

Well-conceived templates should include this type of springboard content to jumpstart the creative process. The simplest way to do that is to just use a .pptx file. No matter how you open it, all of your content appears, ready for you to begin tailoring it for the specific project.

At right are four slides from a recent redesign project that included four slide masters and 25 slides of sample content. Having all of this content as part of the template is standard operating procedure for any job that we take. We consider it an indispensible part of any design project.

The only risk to using .pptx files as templates: if you forget to perform a Save As command before embarking on a new project, you overwrite the template. Make the .pptx file read-only to insure against this happening.

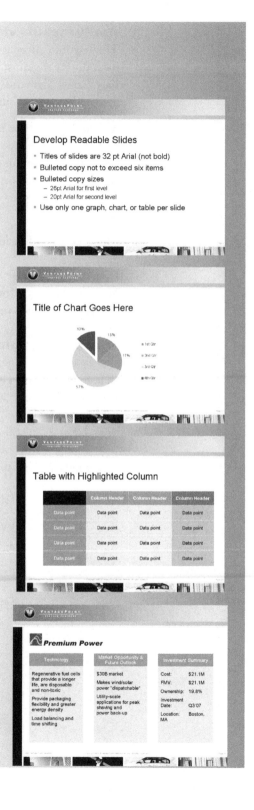

With this placeholder, any slide can now contain notes, instructions, comments, complaints, general whining, and the like. They can be notes to a collaborator or notes to yourself. I have found this preferable to using the Notes window at the bottom, which might or might not be visible or deep enough. On my wide-screen monitor, though, I rarely lack horizontal space so the area to the left or right of the slide is always visible.

Two clicks get you a new slide and a layout

The New Slide command on the Home ribbon does just what you would expect it to do. But if you click the lower-half of the icon, the part with the downward-pointing arrow, you are taken to the now-familiar Layout gallery, allowing you to designate which layout your new slide is to have.

Chapter 10

The Theory
Of the Theme

If slide masters and layouts represent the most significant change from older versions of PowerPoint, the idea of the Theme is the most dramatic, and perhaps the most glitzy. With a theme, you can not only create a fully-branded look and feel for your slide decks, you can extend it out to your other Office documents.

While themes work as promised, we remain as unconvinced as when we first surveyed them that users are willing to make the effort to use them to capacity. It reminds us of the way that most users approach color schemes of earlier versions: with uncertainty and a lack of confidence.

When we first wrote up this part for the second edition, we had it tacked on to the end of the previous chapter and it wasn't until almost press time that we decided to give it its own chapter. The irony here is that now, two years later, we could probably write an entire book on this topic...

10

Just Make It Look Good!

At the simplest level, applying a theme is an easy way to spiff up a slide deck, with easy-to-apply designs that are much more integrated, coordinated, and attractive than the template files that came with older versions. The Design ribbon offers a gateway to 20 themes and you can hover over any one of them to see how the current slide would look with that theme applied to it. You can also get one-click access to dozens of professionally-crafted themes, such as the two in Figure 10.1.

Although a theme is a better starting point than the old .pot files, we'd be happier if you created your own themes around your company branding. Just like the ocean/sunset template, these too are likely to become clichés, and if they do, they don't speak well of those who use them.

One Theme Equals Three Schemes

A theme contains slide masters and layouts, including any that you create yourself, and is further comprised of three distinct elements that together define the total look and feel of a slide deck:

- A set of theme colors, containing 12 color definitions—four more than in previous versions but otherwise similar.

- A set of theme fonts, a simple pairing of two typefaces—one applied to titles and one to text.

Figure 10.1
Two themes from the Office website, downloaded and applied to slides in about 30 seconds.

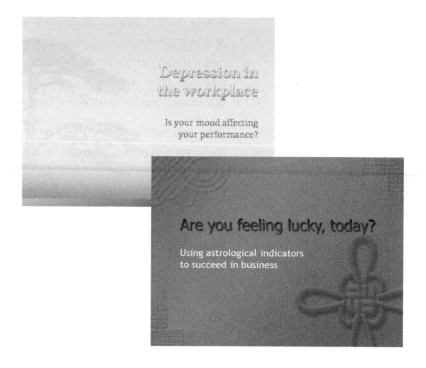

■ A set of theme effects, holding information about fill patterns, outlines, special effects, and backgrounds.

▶ You can apply these theme effects to a slide deck all at once or you can apply any one scheme by itself. The first two schemes mentioned above are user-servicable, sure to be the source of interest to advanced users. More on that soon.

Themes are the next generation of templates and can be used as starting points for new slide decks or applied to existing ones. Like standard .pptx files, they are written in the XML language, making them very portable and pliable. Theme files have .thmx extensions and if you were to study a .pptx and a .thmx file, you would find many similarities in content and structure. In fact, you can tell PowerPoint to load a theme from a .pptx file and it will do so with no backtalk at all.

If you can get a theme from a PowerPoint file, why bother with theme files? Their value is in their portability, to other people and to other applications.

Send a theme to a colleague
If you create a slide deck that is to serve as the model for others, you can save it as a .thmx file (File | Save As | Office Theme) and send it to a client or co-worker. This is similar to sending a .pot file, and our advice from Chapter 9 holds: it is often better to send a regular PowerPoint file than a content-less template file. Nonetheless, when you share a .thmx file with another, you send that person every master, every layout, the color scheme, and font and special effects information.

Send a theme to your Office
The more interesting twist to this is the extensibility with other Office applications. The theme you create in PowerPoint can be applied to a Word document, an Excel worksheet, and Outlook stationery. This is branding on steroids: backgrounds, type choices, color palettes—they can all be standardized across your Office documents.

Each Office app has a Themes button that contains a Browse for Themes command. Use that in your other apps to retrieve a theme from PowerPoint and you're on your way to a more unified look across your documents.

As interesting and as impressive as this intramural feature is, I have my doubts that many users are willing to go this extra mile with themes. Here is why I feel this way:

Figure 10.2
The Colors drop-down is loaded with well-crafted color themes, as well as ones that you can create yourself.

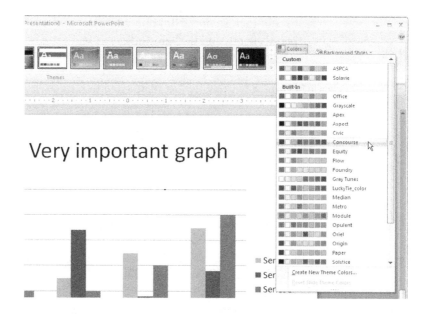

- I have watched for the better part of 10 years now how users wrestle with color schemes, a simpler paradigm than themes. I have concluded that most users are content to create slides that look good unto themselves.

- I wonder how important coordinated documentation is to most organizations. Is it vital that Word files look like PowerPoint slides? Perhaps it is enough that the logo is there. If you think I'm wrong about this, I'd like to hear it.

Even if we all get stage fright around extending themes out to our other Office apps, there is considerable value in being able to coordinate the elements of a slide deck. When you use a properly-created theme, you ensure

48pt Heads in Word?

While it might be appropriate to have large titles on a slide, the same format applied to a headline in a document would constitute Death by Word. And what if you created a theme with a dark background and then used it within Excel—would every cell become reversed out?

No, thankfully.

Themes have many soft definitions built in, so the receiving application can use a bit of discretion. Word automatically dials back the title size when determining point size for Heading 1, and both Word and Excel will adjust colors to work with white backgrounds.

that there is good contrast between foreground and background, that accent colors work well together, and that typefaces are complementary.

The question of color

If you agree with me that the most important contribution of the theme is to ensure better-looking slides, you will find much to like with the reworked color schemes. While colors are integral to a theme, you can deviate from them and not find yourself in design purgatory. If you go fishing in the Colors drop-down menu, like in Figure 10.2, you can choose between a host of color schemes, all of which provide nice complementary and contrasting color combinations.

▷ PowerPoint versions alternate between using "theme color" and "color scheme." They mean the same thing and can be used interchangeably.

You can also create your own color schemes, and this of course, you do at your own risk. If you set a pink background for your white text, no theme is going to be able to save you. Nonetheless, to create your own color scheme, do this:

1. From the Colors drop-down, click Create New Theme Colors. You'll be greeted with an intuitive dialog box for changing each of the colors that make up the scheme.

2. Edit each color swatch as desired and then provide a name for the scheme.

The color scheme in modern versions of PowerPoint is tremendously matured over previous versions, in which color schemes would accumulate like hangers in the closet and discourage users from truly connecting with them. When you save a color scheme now, two important things happen: 1) the scheme shows up, identified by name, in the Custom section of the menu; and 2) an .xml file is created and stored on your computer.

Part Two: The Solution

Unlike with older versions, the color scheme is not document-centric; it will be available across the application, for as long as its .xml file resides in the folder on your computer in which it was created. Any color scheme I make for any project will be available for other projects.

Judging from Figure 10.2, I have files by the name of ASPCA.xml and Solavie.xml on my computer (indeed, two recent client projects). And they are not complete jibberish—here is what one of them looks like:

```
<?xml version="1.0" encoding="UTF-8" standalone="yes"?>
<a:clrScheme
xmlns:a="http://schemas.openxmlformats.org/drawingml/2006/m
ain" name="ASPCA">
    <a:dk1>
        <a:sysClr val="windowText" lastClr="000000"/>
    </a:dk1>
    <a:lt1>
        <a:sysClr val="window" lastClr="FFFFFF"/>
    </a:lt1>
    <a:dk2>
        <a:srgbClr val="1F497D"/>
    </a:dk2>
    <a:lt2>
        <a:srgbClr val="C2C4C6"/>
    </a:lt2>
    <a:accent1>
        <a:srgbClr val="F79239"/>
    </a:accent1>
        <a:accent2><a:srgbClr val="6B2C91"/>
    </a:accent2>
        <a:accent3><a:srgbClr val="9BCD65"/>
    </a:accent3>
        <a:accent4><a:srgbClr val="8064A2"/>
    </a:accent4>
        <a:accent5><a:srgbClr val="4BACC6"/>
    </a:accent5>
        <a:accent6><a:srgbClr val="F79646"/>
    </a:accent6>
        <a:hlink><a:srgbClr val="0000FF"/>
    </a:hlink>
        <a:folHlink><a:srgbClr val="800080"/>
    </a:folHlink>
</a:clrScheme>
```

This is not exactly like reading the cartoons, but many web designers and most programmers will recognize the structures and the statements here. The six characters after the "val=" are the hex values of each color, and you could edit them directly if you were so inclined.

- The slideMasters folder contains the masters.

- The theme subfolder contains a combined color/font/effects information file, one for each master.

XML programmers can build themes completely outside of PowerPoint. Likewise, reckless users can ruin themes outside of PowerPoint.

So create a backup. And don't forget to rename the extension back to .thmx when you're done...

PPTX Files Like to Misbehave When You Email them

Those who regularly cart around PowerPoint files have already discovered that their files behave differently than older version files, and this has everything to do with the fact that they are actually .zip files masquerading as something else. Therefore, email and download links often identify them incorrectly, treat them like .zip files, and proceed to serve up garbage. To address this issue, there is a perfect solution and a bandaid.

The perfect solution is to contact your IT team or your ISP and ask for the Office 2007/2010 file types to be added to the list of kosher formats. In geek speak, this is called a MIME table.

If the thought of that produces a migraine, here are two bandaids for you: 1) Place the V07 file inside of a .zip file (yes, a .zip within a .zip) and send that file off, with the instructions to unzip it on the receiving end; or 2) Rename the .pptx extension to .zip, send it off, with the instructions to rename it back upon receipt.

Of the two bandaids, Door No. 1 is the safer route, given that most people know what to do when they see a .zip file. Door No. 2 involves an easier procedure (renaming as opposed to unzipping), except that it is not clear that this is the course of action unless there are instructions accompanying the file, and many Windows systems remain in the default condition of hiding extensions.

Chapter 11

Creating Shows Within Your Show

If you were to poll 20 experts in PowerPoint usage, it is entirely likely that exactly none of them would list the topic of this chapter as among the most vital. And that is the beauty of writing a book that is designed to be uneven: I can indulge in the arcane and burrow into the obscure, and there's nothing you can do about it!

Lucky you, because while doing all of that burrowing, I have unearthed a topic that is one of PowerPoint's unsung heroes.

You might go several weeks at a time without using it. You might only use it in specific situations. But the fluent practitioners of their craft recognize the creation of the custom show as one of the jewels that combines flexibility with economy of effort.

One File, Many Shows

At its core, the Custom Show engine is a means by which you can create a subset of a presentation. By implication, that means you can also create a superset presentation: you can develop all of the slides that you anticipate that you might *ever* use on a given topic, and then slice and dice them for any given presentation.

By creating custom shows, one presentation file can contain several combinations of slides. Slides 1-5...slides 2, 5, 12, and 80...slides 54, 53, 52, and 10...slides 3, 4, 4, 4, 5, 5, and 6. Any combination, any order, any sequence. Change any slide in the presentation, and it changes for all the custom shows that use it. Imagine the time you could save by not creating multiple versions of the same presentation.

Creating a custom show is not unlike hiding a group of slides, but it is more flexible. While you can only hide/unhide one group of slides at a time, you can create many custom shows:

1. Go to Slide Show | Custom Shows, click New, and devise a name for your custom show.

2. From the list on the left of every slide in the current file, double-click the ones you want to include in the custom show.

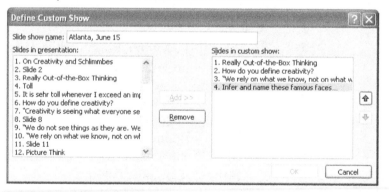

Most of the slides are identified explicitly here, but not all of them. If the slide has a title, this dialog box will show it to you. In this case, Slides 2, 8, and 11 do not; hence the generic identifier for them.

3. Click OK and then Close.

4. To use a custom show, go to Slide Show | Set Up Show.

5. In the Show Slides section, click Custom Show and highlight the name of the show you created in the drop-down list.

The next time you show this presentation, only the slides in the custom show will display. You can also run a custom show directly from the Custom Show dialog.

Less Flotsam, Better Focus

This beats the stuffing out of giving a presentation that is full of slides that you know you won't get to, yet that happens thousands of time every day. Nothing like motoring through two dozen slides in five seconds to detract from your core message.

As bad as that sounds, it's better than what *Presentations* magazine recommended several years ago: for each type of presentation you might give, save the PowerPoint file under a different name and then remove the slides you don't want.

Talk about flotsam! What happens when it's time to update the main content? How many versions of the presentation file will you have to open and change? Granted, tailoring a presentation for a particular client or situation is standard procedure, but it should be done from a single slide deck that you clearly recognize as the most current and up-to-date version of your presentation. That can't happen if you have several different versions, each claiming to function as a base presentation or a template.

And let's be clear here that it really doesn't matter if your template is an actual template file, with a .potx extension, or a plain old .pptx file. As we discussed in the last few chapters, there is no real difference between them. The best argument for using a template file is the insurance against inadvertently overwriting the file because you forgot to perform a Save As. The opposing argument is that it is not very easy to make changes to it when you really want to.

But we don't care on which side of that fence you choose to live: having all of your content in one file is the important tonic here, and knowing about custom shows is the straw that stirs that drink.

E=Makeover x Custom Shows^2

You might know one of my clients: his name is Albert Einstein. Arden Bercovitz does a very good Einstein impersonation and he has been touring the country delivering uplifting and motivating lectures as the brilliant scientist/philosopher.

He appeared at the Presentation Summit a few years ago, but before presenting to a group of presentation pros, he knew that his slides needed an overhaul. He is not a slave to bullets and speaks to his visuals like a pro. But as you can see from his slide master in Figure 11.2, he has not benefited from working with a graphic designer.

De-cluttering his slides and cleaning up his look was not difficult, and Figure 11.3 shows the basic makeover that I performed for him. Just two layouts —one for basic content and one for quotes from the good doctor, with an image of him faded into the background. You'll notice that the standard slide master, the first thumbnail, has no bullet—just centered text.

Figure 11.2
Albert Einstein would probably have designed slides like this back in his day, but the modern-day Einstein wanted a more professional look.

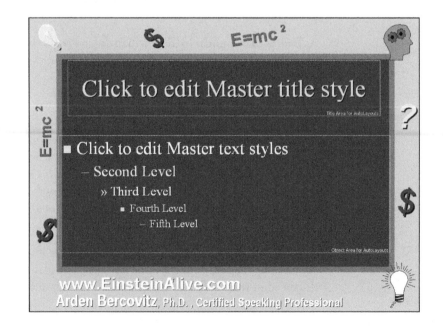

Figure 11.3
No reason Albert shouldn't benefit from a cleaner, more unified look.

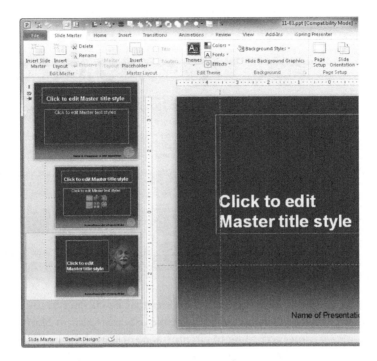

The bigger challenge was accommodating all of his ideas and the creative ways he expressed them. The side-by-side photos of Mona Lisa and Mr. Spock...the coining of "Schlimmbe" (improvements that make things worse), and some great quotes ("The only sure way to avoid mistakes is to have no new ideas").

I recommended to Arden that he prepare for a presentation by acting out the role of Jim Phelps in *Mission: Impossible.* The baby boomers among our readers might remember the classic opening to the television show, right after the tape self-destructed in five seconds. Jim would sit at his coffee table and prepare his IM force. He would browse through the dossiers of several secret agents, figuring out the best match for the specific impossible task ahead. He would invariably pick the same people—television casting budgets being what they were in the 1960s—but the impression created was that he hand-picked just the right players for the team he needed to have.

Arden liked that analogy but was quick to point out that he might change his mind about which slides to use right up to the morning of a keynote. He didn't want to be locked into a specific set of slides.

This has custom show written all over it. As you can see from Figure 11.4, Arden's slide deck is tremendously vast. Just look at the scroll bar along the right edge for an idea of how many slides are in this deck.

Figure 11.4
One presentation file...a lifetime of slides...

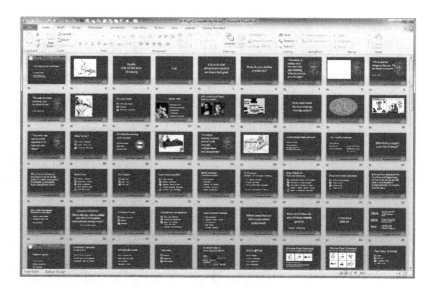

From here, he picks the slides that he chooses to use on a given day. Instead of Jim Phelps' coffee table, he uses the Custom Show dialog box. At any time, according to circumstance or mood, he can modify the custom show to add or remove slides.

Arden could go one step further and build standard shows into his template. As Figure 11.5 illustrates, if his lectures fall into general categories, he can build custom shows for those categories that give him an excellent starting point to building a particular presentation.

Just so we're clear, I'm not suggesting that Arden, or you, work off of the same file for every presentation. That is not realistic—you will surely be adding specific content that suits the client or the situation. Hence, you will

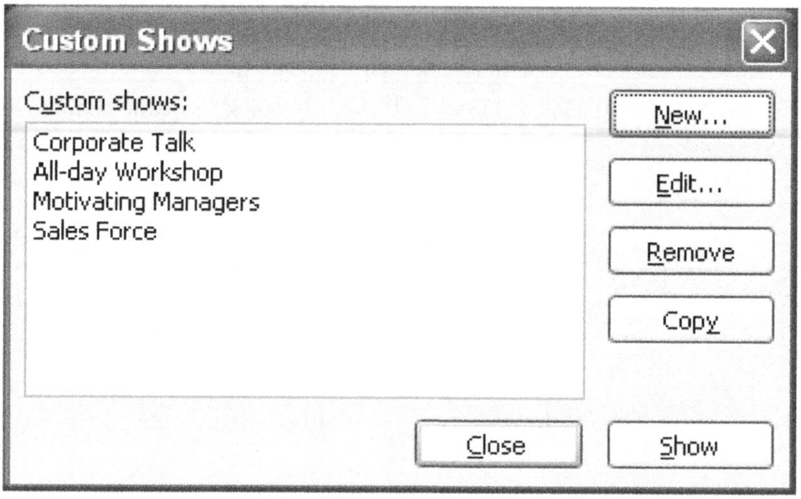

Figure 11.5
If you have a handful of typical presentations you give, you can create generic custom shows to jump-start the process.

invariably be saving your template file under a specific name and customizing it from there.

The key is what spawns this custom file, and the more complete your template, the better your starting point. When you get comfortable with custom shows, you can begin to think like Jim Phelps or the head coach or manager of your favorite team (warning, runaway sports analogy ahead). You have your players and for each game, you assemble the best team you can. Your starting players are in your custom show; the rest are on your bench, ready to see action at a moment's notice.

May your players all be all-stars and may your team win the championship. Groan...

♦

The custom show plays a key role in what we consider to be one of the most powerful and advanced maneuvers available to PowerPoint users. Check in with Chapter 25 to read about how custom shows and a few strategically placed hyperlinks can completely transform the way you might choreograph a presentation.

2. Using the layering commands, place the rectangle behind the text but in front of the photo. The slide should look like it has white text on a dark blue background.

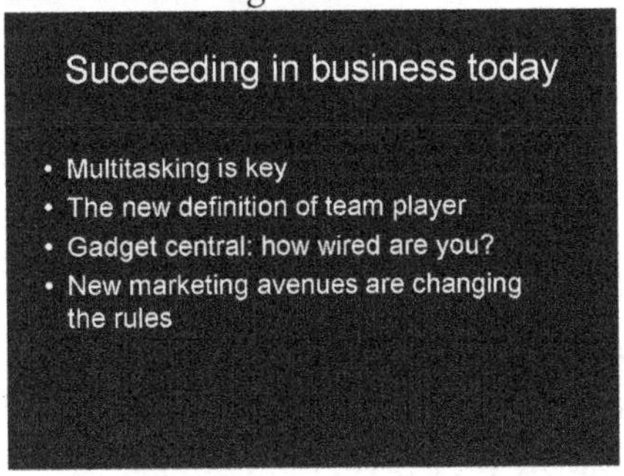

3. Right-click the rectangle and choose Format Shape.

4. Drag the Transparency slider to the right, watching the interactive preview to survey various values. At 10-15%, you can just barely see the photo:

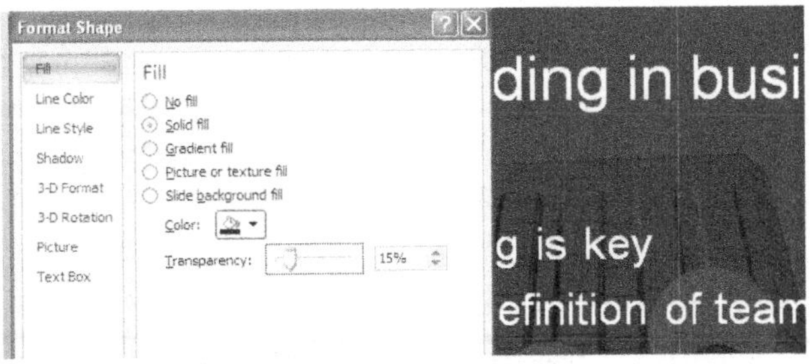

5. Click OK when you have found a satisfactory value. Figure 12.3 shows how a 15% transparency makes the text on the slide perfectly readable.

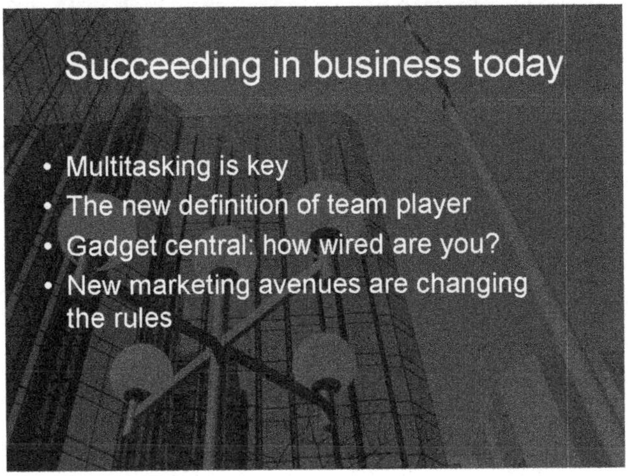

Figure 12.3
A transparent rectangle draped over the photo reduces its contrast and makes it more suitable as a background.

Download 12-03.pptx to see how this effect is created.

Part Two: The Solution

This simple technique of the semi-transparent rectangle has broad implications so I want us to stay here for a couple of paragraphs. Once you know how to tint back a photo, you make it possible to use practically any photo as a background. As we discussed in Chapter 4, overly loud backgrounds are among the most annoying qualities in all of PowerPointdom. With one rectangle, you can eliminate this source of annoyance.

In the steps above, I used navy blue for the rectangle's fill because it matched the predominant color of the photo. I could also have used black (dramatic), white (for a washout effect, to be used with dark text), brown (urban), or green (environmental). In each case when you drape a color over the photo you mute all of its colors and reduce its contrast, making it a suitable candidate for a background image.

Native solutions

With the modern versions come improved graphic support, including effects previously possible only with the use of another shape or an image-editing program like Adobe Photoshop or Corel PhotoPaint or PaintShop Pro.

For instance, instead of draping a photo with a semi-transparent shape, you can apply a tint to the photo itself to create a low-contrast version of it. Figure 12.4 shows the result of 15 seconds spent with the Recolor command within the Format Picture dialog (accessible from the Format ribbon or the right-click menu).

It's worth spending a few minutes with that gallery, as the amount of creative control you can wield over photos is impressive, almost daunting.

Figure 12.4
Modern versions can tint a photo without needing any help from transparent shapes.

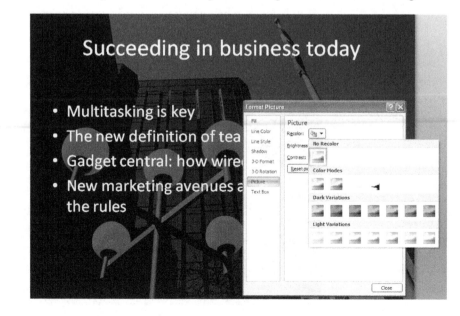

Figure 12.5
A few of the many built-in PowerPoint effects that can be applied to imported photos. Each of these photos was imported as a conventional rectangular image.

From soft shadows to glows, bevels to extrusions, you might feel like the kid in the candy store. The Format ribbon offers numerous presets in addition to the more sophisticated Picture Tools dialog.

Witness Figure 12.5—a slide of imported images. The original photos are all rectangular and unadorned; nothing was done to any of them with outside software. All of the perspective shifts, shadows, cropping, and framing are one-click options from the Format ribbon.

◆

As impressive as this is, for basic photo tinting, we actually prefer our transparent rectangle technique. Yes, it is a bit of extra work, but it is more flexible. You have more control over the color and adjusting the transparency slider is easier to understand than playing footsie with Brightness and Contrast. Furthermore, you can set a gradient transparency that changes the degree of transparency across the span of the rectangle. You can't do that with the photo effect controls.

At the end of the day, PowerPoint's built-in image controls provide more choices for creativity, and that can only be a good thing.

Half transparent, half opaque

There are times when sinking a photo into the background is exactly what you want and other times when a strong photo needs to remain prominent. In the latter case, you can solve major design challenges by applying a twist to the transparent shape strategy.

Figure 12.6 shows one possible implementation, as the text has been confined to one corner and the transparent rectangle shrunk down to fit in that space.

All of Figure 12.6 can be programmed from a layout: the full-screen photo, the transparent rectangle, the title contained within that small space, and the bullets underneath them. You'll need to be heavy-handed with content editing, as many standard-length titles would be too long and you'd be hard-pressed to fit more than four bullets into that space. Hmm, another benefit to this design...

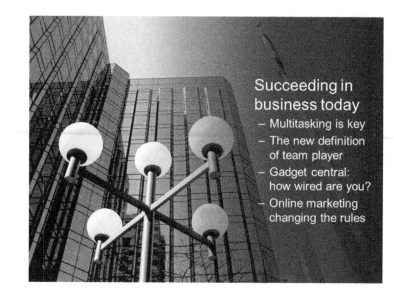

Figure 12.7 shows the use of a gradient transparency, where the level of transparency gradually changes. There are two things worth noting:

- You create a gradient transparency by choosing to blend from one color to the same color, varying the transparency value for each.

- I did not create a rectangle behind the text; instead, I used the text placeholder itself. It can accept a fill pattern and be fitted with transparency, just like any other shape. From the Format Shape dialog, you can set margins and determine where the text resides within the space. Perhaps most important, it means that it can all be programmed onto a layout, which you could see for yourself by downloading the file.

Figure 12.8
This nice effect was created entirely within PowerPoint.

Applying Transparency to Photos

So far, this chapter has focused on applying transparency to simple shapes and placing them atop photos and images. The ante gets upped when we talk about applying transparency directly to the photo. This is not simple stuff, but it's worth the effort as the effects you can create are potentially breathtaking.

Figure 12.8 shows two transparent effects—the basic text and the more elaborate photo—and while the golfer looks like it needs the help of outside software, both of these effects are in fact native to PowerPoint. In older versions, you would have to turn to WordArt to create transparent text; in modern versions, you can apply transparency to any string of text.

But the photo, with its elliptical boundary and semi-transparent quality—the fact that its native address is PowerPoint might be more surprising to you, and it presents an interesting cognitive challenge. PowerPoint can change the shape of an imported photo but it cannot apply transparency to it. You earn brownie points for even trying to solve this puzzle. Let's review a few facts that we know:

- PowerPoint can apply transparency to vector shapes, provided they are closed.

- An ellipse is a closed shape.

- Of the many fill patterns available, one of the options is to fill a shape with a photo.

- Irrespective of what's inside the ellipse, it can still be made transparent. Here's how you would do it:

1. Create an ellipse large enough so that half of it is hanging off the right side of the slide.

2. From the Home or Format ribbon, click Shape Fill to invoke its drop-down menu.

3. Choose Picture and find the photo you want inside the shape.

▼ Download 12-08.pptx to see how we did this.

In this case, you are simply instructing PowerPoint to apply transparency to the ellipse. If the ellipse were filled with the color blue, you would see through to the photo underneath, which would be cast in a blue tint. In this case, we suppose you could say that the photo underneath is cast in a golfer tint. And again, you're only seeing half of the ellipse because the other half is being hung off of the slide. Open the file and you can see this treatment for yourself.

Working with graphics software

As impressive as this is, the real power in these types of effects lies in your intelligent use of an external image-editing or graphic-drawing program. In the age of digital photography, fewer people understand the distinction between the two main types of graphics programs, vector and bitmap. They buy a camera and go on auto-pilot with whatever software is found on the accompanying CD. They tend to gloss over the fundamentals:

- Graphic-drawing software creates high-quality shapes based on mathematics (vectors). The most common programs in this space are Adobe Illustrator and CorelDraw.

- Image-editing software deals in pixels and turns its attention to photos, where you could literally change any one dot of an image. The most

A Gallery of Transparency

Applying transparency to elements on a slide can serve three important purposes:

1. It helps with contrast issues.

2. It helps integrate photos and images into a single visual message.

3. It softens elements and provides elegance.

At its simplest level, a semi-transparent placeholder for text provides integration with text and photos. Compared with the standard treatment of a solid colored boundary for the text, everything about this simple technique says that you gave a moment of thought to how best to drive home the point visually that all forms of travel constitute a significant financial investment (Figure 1) or that a prime piece of real estate could be tastefully developed (Figure 2).

The next two images give away one of our lead author's favorite techniques: the graduated transparency. It can be used to provide a soft border between the text and the photo as in Figure 3 or to eliminate the border altogether as in Figure 4. In Figure 3, it was easiest to create a thin black rectangle over the transition area, traversing from 100% opaque to 100% transparent. With Figure 4, one long rectangle can take care of the entire effect. Few things are more evocative to an audience than when you blend

continued...

Part Two: The Solution

meaningful imagery with simple text messages, and the use of semi-transparency helps you create that blend.

Modern versions support soft edges to photos which makes easier the task in Figure 5. In order to show only two of the edges as soft, we have to nudge the photo off the right edge of the slide and slip it under the footer below it. In older versions, you could only soften one side, using the gradient rectangle technique.

Figure 6 has a lot going on. The vertical text is tinted deep into the ocean and the text box is set with 50% transparency. The soft shadow behind the text box is simple work for PowerPoint, but the soft transition between the two photos needs the deft virtual hand of a dedicated image-editing program.

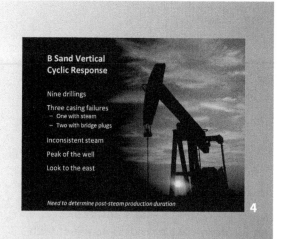

common program in this category is Adobe Photoshop, with Corel offering PhotoPaint and Paint Shop Pro.

Both categories of software have applications capable of creating transparent images that can be understood by PowerPoint. To get technical on you, these advanced programs create an *alpha channel*—an area of data reserved for transparent information.

To get downright geeky, computer monitors display color using the RGB model: all color is divided into percentages of red, green, and blue, and any software program that deals even in rudimentary color reserves three 8-bit channels for describing these three colors.

Professional-grade graphics and image-editing applications work with a fourth channel, the so-called alpha channel, which specifies how a pixel's color is to be merged with another pixel when the two are placed one atop the other. This is also referred to as a mask.

Before your eyes roll into the back of your head, know this: however these programs go about creating this magic, PowerPoint understands it. There aren't many file formats capable of delivering alpha channel information, and most of them are the formats native to the programs that deal in them:

- Adobe Photoshop (.psd)
- Adobe Illustrator (.ai)
- CorelDraw (.cdr)
- Corel PhotoPaint (.cpt)
- Corel Paint Shop Pro (.psp)

PowerPoint cannot read any of these formats, but it does just fine with the PNG (Portable Network Graphics) format (pronounced *ping*). This is the one generic bitmap format capable of containing alpha channel information and all of the programs listed above can export to this format. PowerPoint will also follow alpha channel instructions in transparent TIFF files, but they are not as easy to create and fewer applications offer that export choice.

▶ There is another format that supports transparency, the GIF format, but we recommend against its use. Its limited color palette (just 256 colors) and inability to make more than one color transparent makes it ill-suited for this type of work. Use it if you want to import an animated GIF file.

Figure 12.9
Nothing like a
visible bounding
box to ruin a
perfectly fine
design idea.

Going non-rectangular

When you import a standard image or graphic to PowerPoint, it comes in as a rectangle. A graphic has a *bounding box* that defines its size, and PowerPoint allocates that size and shape for the graphic, irrespective of whether it fills that size. This is why you might have been tripped up by the likes of Figure 12.9, where non-rectangular images import to PowerPoint with white space.

At the core of your challenge is the export of your non-rectangular and/or transparent images with the alpha channel information. This involves telling your software to pay attention to a portion of the photo, not the entire one, and each program will differ in the terminology that it uses:

- In Adobe Photoshop, you use the Marquee tool to define the shape and create a layer from the marquee (right-click | Layer via Cut). Then you use the Save As or Save As Web command, choosing PNG as the format.

Figure 12.13
Complex
transparency like
this can be
accurately
described by the
alpha channel.

Part Two: The Solution

 Download
couples.zip to see
the PNG files
created from each
program.

support for both vector graphics and bitmap images and its ease of use. Figure 12.13 shows one of the choices in Draw's suite of interactive transparency tools, which can be applied to any object. This one is called "radial transparency," where a ring is defined from the inside (completely opaque) to the outside (completely transparent).

This is a complicated effect, in which the degree of transparency is constantly changing across the face of the image. Nonetheless, a PNG file can ingest all of it and PowerPoint can digest it. Figure 12.14 shows the

Figure 12.14
When PowerPoint
imports a complex
PNG file, it figures it
all out.

But Will It Print??

Transparent shapes and images are wonderful for slide shows, but they are hell on printers. Many printers freak out with all of that alpha channel hocus pocus, providing results far below any professional standard you would set. Look at the mess that Adobe Acrobat made over our golfer in the top image. And this is the printing standard of the industry!

Reason No. 72b to thank our lucky stars that the presentation medium is so forgiving. No stars, however, will be of any help or solace if you need to get a clean print of a complex slide. You have two viable options:

1. Save the slide as a TIFF file and print it. By saving the slide as a bitmap, you essentially instruct PowerPoint to depict the image as it looks, not as it was created. This strategy is great for a few slides, terrible for 100.

2. Use PowerPoint's built-in PDF creation tool, which ironically is much better than Acrobat for this type of work. As you can see at left, PowerPoint handles the vagaries of transparency just fine when sending out to PDF.

▼ Download 12-
14.pptx to see the
effect.

potential drama created with these effects. Add a medium-speed fade
entrance to it and you really have something extraordinary.

Raising Your Graphic IQ

It's an annual reality check when I ask patrons at the Presentation Summit
whether they use graphics software. One year, we asked for the difference
between vector and bitmap graphics and the answers were eye-opening:

"Both are graphics; aren't they the same??"

**"That's too complicated—just give me something that lets
me go Ctrl+C on."**

**"When I double-click a photo, some program opens. I just
use that."**

"What's a graphic?"

Furthermore, we find a startlingly high number of PowerPoint users who
settle for the meager tools built into versions 2003 and earlier. To them, a
graphic is a star or a triangle. They take this limitation for granted and that
stunts their growth as creative professionals.

Modern versions offer dramatic breakthroughs in terms of capability, but
not necessarily in terms of understanding. A significant percentage of
PowerPoint users are likely to continue clicking buttons to make things
happen and go on not understanding the field of graphics.

This phenomenon is not limited to those in the presentation community;
we see a world-wide indifference toward creative tools that were once considered *de rigeur*. We note two reasons for this:

- Today, most people associate computer-based graphics with digital
photography, where the hardware purchase is seen as tantamount. Cameras
usually come with a CD of software and whatever (often flimsy) programs
are present on that CD make up that person's creative suite. They just want
something that can work with their digital photos.

- The standard application, Adobe Photoshop, is expensive. Even though
the cheaper Elements version, under $200, would satisfy most needs, the
$699 for Photoshop CS or the $1,800 for the Creative Suite is what gets
their attention in the way of severe sticker shock.

This is why I have been pleased to see Corel make an effort to appeal to the presentation professional with its CorelDraw Suite. For pricing about half of Photoshop CS, you can purchase a bundle that includes vector-drawing and bitmap-editing programs, both offering more power than you'd ever need.

◆

However you get there and with whatever program you choose, becoming proficient with graphic software is key to your development as a presentation designer. Suddenly, you have answers to questions that might have plagued you over the years:

I have a PDF file with text and photos that I want to use; how do I do separate out those elements to import them to PowerPoint? *You open the PDF file in a graphics program like CorelDraw or Adobe Illustrator that knows how to read, recognize, and separate out its parts, and then you export the parts you need as separate files.*

I received a logo from a client and it looks terrible. What can I do to improve it? *You can recreate it in a good vector graphic program, possibly using a tool that will automatically trace the logo for you.*

The client's logo was delivered to me as an EPS file and my version of PowerPoint can't load it. *Open the EPS file in your graphic program and then export it in a different format. (PowerPoint can read EPS files, but not as well as graphic software.)*

The stock photo I purchased of a race car has a terrible background, full of people working in the pits and cars strewn around. What can I do? *You can select the race car, remove it from the scene and place it in a better scene.*

The photo of the girl blowing out her birthday candles has a snot-nosed kid next to her. *Remove him, using the Clone tool of any image-editing program.*

The photo is way too dark. *Adjust the exposure. Yes, you can do this in PowerPoint; we want you to be able to do it in image-editing software, too.*

I want to take the background of my main photo and (pick one) blur it, make it black and white, vignette it, duotone it, recolor it, change its perspective, apply a stained glass to it, add rain, snow, or fog, or do about a thousand other things that I can't yet even imagine. *You get the idea...*

Chapter 13

Thriving with Animation

Chapter Six concluded with the following statement:

> **When done correctly, animation
> can be a beautiful thing.**

Do you recall that? Do you recall reading that and then hurling epithets in my direction? Did you accuse me of hallucinating? After all, when is the last time you remember a PowerPoint animation being beautiful? There are two reasons why the answer might be never:

- Animation might be single-handedly responsible for more PowerPoint annoyance than all the other annoyances combined. Between Edward Tufte and Dilbert creator Scott Adams, PowerPoint animation is publicly flogged more often than our politicians are.

- When done correctly, animation isn't noticed at all.

Good PowerPoint animation is so seamless that you are unaware of it. It reaches its zenith when it allows audience members to become lost in the story you are telling. Therefore, in those rare moments when it is worthy, it rarely gets the credit it deserves.

13

I approach this chapter with the same fear and trepidation that I do our seminars on the topic at the Presentation Summit. This chapter, and the one that follows, will probably be the most widely-read in the book, just as our seminars on the subject invariably play to standing-room-only audiences. I know that your appetite for the subject is insatiable, and that your zeal could send you across the bounds of good taste if you are not careful.

And when that happens, it's my fault. I'm helping you commit Death by PowerPoint. As we said in Part I, your audience members are at your whim with the use of animation, as just about any movement demands their attention. We even go as far as to define it as our Universal Axiom No. 1:

> **When something moves on screen, your**
> **audience has no choice but to watch it.**

They often are not aware of this; it is not always a conscious reaction on their part. They just know that they left your presentation with eye fatigue and a general feeling of being yanked around against their will.

Indeed, this is enormous power you have over your audience and the larger issue is how seriously you take that responsibility. If you consider it a sacred covenant, you are on the road to creating trust with them. If you abuse it, you break trust. So please repeat after me these holy vows of animation:

- I will use animation wisely and appropriately.

- I vow not to offend the sensibilities of my audience.

- I promise not to use an animation technique simply because I just discovered it.

- I swear never to make stuff move on screen just because I like to watch my audience members' heads bob up and down.

Wisely and Appropriately

If you put 10 PowerPoint content creators in a room, you might get 11 opinions about what constitutes "wise and appropriate" animation.

Here is Sandra Johnson's definition: "After you've decided the purpose, then you can determine if and what type of animation is appropriate. Using it in an informative corporate presentation might just help the audience better grasp a complex concept. Bottom line, never use animation just because you can."

Our international editor Chantal Bossé offered the following: "Animate with a purpose...and the purpose is *not* to use all of the bells and whistles.

Meaningful animation helps them focus step-by-step when discussing a complex topic."

I have taken these two great comments and created the following prime directive for use of animation:

> **Good animation promotes increased understanding and appreciation of a topic. It calls attention to the topic, not the tool.**

The goal of any animation should be to highlight a slide's story, being careful not to overshadow that story with inappropriate wizbangery.

Can you learn how to play golf from PowerPoint? What could Figure 13.1 teach you about how to hit a golf ball?

I've been playing golf for over 30 years and to this day, a triple-bogey lurks around every grassy knoll. Golf is way too difficult to learn from a slide full of bullets. A beginning golfer needs to understand the sequence of events that makes up a sound swing, and that cannot come from a bullet slide or even a photo.

But oh, what a bit of smart animation can do—check out Figure 13.2 on the next page, featuring world No. 1 Rory McElroy. This sequence of imagery and captions is one of the finest examples of animation available, even though it is entirely devoid of any of the effects most of us are accustomed to using or seeing. Each image and caption combination appears five

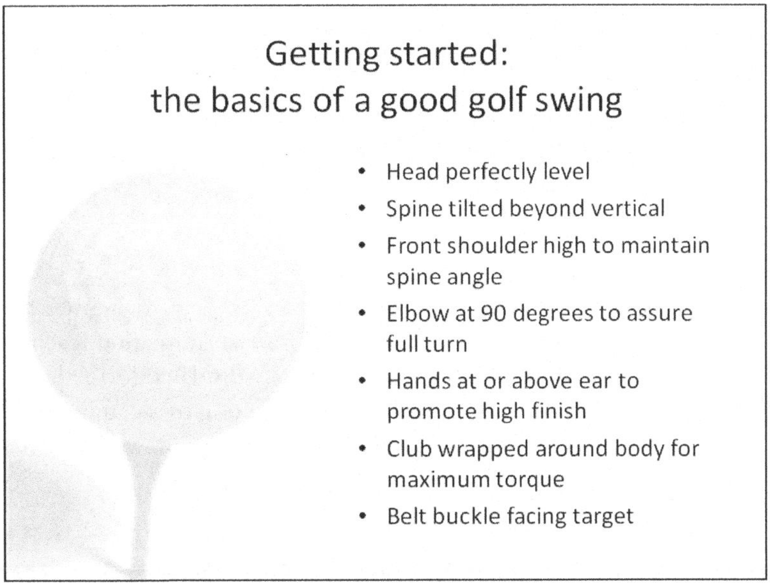

Figure 13.1
Can you learn golf this way? No chance...

Getting started:
the basics of a good golf swing

- Head perfectly level
- Spine tilted beyond vertical
- Front shoulder high to maintain spine angle
- Elbow at 90 degrees to assure full turn
- Hands at or above ear to promote high finish
- Club wrapped around body for maximum torque
- Belt buckle facing target

Figure 13.2
The dynamic of a good swing comes into focus when you see it as part of a sequence. *(Courtesy of Golf Digest.)*

Download 13-02.pptx or watch the video: whypptsucks.com/13-02.mp4

1. Weight evenly balanced between legs, ball positioned closer to front heel.

2. Hips turned but head in same position, and club parallel to target line.

3. Hips rotating toward target, weight moving onto front foot, head in same position.

4. Hips fully open, head behind the ball, still in same position.

5. Weight fully transferred, hips rotated past target line, perfectly in balance.

Click on caption to return to that image.

seconds after the previous, and in so doing, it helps immeasurably in telling the story of a good golf swing. This static image only shows the final image so it doesn't do the sequence justice; download the slide deck or watch the video on your smartphones to see this in action.

This is what we should all aspire to: the simplest use of animation that promotes increased understanding among audience members.

The Sequencing Task Pane?

If you were to ask me, and even if you were to not, I would say that PowerPoint's animation engine was incorrectly named. Too many people equate animation with cartooning or some sort of bringing-to-life experience, and when they expect to apply that to slide elements, the results are often counterproductive.

I wish that the engine were called Sequencing. *Go to the Sequencing task pane to create a build on that slide.* Animation reaches its higher purpose when you use it to strategically display information in the order and the pace most comfortable and inviting to an audience. As we explore specific techniques and strategies for animation, we hope that you continue to ask yourself that all-important question:

How can I present this information so that I increase understanding and appreciation among my audience?

Telling Better Stories

If you are a parent, you have read a bedtime story. And it's a pretty good chance that it didn't read "Once upon a time they lived happily ever after." Good stories have beginnings, middles, and ends. All too often, we do not afford that same luxury to our slides, choosing instead to drop everything on our audience all at once.

That's why just asking the question—"How might I sequence these visual elements in order to better tell this story?"—is so valuable. I almost don't care what the answer is—you're going to end up in a better place than displaying everything at once and making your audience drink from a fire hose.

Take a look at Figure 13.3, a thinly-fictionalized set of slides from one of the largest pharmaceutical companies in the world. These slides discuss two of the company's primary pursuits: curriculum and research. Let's start by

Figure 13.3
An effective animation strategy starts with identifying those elements that should not be animated.

Download 13-03.pptx or watch the video: whypptsucks.com/13-03.mp4:

identifying the elements that are common to all slides: The title, the small running header top-right, the gradient line below the title, and the running footer and its line. These are permanent structures, like the walls of your living room.

Do not animate them. Let them be permanent.

With this decision, you take the first step toward responsible animation by identifying elements that should *not* be animated. Whether they become aware of it or not, your audience members will appreciate having a permanent backdrop that they can count on. Like the walls of their living room.

The first slide introduces six departments that comprise the company's project and they are to be introduced together, not one by one, so as to give the audience appropriate context. Once introduced, small dotted lines emanate from them to the center of the slide, where the company logo emerges.

Once introduced, the logo also becomes a permanent structure on these slides, so no more animation for it.

Now that the relationship has been established between the six departments and the organization, it's time to introduce the two primary concepts to be discussed on these slides, curriculum and research.

Both flow out of the same team (represented by the logo), and this can be represented with simple wipes of arrows and photos.

When it comes time to focus on each concept, the appropriate photo grows in size and text appears alongside it.

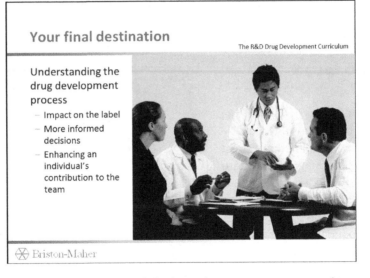

I want to reiterate that while these elements are moving and appearing, it is critical that the permanent structures do not move. That means no slide transitions that redraw the entire slide, like Fly or Push. Resisting animation is just as important to the message and to the storytelling experience as using it.

We see anything responsible for sequencing elements and creating motion as part of the animation scheme, regardless of what PowerPoint calls it. Therefore, a slide transition qualifies as animation.

▶ The use of the Grow/Shrink animation to enlarge the photos merits further discussion—see the next chapter for that.

If you are trying to simulate real motion, that's different. If you are creating a tutorial on how to, say, mail a product back to a warranty center, a motion path might be appropriate to move the product into an envelope and the envelope into a mailbox. Ascend might be just the ticket for simulating stars rising in the dusk sky. And who knows, maybe you really do want to show how a boomerang flies through the air. That's the point: ornate motion should be literal. Use it to literally show motion. Otherwise, stick to Wipe and Fade—they can never hurt you.

Case Studies

We could fill an entire book just on examples of animation; we'll settle for a chapter and a half. The challenge, of course, is to illustrate and explain dynamic motion using a static medium like a book. As always, downloadable files and video sequences help.

Three Ways to do X

Creating lists of topics in a style other than a bland bullet list is an ideal opportunity to use animation to best sequence the information and create the best pace for understanding. In the case of the slide here, there are several ways to approach the staging of these elements, dependent entirely upon the pace that you want to set.

1 This infographic has four elements to it: 1) the title; 2) the three number icons; 3) the gradient shades behind the text; 4) the text.

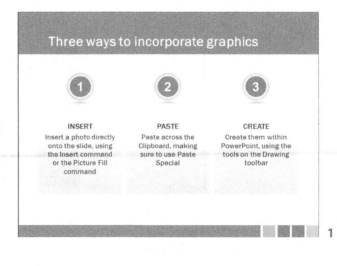

First question to ask: Does this slide need any builds at all? It wouldn't be the end of the world if this slide were all revealed at once—we've certainly seen more egregious examples of making an audience drink from the fire hose. None-theless, this slide presents a good opportunity for smart use of animation.

2 Of the many possible ways to build this slide, here is my preferred way to begin—by revealing the structure and a general sense of the detail. If you only show the three circled numbers first, you risk setting a pace that is too methodical, and if you show all of 1 without any of 2 or 3, you rob the audience of context. In my view, this provides just enough context.

3 The next click provides the detail on the first subject, and subsequent clicks would fill in the rest.

Even though it is not my preferred choice, it would not be wrong to bring in the INSERT, PASTE, and CREATE headings with their paragraphs (instead of before), and that becomes your choice as the author. You get to decide the best way to tell this story.

4 Here is the Animation task pane for this slide. Each text string actually has three animations associated with it—the placeholder, the heading, and the text—and notice that the placeholders are all sequenced first, before their respective text.

▼ Download 13-04.pptx to see this animation in action.

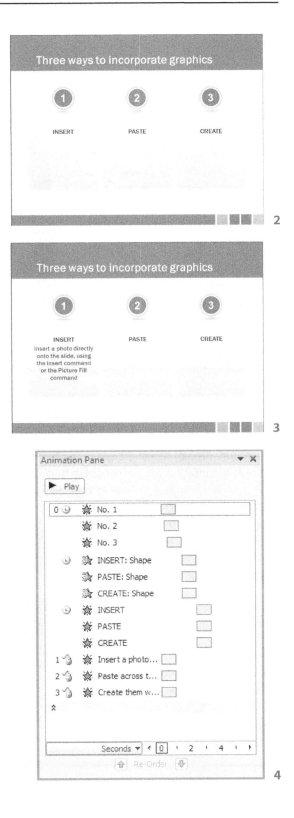

The Off-the-Charts Chart

Few elements benefit more from smart sequencing than data that has to be displayed in the form of a chart or a graph. Audiences are predisposed to tuning out and not absorbing information, especially when they feel as if presenters themselves don't make the effort necessary to describe the comparitive relationship of the data being shown.

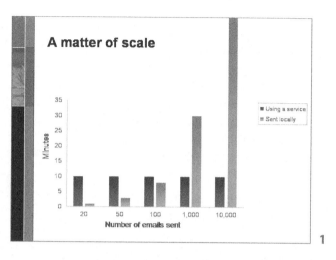

1 At right is a relatively simple chart...with a twist. It tracks the amount of time it takes to send out email two different ways—by yourself using a standard email client, and by contracting with an outside service. The twist here is that the final bar is not part of the graph, but a separate rectangle strategically placed where the final bar would normally be.

There are two critical pieces of information to illustrate: 1) The amount of time to send out email when you use an outside service is the same, no matter the quantity; and 2) The amount of time required to send out email from your office increases exponentially with quantity.

Proper animation of this chart can make all the difference to your audience's appreciation of this point. Most content creators recognize that something should be done to charts like this, but they don't think it through—so instead, they give the entire chart some weird animation, like a box in, or diamond out, or those Venetian blind thingies. Calling attention to the chart is not necessary; it's the only thing on the slide. What is needed here is to *direct* attention, and that requires more thought than Venetian blinds.

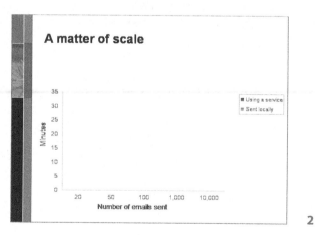

2 I am a big believer in separating the structure of data from the data itself, so whenever possible, I try to show the empty frame of a chart or a table first and then place the data onto it.

3 After explaining what this experiment was all about, I instructed the chart to build "by series" instead of "by category" and I further asked for each element to get its own build. As soon as I did that, every piece of the graph showed up in the Animation task pane. I then asked for all of the first category, Using a Service, to display at once, each wiping up from the bottom. The idea here is to essentially dispose of this part of the story all at once: "It doesn't matter how many pieces you have; if you use an outside service bureau, it's going to take you about 10 minutes."

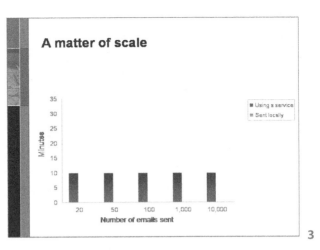

3

4 Then I brought in the second category, stopping after the first three. That showed the pattern and gave audience members a chance to absorb the fact that they are going to start saving time using an outside service once they get past 100.

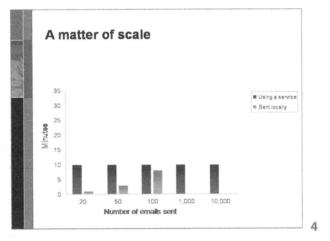

4

5 The next click drives that point home with clarity, so I chose to have it be the only element on that click. Sending 1,000 emails takes so much longer than sending out 100 emails; at this point the audience was left to wonder how we could possibly illustrate the time required to send out 10,000. That was the intrigue I was hoping to create...

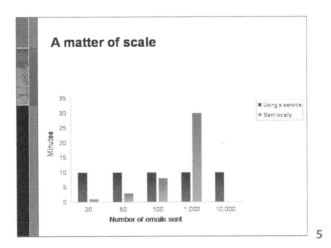

5

6 It became a moment of comic relief when the final bar on the chart wiped slowly up from the axis all the way off the chart, and it was worth the effort. In order to accommodate this, I had to enter 0 for the data point in that category so that the charting engine would still allocate space for it.

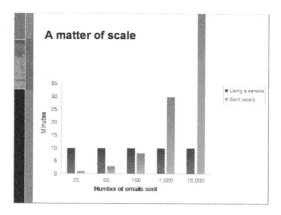

6

7 As you can see, creating this animation sequence was no small effort, and if you have never reverse-engineered a finished task pane, this would be a good exercise. We know from studying the task pane that the story is told in five segments. The first three elements take place on the "zero-th" click—they take place immediately after the slide transition.

The five elements on Click 1 are the entire first category that I chose to introduce all at one time. Click 2 introduces the first three elements of the second category. Click 3 is the fourth element, the data point at 1,000 emails. And you will notice that there is a second element, called Item 10, that occurs right afterward. That is the empty data point for 10,000 emails.

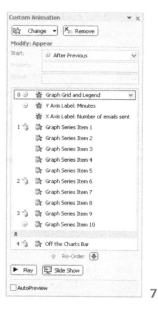

7

Finally, the rectangle that I superimposed atop the graph takes its long journey to the top of the slide.

8 Now for one disappearing caveat to all of this: text quality in animated charts has historically been quite bad, with all versions prior to 2010 displaying noticeable roughness when rendering chart text during an animation. This was resolved in the most current version of the software, but in prior versions users have resorted to ungrouping charts in order to achieve better display quality.

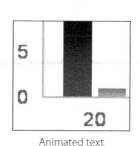

Animated text

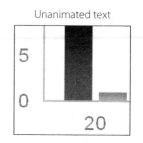

Unanimated text

8

▼ Download 13-05.pptx to see this animation in action.

The Case of the Bloated Slide

There comes a time in the life of all consultants when the client makes them do something that makes their skin crawl. With presentation consultants, it is usually a matter of jamming way, way, way (one more) way too much text on a slide.

1 At right is a poster child for this malady. No matter what I said about the evils of slides like this, my client told me that it was non-negotiable—he was going to speak to the slide this way no matter what.

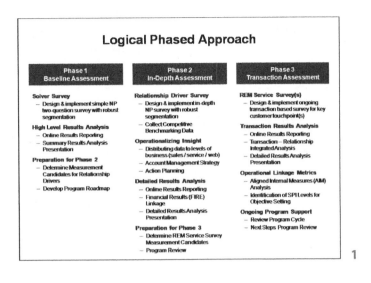

I'm sure I would be preaching to the choir to recite everything that is wrong with this approach. The more intriguing discussion is how can we make a bad situation a little bit better. What can we do with this slide to keep the audience from totally tuning out, and at the same time satisfy the client's addiction to the text?

2 The solution that I fashioned was to introduce the slide with all of the text being mostly obscured by three white rectangles, each set with a small fraction of transparency. This tells audience members not to bother trying to read it, and yet it gives them some idea of what they're in for. I discovered that it was necessary for the rectangles to appear first, so that when the text faded in, it was already obscured.

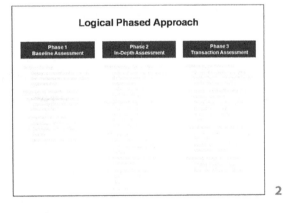

3 With each subsequent click, more of the text is revealed. This sequencing strategy involves a question of what goes away, not

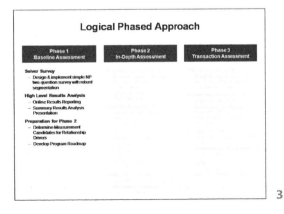

what enters. With each click, a semi-transparent rectangle fades away, bringing clarity to the column of text underneath it.

Let me be clear that I find this solution to be quite deficient; it would be much better to hone and distill the text for the visual and provide this level of detail in the handout. This workaround at least helps focus the audience a bit and makes the data slightly more digestible.

Our creative editor Sandra Johnson points out that you can use the Transparency emphasis animation to dim this text and then undim it (by changing the transparency value to 0). We applaud Sandy's ingenuity, but not the Transparency function's elegance. It applies the effect in herky-jerk fashion, compromising the value of the effect.

The standard objection to this type of treatment is that the slide cannot function as printed material when there are elements placed on top of the text. Good, I say! Presentation slides should not be made to double as printouts. You should create a separate handout, and while you're at it, rotate it to portrait orientation. I'll have much more to say about that in Chapter 16.

▼ Download 13-06.pptx to see this animation in action.

The Trouble with Tables

Creating rows and columns of information is a terrific way to show the linear and gridlike relationship of data.

1 As always, the key is in the presentation: how do you get all of the information you see here properly digested without inducing fire-hose syndrome?

The animation capabilities for tables are all but useless, as the only thing you can do is determine how the entire table enters or exits. Unlike with charts, you cannot determine the animation sequence of the elements within. Too bad, because sequencing the rows and columns of a table is the key to this locked door.

Performance Factors

	Market Position	CEM Program	Customer Experience	Keys to Loyalty Growth
Sustainers	Short-sighted Product Focus	Weak Foundation and Process	Weak Delivery and Relationship	Move out silo'd focus
Optimizers	Long-term Relationship Focus	Eroding Foundation	Strong Product/Svc and Relationship	Sponsorship Account integration
Maximizers	Intensely Customer-Centric	Strong Overall, Superior Foundation and People	Superior Product/Svc, Delivery and Relationship	Keep leveraging information in the context of their business
Innovators	Emerging Customer Experience Focus	Strong Program and Process	Strong Product/Svc and Delivery	Cross-functional ownership Re-engagement

✳ MATRIX

1

Therefore, the first thing to do with a table is "un-table" it: use the Ungroup command to turn it into a collection of rows and columns. Modern versions of PowerPoint have actually devolved in this regard: In order to do that, you must cut it to the Clipboard and then use Paste Special to bring it back as a metafile, after which you can ungroup it. Once you do, you have complete control over the sequencing of the elements, and your first editorial decision is to determine whether you want to present the information down or across. Whichever you choose will govern how you regroup the elements.

2 Assuming you are showing this data row by row, select each row of information (but not the left-most category column) and group it. As with the graph, I recommend displaying the header row and the left column first before the primary content. It would be equally legitimate to decide that you want to speak to just the header row first and then bring in the category column on your next click.

3 Tables are good candidates for the Wipe animation, as text is usually running across or down. The header row would wipe from the left and the category column would wipe down from top.

Then each row would wipe from the left at your discretion.

4 As you can see, the sequencing for this animation is quite simple, with each row (or column) entering as you see fit, in this case each one on its own click. The critical piece of knowledge here is knowing that you can (and must) ungroup the table before you can intelligently sequence it.

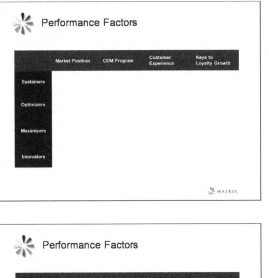

2

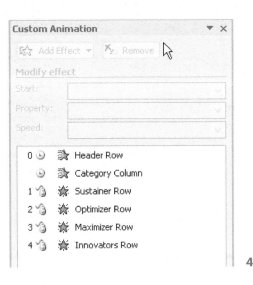

3

4

▼ Download 13-07.pptx to see this animation. The first slide shows the animation by row and the second slide by column.

The Benefits of Effective Animation

When you use animation in this way, you create a completely different experience for your audience members. They are so accustomed to seeing animation used gratuitously, when they see content that has been prepared with thought and purpose, it speaks well of you. Here are a few of the good things that happen when you use animation properly:

Your audience really gets it

As I said earlier, I'm a proponent of separating form and content to promote understanding. Offering up the empty chart is a great way to prepare your audience for the rest of it. Showing just the topics helps frame the conversation before you give the information within each topic.

You control the pace

Most dense slides are displayed too quickly, leaving audience members with the fire-hose feeling. If you suspect that members of your audience are not clear on what it is you're about to show them, you can wait until they understand before continuing.

A Word About Pace

Speed kills, as the adage goes. With presentations, so can the lack of speed. Choosing the proper pace for your animation can often mark the difference between success and failure. When you slow the pace at which your objects appear on screen, you raise the bar of expectation, whether you mean to or not. You send the message to your audience members that this element deserves extra attention. If it doesn't merit that attention, then you are crying wolf. And if you send it to them too fast, you undermine the very reason you use animation in the first place.

My rule of thumb, scientifically proven by nobody, is to animate text at twice the speed at which it can be visually scanned.

On the other hand, complex ideas need to be doled out carefully, so as not to short-circuit your audience. The horizontal axis for a complicated graph should be wiped from the left slowly and you should pause before placing the data points onto it. When you slow the pace here, you assure your audience that you will give them the time they need to see both the forest as well as the trees.

You become more confident

When you prepare a slide with intelligent sequencing, you have control of your audience in the palm of your hand—literally, if you use a wireless remote. Confidence is one of two transferable commodities that can make a presenter more confident. When you are confident about how you handle your technology, you will become more confident about the content of your presentation.

You create trust

This is the second transferable commodity and it's the most important benefit discussed here. PowerPoint audiences are so often on guard in case a presenter does something ridiculous with animation or obnoxious with content, it's amazing that they remember anything. When you take your audience members through a difficult topic with a friendly pace and a well-thought-out plan, you tell them that they can relax, lower their guard, and just take in the information. They can trust that you won't do something stupid and annoying.

And when your audience members begin to trust you with the way you use the software, they will be inclined to trust you with your message, and trust is perhaps the most important emotion of all. It could be the promised land for presenters. How ironic that animation, the tool derided by so many for so long, can be directly responsible for helping you get there.

◆

We spoke in Chapter 8 about the potential insult associated with spoon-feeding bullets. It is an entirely different situation that we are discussing here with dense, chunky data. These slides have to be studied, not just gazed at. Here, you do your audience a service by offering information in a careful and methodical way.

Animation cannot be covered in just one chapter—turn the page and we'll turn up the volume...

Chapter 14

More with Animation

We're as bad as everyone we've railed against or poked fun at: we admonish you to use caution when using animation and then we run wild with so much to say about it, we can't fit it all in one chapter. Chapter 13's focus was on the appropriate times to use animation and the best ways to craft it. This chapter focuses on animation choices that are not mainstream, but potentially invaluable in creating emphasis, elegance, realism, or illumination.

14

Two Animations, One Moment in Time

Once the domain of the experts, the ability to set two objects in motion at the same time has now become commonplace. As with all other matters of animation, that sword cuts two ways, so first, the admonition:

If you think that one object moving across the slide is annoying, imagine two objects running amuck at the same time.

Understanding the With Previous animation event opens many creative doors, and the mechanics are not at all difficult. When you set an animation to start With Previous, you command it to do its thing along with whatever animation was scheduled immediately before it. Standard After Previous animations cannot do this; they won't begin until the previous one is finished. When you use With Previous, you break that barrier. You can still stagger the sequence by adding a delay to one of them, but the fundamental difference is still in place: you can make two or more objects animate at once by employing With Previous.

Figure 14.1
What would happen to this fruit in real life, and can you get PowerPoint to simulate it?

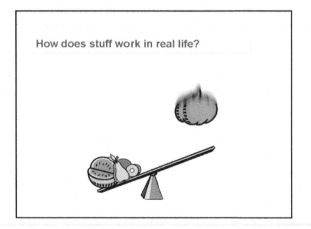

This capability finds its feet when you want to make several objects appear as one system, and I am reminded of the cute demo that we showed at the Presentation Summit a few years ago, courtesy of Julie Terberg, shown in Figure 14.1.

When the pumpkin lands on its end of the teeter-totter, the fruit is going to go flying. "But how will it fly?" I asked rhetorically. "If you're new to animation, it might look something like this..." after which the fruit went flying...one after the other...just as After Previous would do it. People snickered.

Figure 14.2
With Previous is
the key to making
this fruit fly right.

"So then you get a clue," I continued, "and realized that they need to go flying at once...as a group." The second attempt saw the fruit fly off the slide *literally* as a group. It was quite hilarious—they became a big clump hurdling off screen.

As each fruit would make its ceremonious exit according to its own weight, mass, shape, and personality, this was a job for With Previous, as you can sort of see in Figure 14.2 and appreciate more fully by downloading 14-02.pptx.

Unlikely that you'll be sending fruit into orbit in any of your upcoming presentations, but the idea remains: if you want to make motion appear natural and organic, you're probably talking about using With Previous.

Figure 14.3 shows a menu slide created for a seminar on database management. In order to signal that we are diving down into one of these four topics, I faded out the other three. And if you followed the workaround for

Figure 14.3
Animating this
slide With Previous
integrates all of the
parts into a unified
action.

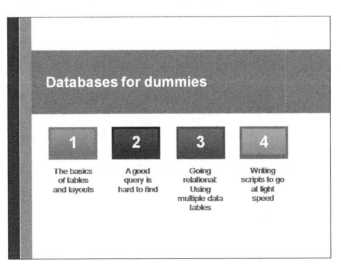

that now-infamous three-column slide last chapter, you already know what we're about to do here: we're going to place semi-transparent white rectangles atop the topics not being discused. Here is how I built and animated the slide to introduce the second topic.

1. I used a slow fade slide transition revealing all four of the topics and the title.

2. I drew rectangles over the topics *not* being discussed, two in all, and set them white.

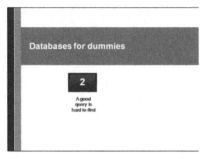

3. I applied a 20% transparency to both rectangles to make it clear that they are subordinate to the current topic.

4. Finally, I applied a fast fade to the rectangles, setting both to With Previous.

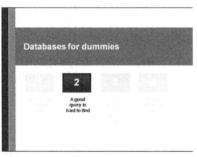

With these elements coming in simultaneously, they create a smooth and refined look, while acting as a roadmap for the presentation.

▼ Download 14-03.pptx to see this animation in action.

This example might not rise to the level of usefulness that we saw in the last chapter. In fact, one reader of the first edition took me to task for this example. Guy Everson from Nebraska wrote in, "Sure, you could use fancy fades to highlight the current point, but why not just point to the one you want to emphasize? Or how about just saying 'On to the second point'? Isn't this the very type of gratuituousness that you rail against elsewhere in the book? How about some consistency?"

What do you think, is Mr. Everson right? Is this more fluff than substance? Is this treatment really warranted? Guy's point of view is legitimate and worth airing. And he is absolutely right that the best way to make a point is often to use your own hands or words to direct traffic. I completely agree with that.

The reason that I do not share the criticism of the technique, however, is because the worst that you could say about it is that it is unnecessary. It does not rise to the level of obnoxious or even annoying. It is just a fade. It does not involve wild motion, and it clearly carries the intention of trying to help guide the audience. So we'll leave this technique in and invite further commentary from Guy and all others.

Part Two: The Solution

Did Animation Win a Case?

According to notorious PowerPoint critic Edward Tufte, PowerPoint brought down the space shuttle. According to our creative editor Sandra Johnson, it prevailed in litigation. And she ought to know: it was her work that might have earned her client's client millions of dollars. For a recent court case, in which a woman suffered paralysis during childbirth, a law firm hired Johnson to illustrate a complicated medical condition at the core of the dispute.

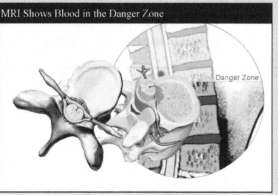

Johnson carefully sequenced the events so that the attorney could explain the situation more easily to the jury. It was effort worth making, as right after Johnson's animations were shown, opposing counsel convinced the defendant to settle. Post-trial jury comments confirmed that they would have likely found for the plaintiff after watching the presentation.

Johnson noted that her clients said they "would never try another case again without PowerPoint."

Figure 14.4
Simultaneous animation helps identify relationships.

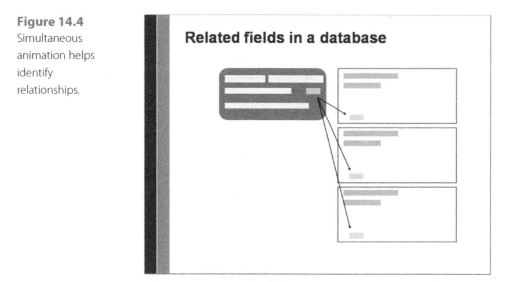

With Previous can certainly do some heavy lifting, also. Witness Figure 14.4, where an intricate relationship needs to be described between elements of a complex database. Relational databases are difficult concepts for many and you cannot just talk your way through a description of the theory behind them; you must create a visual in the minds of your audience members.

Sending several objects onto the slide at one time is key to showing which ones relate to which other ones. First, the main record of the database appears (the one on the left), and soon afterward, the frame for the related records appear, to indicate that *something* else is part of this virtual ecosystem.

Next, the parallel fields of these related records are displayed, together. Then, the critical field for each related record that pivots around the main record displays, in a different color for emphasis. Finally, simple arrows emanate from the main record, again all using With Previous. The simultaneous quality of this animation is central to its ability to describe the dynamic relationship.

"With Previous" Can be Good P. R.

When the Port of Long Beach engaged me to help one of its executives with an upcoming presentation, I learned first-hand the tightrope that is walked when a heavily-trafficked seaport needs to demonstrate that it also has concern for environmental issues.

In this slide, the environment is identified as merely one of the Port's three challenges, when really, this presentation is about to turn most of its attention to the environment. In effect, the topic is about to be promoted from just another bullet point to a main topic.

So we decided to first make that point visually, with the bullet literally becoming the title. This involved three simultaneous animations: 1) The line of text moves up toward the title; 2) It grows larger to match the size of the title; and 3) The title disappears as the bullet text arrives in its place.

The more significant metamorphosis occurs on the next slide when the photo of the cargo ship at sunset gives way to a peaceful seagull and a montage of photos of birds peacefully taking up residence at the Port. This involves several carefully-choreographed pieces of motion, all working in concert.

This transformation takes about 20 seconds from start to finish, and I cautioned my client to make sure that he had something prepared to say during that time, lest he just start watching the slide morph and the effect would be lost.

▼ Download 14-05.pptx to see this animation.

1

2

3

Please Leave by the Exits

I haven't forgotten the first time I saw it. A medal deserves to be awarded for the most elaborate workaround by someone who never knew that an object's departure from a slide could be choreographed as readily as its entrance. Without knowing about exit animations, he went to hell and back to compensate.

Without knowing about exit animations, when it was time to show the next example, he created rectangles the color of the background and faded them atop the old examples. He used rectangles like erasers...except he was not really erasing the examples; he was just covering them up.

He constructed a labrynth of these eraser rectangles, each one entering right when it was time to make an object disappear. This slide involved about 75 objects entering the slide, half intended to simulate the disappearance of other objects.

It was a mess.

It was a masterpiece.

And it was largely unnecessary.

As many of our readers know, the better course of action would have been to apply exits to the old objects either right before or at the same time new objects appear.

If you know how to animate, you know how to create exits—you just choose Exit instead of Entrance and do everything else the same. At the risk of oversimplification, there is nothing complicated about applying exits to elements of a slide.

When to exit, when to transition?

To be honest, the biggest hurdle to using exit animations is in knowing when *not* to use them, and Figure 14.6 frames the potential dilemma that content creators face. This slide is part of a promo for a reopening of a downtown restraurant and it starts with a stack of four photos depicting the great food and service offered. Three of these four photos will exit, revealing the text underneath. That text has a few simple builds associated with it.

This is not a terribly complicated animation sequence, but if you create a slide with exits, it will likely require you to create, format, and animate text while it is underneath the photos. You will probably get adept at using Tab to cycle through the selection of objects and you probably have fallen in love with the Selection Pane (see Page 137). But no matter how facile you get at these tricks, your internal slide plumbing will work against you.

Figure 14.6
On this slide, three of the images exit, revealing the text underneath. Working on the text while it is underneath the photos will become tedious. Better to seek an alternate strategy...

It would be better for your sanity to have the text reside on its own slide, and this suggests a fundamental technique that accomplished content creators turn to regularly. I refer to it as the "stealth transition"—one slide changing to another without the audience noticing it.

▼ Download 14-06.pptx to see the effect created both with exit animations and with a slide transition.

In this case, you would not create any exit animations. Instead, you would use a Fade Smoothly slide transition, but the photo of the server would be present on both slides. This would give the appearance that the three photos have faded away, leaving only the woman. Then you would build the other elements how you see fit, doing so in the comfort of a dedicated slide, not one that has layers upon layers of elements.

The advantage to the transition-instead-of-exit approach is more comfortable content creation. The disadvantage is less control over the

Figure 14.7
This dramatic and sweeping montage of photos can only be created with exits.

action, because your transition choices are more limited than your animation choices.

Figure 14.7 offers a situation in which exit animation is the *only* way to achieve the desired effect. In this homage to the sea, the background scene slowly drifts to the right, while other evocative photos appear and disappear in sequence. This must be done on one slide, because the background image is constantly in motion throughout the experience. It's exits or bust! There are three other things to note about the screen image in Figure 14.7:

- You can't see the Zoom toolbar, but it reads 33%, meaning we are zoomed out quite a bit.

- We have created a temporary dotted white line around the slide to give you a sense of scale and proportion (the background photo is much larger than the slide).

▼ Download 14-07.pptx to see this mosaic of images.

- The Animation task pane indicates that three of the elements scheduled to fade in promptly fade right back out afterward (exit animations have lighter-colored icons).

Using the Advanced Timeline

Anyone who has ever used non-linear video editing software such as Adobe Premiere or Windows Live Movie Maker would look upon the Advanced Timeline available in the Animation task pane as something akin to nursery school. Advanced? Hardly.

That said, sometimes we animators don't need anything more than nursery-school tools, yet a vast majority of PowerPoint users never use the Advanced Timeline, and according to our informal surveys, as many as 70% do not even know that it exists.

Right-click on any of the entries in the Animation task pane and choose Show Advanced Timeline. That brings up a chronological display of the animation sequence for the current slide. Advanced or not, it often beats the stuffing out of having to right-click on every animation and work a dialog box. By sliding those orange bars around, you can

- Set the moment when an object begins its entrance

- Control how long its entrance lasts

- Choose how long it will reside on the slide

- Determine when it will begin to exit

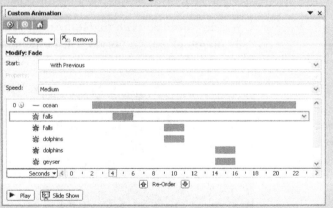

And as you can see here, you can also stretch the task pane to show a much longer duration without scrolling—in this case, we are seeing across 22 seconds, the length of the montage in Figure 14.7.

No element is an island, and that is especially true when a slide has elements set to With Previous or with elements whose exits are tied to the entrances of other elements. Advanced Timeline shows you those relationships with more clarity.

The Path to Motion

Many PowerPoint users overlook the Motion Path option for animation for three reasons: a) they view it as redundant to what Fly can do and they already know how to use Fly; b) working the motion path controls can make even the most accomplished user feel like a moron; and c) isn't all animation motion? Why should you bother with something called Motion Path?

While it's true that some of the animation choices can mimic a motion path, and while it's equally true that the tools can often make you feel foolish, sometimes you just can't beat a well-executed motion path, especially if you learn a trick or two...

Fly moves in one of a few straight-line directions, and arcs, ascensions, and some of the other more dubious animation choices are similarly limited. But with a motion path, you can move an object from any point and to any point, without restrictions. And combining motion with other animations is exceptionally powerful.

Figure 14.8 offers a rudimentary example of motion's value in basic tutorials. Not many people in our user community would need to be taught how to place a CD into a CD drive, but there are plenty of new PC users who would welcome this level of hand-holding. Thanks to a motion path, this CD will literally move directly atop the holder.

If you download and run this animation, you will see that the CD lands right on top of the tray...or does it? Please don't look too closely, okay? We don't really have a clue where it ends up. After about seven or eight tries of

Figure 14.8
Better hand-holding through Motion Path.

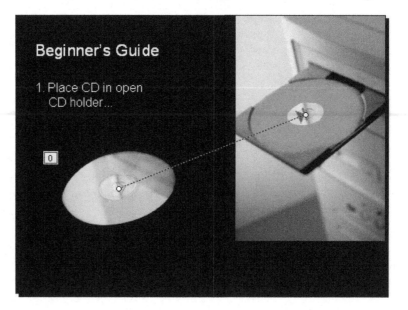

tweaking the ending arrow and then playing the slide, we achieved something that perhaps rises to the level of passable.

One of our longer-standing objections with the software is its lack of coordinate points for animations that change the size or position of an element. You can't even eyeball it because while editing the slide, the element is in its starting position, not its ending position.

Throw motion in reverse

Because of this shortcoming, there is a semi-elaborate workaround that is often worth the effort. It involves a little-known ability to ask for a motion to go in the opposite direction. At the Path dropdown on the Animation task pane, choose Reverse Path Direction.

Download 14-08.pptx to see the techniques for using motion paths.

With that setting, when you extend the line out from the element, you are defining its staring point. Now you can use your nudge keys, which, in conjunction with Shift and Ctrl, give you tremendous control over object placement. You can also use the coordinates built into the Size and Position dialog box to get the ending location of the object just right. Meanwhile, you'll be approximating the object's starting point, but that's okay in this case (and most cases), as the starting point is rarely as important as the destination.

But here's the tricky part about this strategy: when you show the slide, the object initially appears at its destination. Then when you begin the motion path, it suddenly jumps to its starting point and moves back to its destination. In the case of the CD and the computer, the CD initially appears in the tray then jumps out into the open space, then moves back to the tray.

This can be solved by one of two techniques that are more easily understood by watching than by reading about them, so we suggest you dissect them in 14-08.pptx. In general:

- You add an entrance fade to the CD and you begin its motion simultaneous to that entrance. As long as the motion begins at the same time, the CD will not appear in the tray. This technique is shown in the second slide of the file.

- You make a copy of the computer and place it on top of the CD. As soon as the motion begins and the CD jumps to the starting point, you make the computer disappear. See this effect in the third slide.

This is really geeky, we know. But figuring this stuff out makes you feel on top of your game. As you get more of these geeky little victories under your belt, you'll begin to feel as if there is nothing that you can't simulate or replicate with PowerPoint animation.

Zoom!

For instance, it took a geek to figure out that you could couple the motion path with a Grow emphasis and simulate the feeling of flying over a landscape. Figure 14.9 shows a nice aerial view over a waterway, and if you study the screen image, you will find two clues for what is about to happen:

- The motion line on the photo heads past the lower boundary of the photo, indicating that this photo is going to move a lot.

- According to the Animation task pane, the photo will also grow in size by 500%.

In other words, as the photo is moving down (which is the same as you moving up over it), everything will be getting bigger...just as it would if you were flying toward the bridge in a helicopter.

 Download 14-09.pptx to see the effect and to see how we end up with a good-quality image. We included slide numbers for your reference.

There is one important finishing touch necessary: PowerPoint does not actually upsample the photo, so its zoom is going to be heavily pixilated. This does not become objectionable until the zoom stops, so I find it necessary to immediately replace the zoomed image with a static image, sized and positioned to be identical to the final zoom.

Would that PowerPoint provide coordinates for this final location, but I've already belly-ached about that. So once again, you just have to tweak and adjust. Using a round number, like 500%, makes the sizing part easy. Nudging it to the finished location is just trial and error.

Figure 14.9
Add a Grow to a Motion Path and you get a helicopter ride.

▶ Another way to zoom: Insert the picture at the size you want it to be after you zoom in on it. Add an immediate shrink animation to shrink it to the size you want it most of the time. Now, add another grow animation to put it back to full size. The end result: Smoother zooming and less pixilation. You decide which form of elbow grease you want to employ.

Modern Aids to Animation

While the Animation task pane and the engine's capabilities have remained largely static over the past few versions, there are several additions made with version 2007 and one in 2010 that could yield big dividends. And because they go largely overlooked, we treat them like news here.

1. The Selection and Visibility Pane

Objects that you create or import can be renamed, and the name that you assign to it displays in the Animation task pane. No more Rectangle 46 or Picture 14! This makes identifying an object's animation settings in the task pane infinitely easier. From the Home ribbon, click Select on the far-right of the ribbon to access the Selection pane. From here, you can not only rename objects, but select them, relayer them, and hide them (more on that one soon).

Here is what the pane looks like for the slide deck shown in Figure 14.6. As you can see, you can choose to name elements based on location, content, or source. For the serious animator, this is huge.

2. Hide and seek

The eyeballs to the right of each object in the Selection pane act like a toggle to show or hide it, and this too has major-league implications for those who create complex animations. I will refer you back to the discussion about the relative merits of working with many elements on a slide or creating stealth

Selection and Visibility

Shapes on this Slide:

Lower-Right Photo
Lower-Left Veggie Wrap
Top-Left (from photos.com)
Promo Text
Headline
Address
Name
Bottom Bar
Transparent Overlay
Server

Show All
Hide All   Re-order

slide transitions to help you keep everything straight in your mind.

The ability to hide objects on top of others is a game-changer for those who regularly face this decision. It will now be much easier to keep a group of elements that comprise a complex animation sequence all on on slide. Just remember to unhide them before you run the show, okay?

3. The Change Picture command

Animating groups of photos is much easier in modern versions thanks to the ability to replace one photo with another and retain the animation qualities of the original image. In earlier versions, this requires a semi-convoluted maneuver in which you create a rectangle and fill it with the photo. Any animation that you apply to the rectangle is maintained, irrespective of what fill color, pattern, or photo is inside.

Modern versions allow you to employ that same strategy but without the Shape Fill gyration: right-click any photo to see the Change Picture command. See our upcoming case study for a real-world example.

4. Animation Painter

Introduced in version 2010, you can now pick up animation attributes from one object and apply them to other objects. Select the object that contains the animation, invoke the tool, and click on the object you want to have receive it. They must be on the same slide—that's the only requirement. While this falls short of a set of styles that I wish we could define and apply, the Animation Painter is quite handy when you would rather not reinvent wheels or spin your own wheels.

Solavie: Environmentally-Aware Care Products

When one of our clients had an opportunity to pitch her product to the QVC shopping network, we knew that we had an opportunity to help them tell their story in an engaging and dynamic way. Theirs is the story of hair and skin care products that are specially formulated to work in specific environments—six in all.

1 One of the first slides in the deck involves a complex metamorphosis of the small round icons that represent the six environments served by the product. In turn, each of the icons moves, grows, and eventually fades into the larger rectangular shape, after which the text for that environment displays.

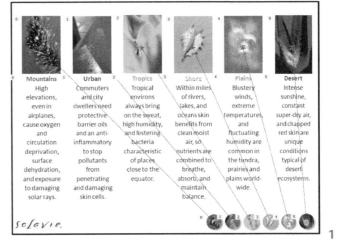

Fine-tuning the timing, precision, and synchronization was no small effort; it took me over an hour to create the first one, and then I pondered the specter of recreating it five more times. To be honest, I'm not sure that I would have attempted this in older versions of PowerPoint. I certainly could not have justified spending half a day on this effect, nor in good conscience billed the client for that time.

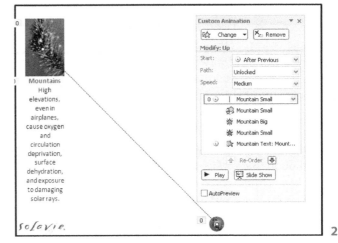

2 But modern versions allow for this slide to be crafted in an entirely different way. I spent the requisite 60 minutes getting the first one perfect, and as the Animation task pane shows, I carefully named each object, in this first case: Mountain Small (the round icon), Mountain Big (the larger square image), and Mountain Text. You can see that there are three animations applied to Mountain Small: a motion, a grow, and a fade out.

In older versions, I would have to either recreate the elements and their effects for each icon or try my hand at one of several after-market animation-cloning tools. Like I said, I probably would have just given up on the whole idea.

3 Instead, I made a duplicate of the Mountain Small icon and immediately renamed it to Urban Small. I duped Mountain Big, also. With identical proportions, the only part of the animation that needed to be tweaked was the motion path, and that required no more than about three or four minutes.

Notice how the task pane shows the descriptive names, allowing you to know immediately what animation goes with what object.

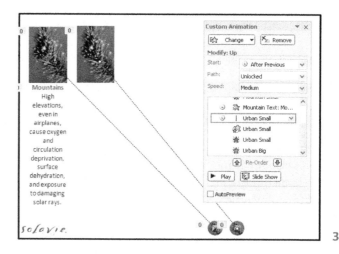

3

4 The promised land for this operation, however, is the Change Picture command, shown here being used to turn the duplicated mountain image into the urban photo. All animations originally in place remain when one photo is swapped for another. The same will be done for the small round icon, resulting in dramatic savings of time and effort. Your mileage might vary, but I found this to be a cleaner solution than the Animation Painter.

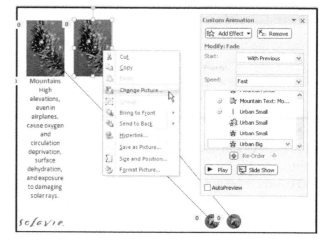

4

5 The Selection pane's ability to hide objects came in very handy here, even though there were no overlapping objects. These animations occur in sequential order and that normally makes editing the last few of a sequence quite tedious, as you mindlessly wait for the ones before it to do their thing. But as you can see here, the ones earlier in the sequence have been hidden, making it much easier to test the last few in the sequence.

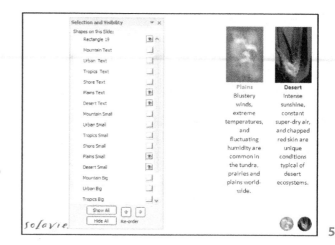

5

6 Finally, let's take a look at the Animation task pane for the finished slide. Have you ever seen anything so clean, organized, and approachable? Gone are the arbitrary names that serve only to confuse. When allowed to create a naming scheme that makes sense to you, you guarantee an easier time sifting through the many elements that make up a complex animation.

I particularly appreciate that objects that are hidden with the Selection pane are temporarily removed from the Animation task pane.

These three factors combine to make the creation of complex, multi-object animation a pleasure instead of a chore.

Now if we could just get keystroke commands for adding the animation effects, I'd never ask for another thing as long as I live...

▼ Download 14-11.pptx to see how modern versions of PowerPoint handle the creation of this complex animation effect.

Part Two: The Solution

Be Conspicuous in Your Tastefulness

As we arrive at the end of two very long and substantial chapters, I will reiterate what the most important feature is of PowerPoint animation.

Restraint.

Your audiences have seen it all. They've watched the flying bullets, the ridiculous transitions, weird things dissolving into weirder things. Just by standing in front of them and having a slide projecting onto a screen, you have already made a first impression, and through no fault of your own, it might be a negative one, so pervasive is the reputation of a "PowerPoint presentation." Some in your audience will have already concluded that you are probably going to be one of the countless thousands of people who will do stupid things with their slides or put them to sleep with incredibly boring content that provides no insight into the subject at hand.

Why would they think otherwise? They've seen this all before.

Every time you resist the use of a wild animation or some other gratuitous effect, you score sensibility points with your audience. You tell them "I could have done something stupid here—you know because you've seen it a thousand times—but I have consciously chosen not to do that."

You couldn't buy that kind of impact with all the animation in the world.

When they see that you are using animation to help tell a compelling story, they might realize how unusual the presentation is. When your slides illustrate points so cleanly and dynamically that audience members reach a higher level of understanding, you know you've got them.

Every presenter who has ever stood before an audience has some degree of ego on the line, and for most of us, there is some element of showing off that takes place.

Show off your sensibilities. Show off that you understand understatement to be its own form of emphasis. Show your audiences that you appreciate that restraint is a special form of respect and they will remember the time they spent with you for years.

Part Three

Survival Skills for the Non-Designer

In any one of my typical seminars, there are between 35 and 80 people in the room when I ask the question: "How many of you consider yourselves to be professional designers or illustrators?" That question usually evokes between zero and one hand to rise. Of the many bridges that people take to their involvement with presentation content creation, very few of them travel across the arts. Slide creators must rely on their imagination and guile and an often-mysterious sense of what makes good content.

We think it an affront to the profession to imply that graphic design mastery can be achieved by reading five chapters. Nonetheless, there are strategies and perspectives that we think can help you and we will uncover them here.

Chapter 15

The Meaning Of Design

On the topic of design, I would like to start with the most important piece of advice I know. If you were to stop reading after this page, if you were to burn this book, or do something even more violent like give it to an Apple Keynote user, I would be confident that you had received the most important message of all.

Are you ready? Here it is...

You are the presentation.

15

Did that piece of advice surprise you? Here is my second-most important piece of advice:

It's not about you.

And the third:

Get away from technology.

This probably sounds like quite a contradiction—you are the presentation, but it can't be about you, and let's talk about PowerPoint but please leave the computer. And what does any of this have to do with design, anyway?

In fact, it has everything to do with design, and the likelihood that many of our readers might be confused by that underscores the point that most people don't really understand what design means.

To most people, the word *design* refers to how something looks. To most people, these phrases are synonymous:

When people say	They usually mean
That is a well-designed slide.	That slide is pretty.
That is a poorly-designed slide.	That slide is ugly!

When people hear the word *design*, they usually think of *decoration*. But that's different. Design is more fundamental, and I refer you to the Urban Dictionary's definition:

> The process of originating and developing a
> plan for a product, structure, system, or
> component with intention.

Structure...plan...intention. These are the essential concepts of something that has been designed. You can have the prettiest slides on Earth, but if they do not represent purpose and forethought, they cannot perform the heavy lifting of a presentation that moves an audience. The best you could hope for from them would be a sugar high, not a genuine reaction with a lasting impression.

Designing a Presentation

With this definition in mind, the notion of what it means to "design" a presentation takes on an entirely different perspective. It begins far away from any particular slide. Let's return to the three principles that I identified as most important to good design...

1. You are the presentation

Among the tens of millions of presentations delivered since the mid-1980s, do you suppose that, even once, a single member of an audience has ever entered a boardroom or ballroom thinking, "I sure am looking forward to seeing the speaker's slides..."?

Nobody does that. That's not why people attend a presentation, and if you are the one whose presentation they are attending, you need to understand this before you can even have a conversation about what creates success.

They are there to hear you. They are there because you have expertise in a subject that matters to them. They are there with the hope that you will improve their life in some way.

When new clients begin a conversation with "Here is a printout of my presentation," I immediately correct them.

"This is not your presentation," I reply with noticeable disdain for the pulp that has been placed in front of me. "This is a printout of your slides. Don't insult yourself."

It might be just semantics. It might be a small thing to them, and they might think I am being too anal about it. On the contrary, if you are that new client of mine, it suggests to me that you might have your priorities wrong. It is an immediate red flag that you might be asking your slides to do your work for you. And that never ends well.

You are the presentation, not your slides. No worthwhile discussion about the design of your presentation can take place until you understand, appreciate, and embrace this notion. The job of your slides is to help you tell your story. They must take a subordinate position to you, because none of your audience members cares about them. They care about what you have to say.

▶ As always, this argument presumes that your presentation is to be delivered live, either in front of an audience or in a webinar. In the case of a presentation file that is delivered electronically, the slides *are* the presentation. That changes everything. See Chapter 17 for more on this subject.

2. It's not about you

The notion that you are the central focus of the presentation does not imply that the presentation is supposed to be about you and about how great your organization is.

We wrote about this in Chapter 4 and it warrants elaboration. You need to find a way to make your presentation about them. Your audience members enter the room because, yes, they want to hear what you have to say, but more to the point, they hope and expect that you address the issues and concerns that matter most to them. They don't enter the room caring about you except in so far as you have something to say about an issue of theirs.

Your quickest path to engagement is to identify, understand, and speak to their issues.

Let's be more direct about this. Your audience members do not start their day caring that your company's mission is to proactively create market opportunities in high-growth sectors. They do not care that you are the leading supplier of distributable commodities when evaluated on a quarterly basis. And they don't care about all the wonderful clients you have.

No doubt you would like them to care. In fact, it might be your primary objective to make them care. But the burden of caring is yours, not theirs. You have to care first.

This has far-reaching implications for how—here comes that word again—how you design your presentation and the slide deck you create for it. If you begin your presentation talking about how wonderful your company is, a combination of four things is likely to happen:

■ Audience members will stop listening.

■ They will figure out that your focus is not on them and they might become resentful.

■ They will be on guard for the rest of the presentation because it already feels like a sales pitch to them.

■ They will listen with their ears but not with their hearts or their gut.

And yet, as we have noted numerous times across these pages, most presentations are structured this way. Most presentations are hard-wired to fail at the ultimate objective: reaching out to the hearts and the souls of an audience.

Good design of a presentation begins with the central question: what does your audience care about and how can you connect with their pain and their passion?

If you care about their passion, the chances are much higher that they will care about yours, and that is the best-case scenario. Now, instead of you having to hit them over the head with your mission statement, unique services, history, clients, yadda yadda, as you near the end of your presentation, they just might be asking you about those things. Welcome to the promised land.

3. Get away from the computer

We covered most of this point back in Chapter 7, so we'll be brief here. Your best ideas usually come when you can freely associate them with other ideas and other people and toss them around in an interactive setting. Most people are more creative when they can do that.

As wonderful as computers are, they do not promote that type of creative thinking. They might be unrivaled in their ability to help you express those great ideas, but more often than not, they serve to inhibit your having the ideas in the first place.

So start designing your presentation away from the computer.

- Instead of a keyboard, get a yellow pad and a pencil.

- Instead of Outlook and Facebook pinging you every few seconds, put on your favorite music.

- Instead of clutching the mouse, pour yourself a glass of wine.

Create an environment in which you can freely think about how you want to deliver a message. Don't think about bullet points, slide masters, or fast fades on clicks.

Just you and your ideas. How can you best engage your audience? What do you want them to feel about your message? That's the basis for good presentation design.

Design vs. Décor

Let me share with you a spirited debate that took place a couple of years ago between members of the Presentation Summit conference team. It had to do with the name of one of our seminar tracks, Design and Décor. One of the presenters on our team, Nancy Duarte, familiar to many of you, fired off the first salvo:

> Can you substitue the word décor in the track name "Design and Décor?" There is a huge difference between them and decorating a slide is bad.

Decorating a slide is bad. I didn't know that; I'm still not sure I know that. I wondered if Nancy was reacting to a potential situation that she has probably seen countless times, in which a client or colleague only wants to pretty up a slide, without regard for how the slide deck functions, how it was built, or above all, what message it is trying to communicate. So I pressed on a bit:

> The point of the track name is that designing a presentation and decorating a slide are two very different things. Slide decoration is not an intrinsically bad thing, unless it is done in lieu of design. Décor is necessary; the problem is that many people don't understand what the word "design" means and when they hear the word, they immediately think of décor.

That wasn't good enough for Nancy, who pressed her case a bit, too:

> Décor is simply for visual pleasure. If you look at dictionary.com they even use words like "decorative baubles" to describe it. Whereas the word design has its origins in the word designate. That means there is an intentional way to designate or display things for optimal visual and cognitive intake. Randomly placing baubles in places because you like them there is very different than thinking through hierarchy, purpose, and intentional arrangement of the information.

I thought back to the days when interior designers were called decorators. We had a terrific one who might have taken issue with the suggestion that she dealt in baubles of visual pleasure.

But it was when I spoke with Julie Terberg about this that the issue came into sharper focus. Also a prominent presenter at the conference, when Julie performs makeovers, she often does not have the luxury of being able to scrutinize the message or revisit the foundation of a slide deck. Sometimes, she's just in rescue mode! Yet she too bristles at the idea of being the decorator of slides.

> I never use the word décor. I would use the term embellishment or design element. I like to try to create a cleaner layout, simplify, create consistency, pick up elements that might be pleasant already.

But that's décor, I argued.

> I don't agree. They are graphic design pieces. Décor says that you are fancying it up, sometimes to excess. It has a negative connotation. We don't want to just fancy them up.

Julie put her finger on it: The word has a bad rap. In far too many cases, the only help that a bad slide deck gets is a futile attempt to get prettied up. The quintessential lipstick-on-a-pig situation. So it's no wonder that the mere suggestion of taking into account the aesthetic nature of a slide deck is met with scorn. And you and I know this all too well: the words "PowerPoint," "slides," and "giving a presentation," are often the subject of derision.

Despite the strong opinions of two friends and colleagues whose work I respect and admire enormously, I am going to maintain that attending to the appearance of a slide is not a bad thing; in fact, I think it can be a good thing. But where the three of us agree is that it should never be the only thing.

The next few chapters, in fact, dive into the particulars of slide design (as opposed to presentation design), and I will remind all of us that the underlying foundation to good slide design is that the slide contributes to the tone, direction, and core message that you established when you sat down, away from the computer, to design your presentation.

The Triad of Presentation Design

A presentation is made up of three things:

1. What you say

2. What you show

3. What you give

These three things are so important to the presentation experience that it is incumbent upon you to think about how you can best deliver each one. While the gray area of all of this makes up the wonder and the beauty of our profession, what I can tell you with black-or-white certainty is that they should not be the same thing.

Each deserves your time and attention.

Chapter 16

Too Much Text!

My friend and colleague, Dave Paradi, conducts a biennial poll on the aspects of PowerPoint that annoy people. Most people talk with abstraction about their objections with the software; Dave actually finds out and quantifies it (thinkoutsidetheslide.com/survey2011.htm). And since 2005, the issue of text on a slide—too much text, to be specific—has never *not* been ranked in the top three of PowerPoint annoyances.

So this topic strikes me as the ideal place to begin the discussion on slide design. And because I'm not actually a graphic designer by trade, I will not attempt to create jaw-droppingly beautiful slides that might inspire and intimidate you.

Instead, my goal for everything we do in this chapter and the ones that follow is to make you think *hey, I can do that*.

16

Why Do We Create So Much Text?

We identify four legitimate reasons why well-intentioned content creators feel compelled to overload their slides with text. Some are easy to resolve, others not so easy—and in all cases, the text creates one of the most insidious barriers to a presenter being able to connect with his or her audience.

Here, for your reading enjoyment, are The Four Reasons Why Excessive Text Can Ruin Your Day.

1. You do not know any better

We spoke about this way back in Chapter 1 when we sketched one of the typical profiles of the PowerPoint user: the person who comes to the software from other Office apps and has no idea that a quick copy-and-paste from Word could lead to Death by PowerPoint.

If this is you, you're easy. You have not yet formed a multitude of bad habits. You simply followed your instincts and thought that the stuff you wrote in Word would work as well in PowerPoint. You simply need to learn about the foundation of what makes for good presentation content, and with few preconceived notions already in place, that training would likely go quickly and without trauma.

You are the easiest to address. You create slides like the one in Figure 16.1 (repeated from Chapter 2) because that is the only way you have known how to tell a story or deliver a message. You don't have bad habits; you have no habits, and that is a much better thing.

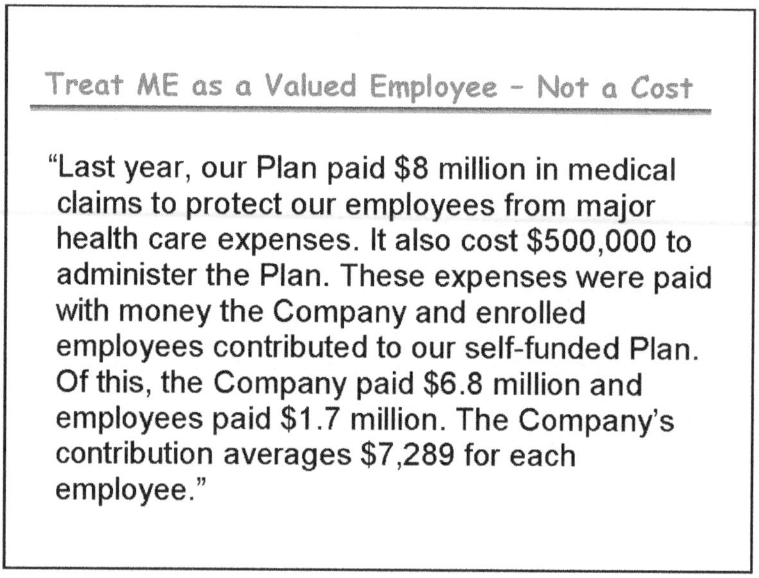

Figure 16.1
A person with no experience whatsoever with presentation design is liable to overcreate his or her slides.

Treat ME as a Valued Employee – Not a Cost

"Last year, our Plan paid $8 million in medical claims to protect our employees from major health care expenses. It also cost $500,000 to administer the Plan. These expenses were paid with money the Company and enrolled employees contributed to our self-funded Plan. Of this, the Company paid $6.8 million and employees paid $1.7 million. The Company's contribution averages $7,289 for each employee."

Figure 16.2
Can one slide sum up everything that is wrong with presentation visuals? Maybe so...

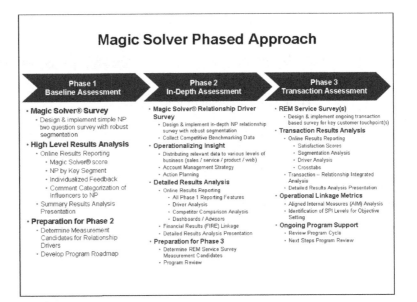

2. You are addicted

Your situation is more complicated than the person who simply doesn't know any better. You might very well know better, but you cannot help yourself. You do not feel comfortable unless everything you want to say is displayed before you. You don't believe you can function...you become paralyzed...you feel naked. Without your safety net of a fully-composed script being projected before you, you lose your composure and your poise.

Figure 16.2 will look familiar to those who read Chapter 13. It is the quintessential poster child for the too-much-text syndrome. My conversations with the client who created this slide were, all at once, educational, amusing, exasperating, and telling:

Me: Why do you want all of that text on the screen?

Him: I just feel more comfortable with it.

Me: What if we kept all of the high-level ideas but removed the detail?

Him: That would not be acceptable.

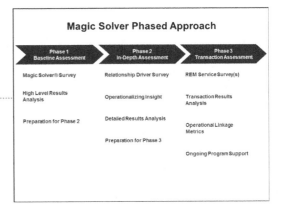

Me: How about if we compromised and created two levels of text?

Him: No, I want all of it to be shown. I concentrate better with it there and I'm more comfortable, knowing that even if I forget something, they'll be able to read it.

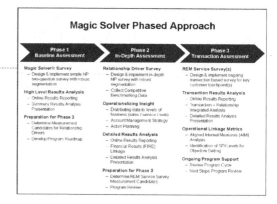

Although I didn't have the heart, it was my obligation as his hired consultant to find a way to tell him that his audience will never be able to read all of it, and worse, they cannot give him the attention he deserves with a backdrop of all that drek. He listened, nodded, and then said, "Well, that's my style and I'm not going to change it."

It might as well have been crack cocaine we're talking about here—he could not function without it. He was addicted. And I had no opportunity to conduct an intervention—he let me go a few weeks later.

Are you like my former client? Do we need to send you through detox? And what does detox look like with respect to text addiction? I actually have some experience in this matter...lucky me...

1. The first time you, the addict, try to deliver one of your standard presentations without your usual verbose slides, you feel awkward and lost. You don't know what to look at, you have difficulty keeping your train of thought, and you get thrown off by the fact that your audience is (perhaps for the first time) looking at you.

2. The second time is a bit better, as you realize that you must compose your thoughts from what you know, not from what you can read on the screen. It is still scary for you but there are moments when you connect with audience members in a way that you never had before. You actually made eye contact! You want to feel that way again.

3. By your third attempt, you own it. You are more comfortable sharing ideas that come from your heart and your experience and you not only enjoy the better contact with the audience, you begin to crave it. It's like a high.

You realize what I'm suggesting here—you have traded one addiction for another. The feeling of true audience engagement is so intoxicating, it is not long before you feel as if you cannot live without it. You're still addicted, but to something healthier. This is a good trade.

3. You want your slides to double as handouts

You are not going to like me for this discussion, because while trying to improve the quality of your work, I'm going to hurt the quality of your worklife. I'm both mindful of and sympathetic to the demands that are placed on presentation designers and creators in today's workforce. Your deadlines are often ridiculous. Nonetheless, I must tell you this:

> **In 17 years as a presentation consultant, I have not once seen a slide deck that successfully functions as both compelling visual content and informative written material. Not once.**

There is just no getting around it: if you create slides for your presentation that follow the ideas laid forth in this book—or the ones authored by Garr Reynolds, Nancy Duarte, Cliff Atkinson, or countless others—those slides will necessarily fail as printouts. And if you create slides that contain fleshed out thoughts for audience members to review afterward, you create instant Death by PowerPoint were you to project them.

These two purposes are hopelessly disparate—the twain shall never meet. And yet you are likely one of tens of thousands who attempt it on a weekly or maybe even daily basis.

My clients and my readers never like to hear it, but it is nonetheless my duty to inform them that they must create two documents in order to do this right. Stay tuned, however, for a creative solution that assuages some of the pain.

4. You are required to

We acknowledge that there are circumstances in which a presenter feels compelled, or is literally required, to read a passage of carefully-composed text and display that same text.

I refer you to Page 9 for the two universal axioms of PowerPoint that describe what happens if you attempt this without special training. There are few things in life more annoying than when a presenter displays fully-formed sentences on screen and then proceeds to read them. And yet, in our travels, we have identified numerous situations in which that very practice is required:

- An annual shareholders meeting, in which the presenter has a fiduciary responsibility to report both visually and verbally.

- A pet-adoption clinic that offers an orientation for new pet owners, including lots of DOs and DON'Ts.

- An airline's maintenance training program, in which proper procedure and protocol are of paramount importance.

In these cases, ensuring that the message is delivered takes precedence over the elegance of that delivery and we do not fault department heads for erring on the side of over-delivering a message, rather than under-delivering it.

And yet, we know what happens to audience members who get hammered with text—they tune out. Therefore, we refer you back to the sidebar on Page 44 and to the case study later in this chapter for our recommendation on how to deal with this reality.

Case Studies in Text Reduction

Several significant phenomena take place when you succeed in reducing the amount of text that appears on your slides. Here is a digest of the discussion back on Page 40 where we introduce the Three-Word Challenge:

- Your slides are friendlier.

- Your pace improves.

- You create intrigue.

- You learn your material better.

There is one other important benefit: you become a better slide designer. It is entirely possible that the reason you do not feel confident designing a slide is because you have never had the opportunity. The most accomplished artists wouldn't fare well when faced with slides that contain five and six bullet points, all complete sentences. But when you open up some real estate, you give yourself the opportunity, perhaps for the first time, to think about how an idea could be expressed visually.

That would be a liberation—a deliverance!—for you and for anyone whose PowerPoint career has been defined by excessive text.

The following accounts are proof positive that reducing the amount of words that appear on a slide creates a more rewarding experience for everyone concerned.

Southern California Edison and the Postage Stamp Syndrome

When the largest utility company in the western United States contacted us for presentation help, we knew that we would see some old habits that would die very hard. Edison's "Enterprise Resource Planning" rollout proved to be a difficult initiative to explain.

1 Slides like this one didn't help. I asked why there was a little photo of a man staring off the slide (I was more diplomatic than that), and the answer was telling: "We wanted to break up the text a bit."

My clients' instincts were correct about providing relief from the text, but adding a tiny photo isn't the answer. In fact, a photo like this serves only to add to the visual clutter. I call this the "postage stamp syndrome"—one of several knee-jerk responses that we regularly observe to the problem of too much text.

2 We insisted that the creative team at Edison take the Three-Word Challenge and they were equal to the task. Look at all of that fat that they identified...

3 Immediately upon removing the excess verbiage, one of the team members said, "Wow, look at that poor guy stuck in the middle of nowhere." Indeed, the postage stamp seemed even more out of place when swimming in all of that wonderful white space. It was as if he were now screaming out to be made larger and more prominent.

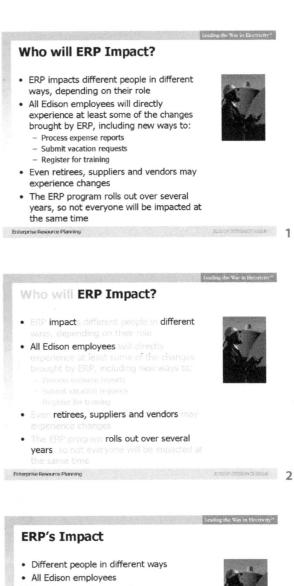

4 Once we sized the photo to its full height, it became even more apparent that having him looking off the slide was not such a good idea. When he was just a postage stamp, my clients barely even noticed him. But with the opportunity to actually see elements for what they are, the Edison folks began to think more like designers.

5 Moving him to the other side of the slide was the cognitive leap that had the biggest impact, and I remember well the "a-ha" moment that occurred when that move in turn suggested that the text be shifted to the right. At this point, the slide would have been deemed ready for its debut.

6 I suggested two additional tweaks—moving the headline into the photo and removing the bullet characters from the text. The first serves to integrate the two elements better and the second reflects my general desire to remove bullets when they are not needed. With a short list like this, I believe that the bullet characters serve no real purpose, and the slide looks less "PowerPointish" without them.

4

5

6

7 It didn't take the design team long to seek other opportunities to create a better visual impact. The very next slide was another paragon of text excess, screaming to be delivered from its purgatory.

8 Distilling this slide was easier—practice makes perfect—and the presenting team acknowledged that they could do just fine with the key talking points.

Getting buy-in from the presenters to undertake this kind of paradigm shift is vital. We also find it is easier to get their endorsement than you might think. They usually welcome the opportunity to be different and distinctive.

9 The new slide design practically presented itself. This photo was purchased from photos.com and the areas of open space were perfect for the remaining text. Using the simple drop shadows helped readability in areas where there was not high contrast.

▼ Download 16-03.pptx to see the progressions of these two redesigned slides.

Leading the Way in Electricity™

What Challenges do ERP Systems Address?

- Many separate systems which cannot share data
- Outdated legacy (existing) systems that cannot support growing business
- Lack of data consistency — multiple entry points and no single "version of the truth"
- Automation – some areas still rely on lots of manual processes
- Strong businesses need to integrate business functions across the enterprise

Enterprise Resource Planning

7

Leading the Way in Electricity™

What Challenges do ERP Systems Address?

- No data sharing
- Outdated systems
- Lack of consistency
- Manual processes
- Integration

Enterprise Resource Planning

8

What Challenges do ERP Systems Address?

No data sharing
Outdated systems
Lack of consistency
Manual processes
Integration

9

Part Three: Design

When is a Bullet Not a Bullet?

US Airways had long felt that its course curriculum could stand improvement, and this part of the book is peppered with examples of the time that we spent with the maintenance training team.

1 We encountered many slides like this one, in which a subtitle was formatted as a bullet, undoubtedly because that is the default layout for new slides. But a bullet implies a list of points—you cannot have a list of one.

2 As we began "three wording" the text, we realized that the first bullet did not even need to be a subtitle. It was superfluous altogether, so we eliminated it.

3 If ever there is an organization that owns compelling visuals, it would be an airline. This was one of countless aircraft-in-the-sky photos at our disposal. With the clouds providing an uneven background, we formatted the text placeholder with a touch of additional white (white fill, transparency of 65%), just enough to ensure readability.

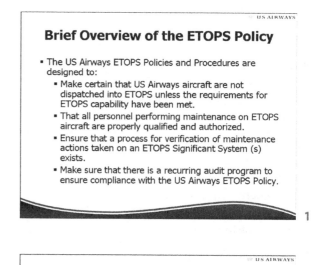

City Managers Just Want to Get to Bed Earlier

When the City of Chino Hills (about 30 miles east of Los Angeles) brought me in to help with presentation design and delivery, I asked a simple question first: "What part of the process provides the most stress?" The answer was quick and unequivocal: "We don't want the city council to always be mad at us."

1 The source of said ire? Slides like this one, often shown after 11:00p during long city council meetings. The slide number at the bottom-right is a clear indicator of the problem: city managers were trying to create a single deck for show and for print. See my earlier rant about how impossible that is. All of the information on this slide, by the way, was already emailed to councilmembers the day before and given to them when they entered the chambers. And now, nearing midnight, they have to look at it again. Imagine their thrill...

2 The makeover began with the ineffective border that did not start at the slide's edge and poached too much space from the content area. I also turned the title into a header. "Heritage Professional Center" is the development in question, but the slide is really about the proposed agreement. That should be the title. Finally, I found the city's logo on their website and integrated it into the running footer. And no slide number!

3 Those changes produced this result, which might be more attractive, but will do nothing to assuage the ire of city council members who want to get to sleep before midnight. So keep reading...

▼ Download 16-05.pptx and view it in Edit mode to see how this solution was designed and implemented.

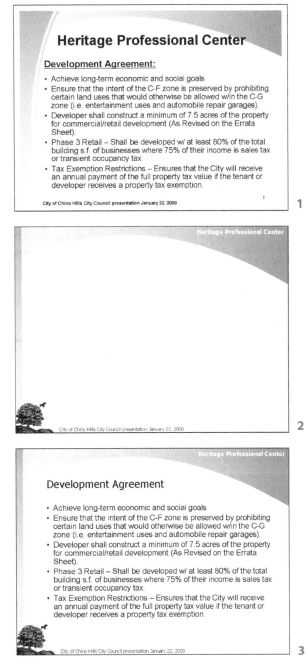

Part Three: Design

My redesign did not stop with a couple of new slide masters—I also made a stop at the Notes master, a part of the program that most users ignore. After all, who cares what the notes look like; they're just for your own purposes, right?

4 I am suggesting here an altogether different use of the Notes page: use it for handouts. You can design the notes master just as you would the slide master—here you see the graphic element atop, the tree logo and running footer, type set in a serif typeface (this style is for print), and a page number. Notice that the slide thumbnail is gone altogether; it would be your option to remove it or to integrate it into the design of this page.

5 Moving the text from the slide to the Notes page is incredibly easy, thanks to the small notes window normally visible below the slide.

Just copy and paste from the slide to the window...

6 ...And then begin three wording the slide. Now this slide won't offend the sensibilities or strain the tired eyes of city councilmembers.

7 Meanwhile, how's this for a professional-looking handout? Once the master was designed, it took all of 30 seconds to copy and paste the text and set the title in bold.

This is the way that every handout should be done—as a separate document. Using the Notes page to create the printed handout at least allows you to create both documents in the same PowerPoint file.

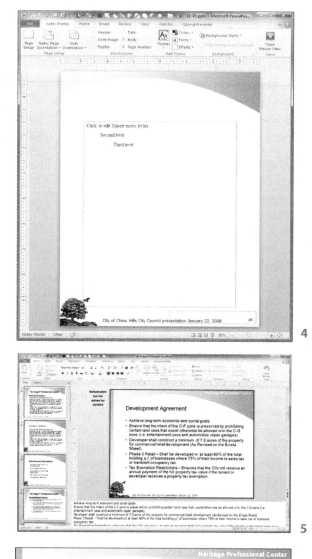

This became almost cookie-cutter-like for the city managers, as the three images below illustrate: the original slide was given a new design, the text was sent to the Notes page, and then the slide was reduced to key points.

And everyone got to bed on time.

▶ If you use the Notes master this way, make sure to save the file as a plain PPTX file, not a POTX template file. The Notes master is not preserved in template files so all of this nice design work would vanish.

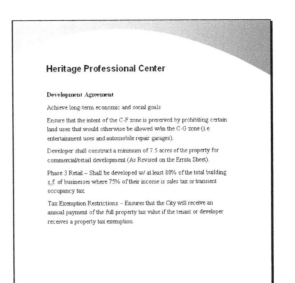

Display Every Word, Say Every Word...Just Not in that Order

Satmetrix is a client in San Mateo CA, about 15 miles south of San Francisco. Company reps dive deeply into the world of customer experience, feedback, and ongoing relations. They use sophisticated analysis and software, not just warm and fuzzies. They brought me in because their slides reflected that philosophy to excess. (As their work is highly sensitive and competitive, all of the content in these slides has been altered and rendered meaningless.)

1 This slide is a poster child for many of the problems that we discuss in this book. The larger issue, however, is that company officials believe that because this information is so vital to the audience, presenters must say it out loud, as it is displayed here, *and* show it on the slide. We refer you to Page 9 and Universal Axiom No. 2.

2 After the makeover and a bit of organizing of the content, the simple solution was to apply a touch of animation. Here, the slide displays just the three main categories of ideas that these points represent. Now let the presenter recite all of the content. Word for word, if necessary. Of course, now the presenter can't just read the slide; he or she needs to be better prepared than that.

3 When done, one click brings in all of the required content, satisfying the brass. But when you say it all first and *then* display it, it is not nearly as bad as displaying it first and then reciting it. See the sidebar on Page 44 for more on this topic.

▼ Download 16-06.pptx to see how this simple animation can be so helpful.

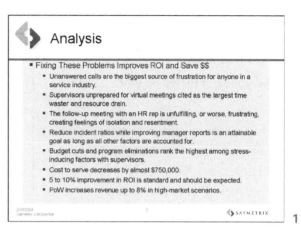

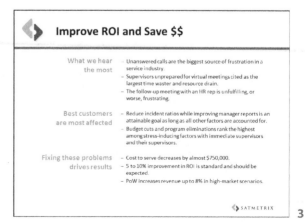

Chapter 17

Designing Presentations for Remote Delivery

The last time I felt like this was in 1999. We asked at the CorelWorld User Conference who in the audience owned a digital camera. Just three years after its introduction to consumer markets in the United States, over three dozen hands rose in a room of about 250.

"This is going to be huge," I said to a friend from Corel Corp., begging the real question as to why I couldn't leverage that prescience into a home with a Beverly Hills or Central Park address. Irrespective of my own lack of investment acumen, indeed, digital photography became THE killer app of the 1990s and early-2000s.

There is a killer app upon us in the presentation community. Presentations are slowly freeing themselves from the traditional constraint of notebook/projector/screen/person. Leading this charge are webinars, portable devices, and social networking sites. The next two chapters examine and speculate on the unique demands of designing for these emerging presentation destinations, starting here with the exciting yet daunting proliferation of the webinar as an alternate presentation medium.

We Try Harder...

For the better part of 16 chapters, you have had to read my badgerings about getting out from under your slides, not letting them derail you, and reducing the amount of text they contain.

Well, not so fast.

As we define and discuss alternate ways to deliver a presentation, the common characteristic that these alternatives share is their nomadic quality. They deliver a message without a warm body in the room. The most important component to all great presentations has been removed from the formula. You. You are missing!

Slides that you prepare for electronic delivery will now have to represent you in a way that has heretofore been regarded as impossible or unacceptable. Your slides are going to have to be smarter and they are going to have to try harder. They are going to have to become the presentation. That changes everything.

Delivering a Presentation File Electronically

The simplest incarnation of the remotely-delivered presentation is the PowerPoint file that you send via email or make available as a download. In this case, we will retreat from none of our admonitions about gratuitous animation or stupid transitions—that's still a one-way ticket to amateur land.

There are a handful of other considerations that must be addressed with the self-running PowerPoint file:

Typefaces
Your slide deck will run on someone else's computer and will be at the mercy of that person's typeface collection. Best to play it safe and use a sans serif face that is universally distributed, like Arial, Verdana, Tahoma, or Calibri.

Security
You will be doing more than showing your slides; you will be giving them away. Make sure that your Notes pages do not contain confidential, compromising, or embarrassing information. My mind invariably drifts to the pharmeceutical conference I once worked. A slide deck was being delivered to the organizer for queueing on the presentation computer. The file opened in Notes view (files remember the view settings present during the last save) and there on the title slide was the following directive: "Make sure to use all of the proactive verbs that PinHead demands." We're not sure who was represented by this less-than-flattering moniker, but we're pretty

sure that the employment status of the presenter suddenly became dependent on the sense of humor of he whose hatsize came under scrutiny.

More at issue here is the fact that all of your presentation content is available to be looked at, extracted, and distributed. Yes, you can password-protect the file and disallow saving, exporting, and printing, but it's better for your peace of mind to just build a bridge and get over it. The more restrictions you place on the file, the more unfriendly you make it, and someone hellbent on getting at your content will do so anyway. Our advice? Scrub the file of anything sensitive and send it out without restrictions. If you're squeamish about your audience being able to get a cursor on your text or graphics, send them a PDF file instead. The tech savvy will still be able to extract what they want to, but most won't bother.

Version

Version 2007 now enjoys wide-spread saturation in the businessworld, but the same cannot yet be said about Version 2010. Fortunately, there are few differences between the two worth discussing in this context, but if you were informed that a large share of your recipients are still using version 2003, that would be a game-changer. You'll need to ask yourself just how married you are to those cool drop shadows and reflections. They might become a shipwreck.

Voice

Here you must address the most fundamental question of all: how will the slides be narrated? The fact that you won't be there alongside them does not absolve you of the responsibility of determining what type of voice to offer. This is usually done one of three ways:

1. Allow the titles of each slide to lead the way. This is the easiest approach, technically speaking, but requires that your titles be descriptive, clear, and inviting.

2. Apply a "textover" (I might have just made up that word). Integrated with the slide's build is text that is clearly recognizable as the narration of the slide. This requires an additional element beyond using the title, but I nonetheless find it easier to create and better received by the audience.

3. Adding a voiceover. By integrating audio clips, you bring back the idea that a human presenter is leading the way. This is obviously the most labor-intensive. Is it worth the effort? You tell me...keep reading...

Part Three: Design

A Case Study in Choosing Narration

A primer on digital photography provided the perfect backdrop to experiment with adding narration to a slide deck that was to be delivered electronically.

1 When shown, this slide deck begins with a menu offering the three choices outlined on the previous page. Each of the three headings is a link to a custom show set to show and then return to this menu. All slides past the menu are hidden, so the only way to access them is to use this menu and click one of the headings.

2 This slide relies on the title and the animation to describe the value of framing your subject(s). After the title appears, when the viewer follows the <space> prompt, the black rectangle appears and the photo crops to it. After that, the story of this slide is over and the "Press <space>..." line at the bottom appears.

3 This next slide employs "textovers"—strings of text that appear in the animation sequence along with the crop. It is more dynamic than just using a title, as it simulates a narration, but without the overhead and effort of creating and embedding audio clips.

▼ To follow this case study, download cropping.pptx.

Figure 17.2
This slide is made friendlier and more navigable by the links along the bottom. But not all links should be created equal...

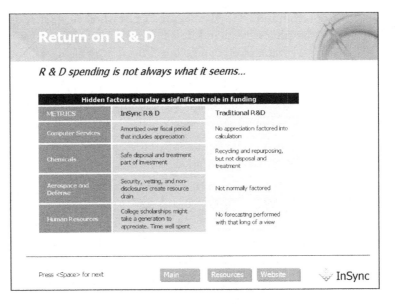

positioning that way, but it would likely frustrate you in all but the simplest of slide designs. The three links at right are fine to be placed on a master or a layout because you want them to always be visible, always available, always clickable.

But you need to be more strategic with the "Press <Space>" prompt, as it should appear only when all sequencing has completed. If it is on a layout, it can only follow other elements that build on the layout. All slide elements would come afterward and that would confound you.

If you were determined to use the layout for your user prompts, you could use a text placeholder instead of static text. That way, you can manipulate its position in the animation sequencing. The tradeoff: You would have to enter the "Press <Space>" text on every slide, because placeholders are empty by default.

If you just want a persistent button that advances when clicked, go ahead and build that on a layout. But then, most users know how to advance a slide deck, so how much value is it really bringing to the experience?

Our conclusion is that the most helpful on-screen cue is one that tells you, the viewer, that: the current idea on display is over, and when you are ready, press a key or click the mouse to move to the next idea.

Verbosity

All that stuff I told you about the three-word challenge and putting your slides on a diet? Well, you can forget about that when your slides are called upon to do the heavy lifting. When the text on a slide is the only way to communicate a verbal message, a whole new set of design principles assumes command. It is more critical than ever that your slides engage the viewer and that you control the flow of elements. You are capable of being brilliant; it's not so easy for your slides to be. There's a limit to how good presenterless slides can be. So in a way, you work from a disadvantage when you design and create self-running presentations. How best can you overcome that disadvantage?

Figure 17.3
Viewers of this slide will need to read this text for themselves. Can its readability be improved?

Figure 17.4
Opening up the line spacing and dividing the text into three chunks certainly helps.

Figure 17.3 is a slide about a municipal pet adoption program. As a self-running presentation, it has a lot of work to do—it must explain the program, generate interest, and include a call to action.

If this were a live presentation, this block of text would define the worst kind of Death by PowerPoint. Is it any better as a self-running presentation?

Only marginally.

Just because a self-running presentation makes it acceptable to include more text on a slide, it does not follow that a solid block of text is going to be welcome. Just the opposite; now that you have to have it there, it is even more vital to make the text as inviting as possible.

Figure 17.4 is better, with the copy in three distinct sections, the margins narrower, and the line spacing opened up. And if the corporate brass allows something so unique, Figure 17.5 is better still. Two things:

- Note that Figures 17.4 and 17.5 both have navigation control. Even something as simple as the one word in 17.5 is sufficient.

- Including a lot of white text on a black background is risky, however dramatic it looks here. Readability suffers with reversed-out text and it would be hell to print. A slide like this one is near the threshold of tolerance for white text. Anything more dense, and I would argue against its use.

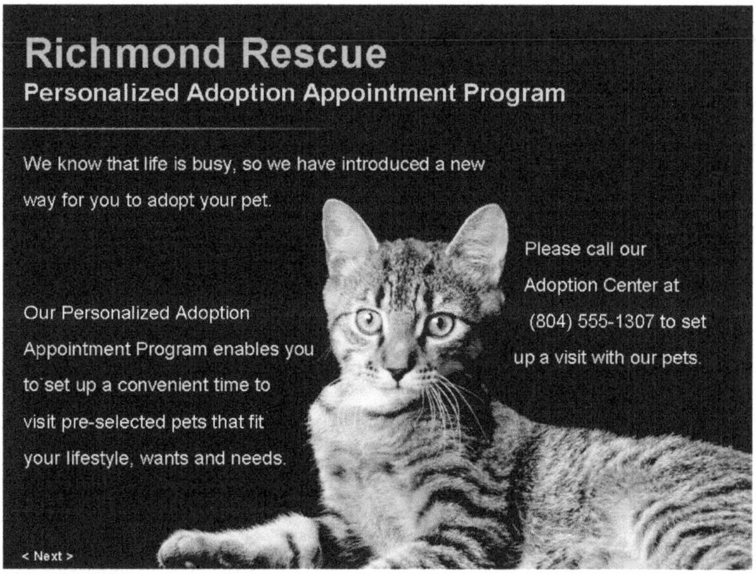

Figure 17.5
There is no reason why you still can't look for a big evocative photo to blend with your text-based message.

Richmond Rescue
Personalized Adoption Appointment Program

We know that life is busy, so we have introduced a new way for you to adopt your pet.

Our Personalized Adoption Appointment Program enables you to set up a convenient time to visit pre-selected pets that fit your lifestyle, wants and needs.

Please call our Adoption Center at (804) 555-1307 to set up a visit with our pets.

< Next >

Preparing Webinars

The notion of delivering a seminar from your own home or office, attended by people in their own homes or offices, was gaining traction before the bottom fell out of our economy. As travel budgets are getting sliced into smithereens, the webinar is becoming even more popular.

In most cases, preparing a webinar does not require that you learn new software, only that you use PowerPoint in different ways. As with the remotely-delivered presentation, the different medium suggests several shifts in strategy and this section of the chapter will define and discuss those strategies.

The bandwidth variable

The single biggest influence on your experience as content creator and/or presenter of a webinar is the performance drag created by your Internet connection. Little is more frustrating than watching your carefully-crafted fades and morphs become reduced to pathetic spasms of pixelation by the rush-hour traffic that we refer to as "latency."

For this reason, you should forego ambitious forms of animation. As bandwidth increases, webinar plumbing improves, and by the middle of 2012, we have come to expect that Fade, Wipe, and simple motion will perform acceptably. There are several mitigating factors, however:

All fades are not created equal

A one-second fade from one conventional slide to another is not the same as a four-second fade from one full-screen photo to another.

At worst, the fade will not come off as planned, and it will resemble the basic Appear, so the risk is not terribly high. But if you were counting on that fade to create drama and impact, the result will likely disappoint you. Use Fade to soften and smooth transitions, and if a latency storm hits, it's not a disaster.

Where do the slides live?

Your webinar service provider probably offers you two choices when presenting: You can either upload your slide deck to your provider or you can run your slide deck from your own computer and ask that your screen be shared.

Uploading your slides ahead of time will usually result in measurably better performance, but the cost is high: you must send your content well ahead of time and be willing to not deviate from the visuals you have prepared. I go kicking and screaming to this choice, insisting that we first try sharing my desktop. I greatly prefer having the flexibility of hyperlinking to a related topic or a software demo, and I willingly trade a bit of performance for that. Performance has to be dreadful for me to concede that.

What are you showing?

If you are just showing slides, demands on your provider are known and predictable. If you are demonstrating software, that's different. Now the audience must track your cursor and watch you pull down menus and execute commands. That is more taxing. If you are planning to demo software, you *must* share your desktop and accept the drop in performance.

It used to be that online services would request that you not even run your slides in Show mode, asking that you instead step through them in Edit mode. In that case, the only way to create a build is from one slide to the next. Those of us on the bleeding edge of all of this used to create our builds that way to begin with, just so we could be prepared for any scenario.

Times are better—we don't have to do that anymore. And you can pretty much count on being able to build simple sequencing to better describe complex relationships and systems. Just stick to simple fades and wipes and you should be fine.

Even with your slides free of excess motion, the very act of advancing from one slide to the next will take place for your audience more slowly than what you will see on your own computer. This is why we always recommend that you request two nodes into the webinar from your location—as host and as guest. If you have a notebook PC or a netbook at your disposal, log on from it as a guest and have it next to you as you deliver your content. You will then see exactly when a latency storm hits so you can adjust your cadence and pace accordingly.

▶ We wish that we could report that your second login could be your iPad, but too many webinar services are Flash-based. We have had luck with connecting to webinars with Android tablets and phones. Watching an entire webinar on a smartphone is only for the youngest of urban professionals, but if you are just monitoring the speed of the display, that's a bit more plausible.

Strong voice, strong visuals

Listening to a disembodied voice is never as engaging or as vital as when watching a live presenter. No eye contact, no watching lips move, no absorption of gestures—these all suggest that your voice has to carry the day. You need to find occasions to raise your voice, opportunities to create emphasis, and times to stage dramatic pauses.

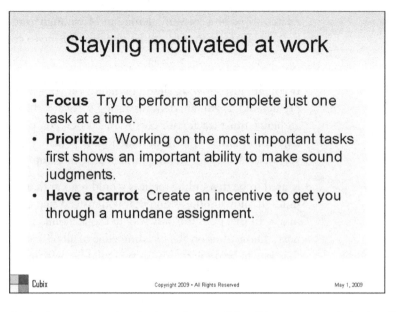

And whatever you do, don't read your slides. It's even more irritating for an online audience than it is for a live one. At the same time, it's much easier for your webinar audience to give up on you if you commit Death by PowerPoint. They're just one new email or text message away from tuning you out if you become a drone.

Figure 17.6 is a run-of-the-mill slide for a webinar discussing strategies for better workplace performance. If this slide appears like this, Universal Axiom No. 2 immediately rears its ugly head, as you feel the overwhelming compulsion to read the slide.

Say goodbye to half of your audience in 10 seconds. The only thing worse than watching a presenter read this slide after you have already read it is listening to a disembodied voice read it after you. Your audience would tune out, determine that you are an inane drone, and you would deserve it.

Audience engagement is a much more fragile commodity on a webinar, so the stakes are higher.

This is the best opportunity ever for you to substitute big, strong visuals for your text. Even if you are addicted to reading text word for word, you can get away with it on a webinar—nobody sees your script.

These slides will prove much more effective to the fleeting attention span of a webinar audience.

1 This first image is one that even non-golfers can relate to—who would not rather be anywhere than at work?

2 The next slide introduces the three key objectives that you want them to focus on, and it is here where you make your case. If you have to, read your script word for word.

3 And when you're done, then reveal the rest of the copy. As we discussed in Chapter 8, saying it before displaying it is a much better experience for your viewers.

If the webinar organizers intend to create PDF files from your slides and send them as handouts, try to persuade them to let you create them instead. A progression like this one is great for visuals, but tedious and annoying as three separate pages of a handout. Better to use the strategies discussed in Chapter 16 and craft a dedicated set of handouts.

1

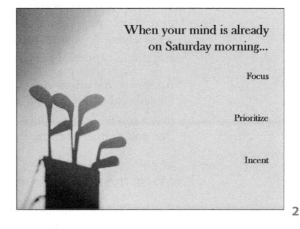

2

3

They're going to multitask...get over it

It is the dream of every webinar leader that he or she is so captivating and engaging that every member of the audience is riveted to the browser window, hanging on every word.

Emphasis on dream.

It is not necessarily a reflection on you or commentary on your webinar skills if the attention of your audience members wanes. They are in their cube or home with their iPhones, not in an environment in which it is rude to check their emails and texts. Not to put too fine a point on it, but during a webinar that you host, you are not a speaker so much as you are just another application window. Sorry if the truth hurts.

You have two choices: fight it or accept it. If you try to compete with the distractions, you might find yourself just pumping up your volume to the point where, as we discussed last chapter, in your attempt to emphasize everything, you will be emphasizing nothing.

Accepting this situation does not mean conceding; just the opposite. Understand that while you are talking, audience members might be listening to you while watching something else. Or as you have moved to a topic that doesn't interest them, they are waiting for the next topic.

So give them easy-to-follow cues that tell them that they should regroup and return their attention to you and the webinar screen.

- State prominently: "Okay, for our next topic..."

- Use conspicuous segue slides when transitioning to new topics.

- Ask a rhetorical question or make a controversial statement.

Then when you have everybody's attention, respect it: Use the inverted pyramid approach that journalists and reporters user to deliver the most important parts of the new topic right away. Let people take it in at whatever pace they want, and if they then choose to return to that spreadsheet they were working on, don't take it personally.

If you try to make everything important, you cry wolf. If you reserve this type of emphasis for transitions, your audience members will appreciate the cue and will indeed stop what they are doing and pay attention to the new topic.

If only for a moment...sigh...

Chapter 18

It's Nice to Share

Let me start this chapter by quoting a passage from the second edition: "Twelve months ago, few of us were writing on anyone's walls and nobody was following anyone's tweets. It wouldn't surprise me if, 12 months from now, we are uploading slide decks to the cloud and sending links to them. I am certain that these [few] paragraphs on this topic will make up an entire chapter in our next edition."

Welcome to that chapter, celebrating all of the ways that we can distribute slides and presentations in our wired world. The sun never sets on the opportunities before us to share, distribute, and collaborate, and I am equally certain that new opportunities will present themselves before even the first copy of this third edition rolls off the press.

So until then, here is an overview of a few of the many opportunities and technologies that enable us to share our work more simply and more capably.

18

Look to the Sky

Few recent buzzwords have taken root as firmly as cloud computing. As Internet connectivity and bandwidth improve, it has become incresingly trivial for us to send content to places other than our own computers and local networks.

Aside from the obvious safety benefits of having your important data in more than one location, presentation content creators can distribute their work in a variety of ways. All of it stems from the emergence of "the cloud," which is just a lofty way to describe data storage on servers connected to the Internet.

In this overview, we first want to make the distinction between services that act as simple receptacles for your presentations (like data backup services), and services that act as a host and a distribution center for your presentations. And we'll start with the latter.

At your service

There is no shortage of organizations that would like you to park your presentations with them for easy distribution and viewing. And in order to ensure universal web viewing, these services all translate native PowerPoint format into something more universal—usually Adobe Flash, which adds a layer of complexity to the discussion, given Apple's continued refusal to support the Flash format.

Most of these services share the following characteristics:

- Support for direct upload of native PowerPoint (.pptx) files

Figure 18.1
authorSTREAM is quick on the upload and wide on compatibility.

Figure 18.2
BrainShark's iPad viewer is top-notch, barely breaking a sweat with our torture test shown here.

- Unique URL assigned to presentation

- Code available to embed in blogs, websites, and social sites

- Replication of PowerPoint animation

- Inclusion of audio and narration

- Compatibility with iOS products that do not support Flash

We know that as soon as we start listing them, our list will be out of date. No matter, here is an already-incomplete list of a few of the more prominent outfits with whom you can share your presentations. Listed here in alphabetical order.

authorSTREAM

One of the many Flash-based hosting services, authorSTREAM is in pursuit of one of the easiest experiences for PowerPoint users looking to share their work. The company freely distributes authorSTREAM Desktop, a tool whereby you can quickly upload slides to the company's site and have them be automatically available for viewing and shared by social media.

authorSTREAM claims full compatibility with all mobile devices, despite its roots in Flash. Figure 18.1 shows a presentation being hosted at the site displaying accurately on an iPad, an iPhone, and an Android phone.

BrainShark

Sporting one of the cooler names in the industry, this outfit offers several services, all around making online slides smarter and more useful. To any

Part Three: Design

Figure 18.3
Docstoc is like the supermarket for business documents. Browse the aisles and pick what you need...

PowerPoint deck you upload, you can add sound and narration, and also track how wide an audience it attracts. "Create, Share & Track" is the company slogan.

Also turning heads is SlideShark, an iPad viewer for native PowerPoint files that actually works. Figure 18.2 is somewhat of a torture test, with four ornate typefaces, close alignment of images and text, and carefully synced animation, all of which performed with SlideShark as if it were taking place on a Windows notebook.

Docstoc

This site wants to be regarded as the ultimate clearinghouse for business documents. You don't just upload your documents there; you make them available for sale. You don't just visit the site to view people's work; you also go there to purchase them for use as templates and guides for your own work.

Figure 18.3 shows a typical document available for sale. There are many free documents to peruse, as well; in fact, most of the PowerPoint files at the site are free, including entire archives from companies. There are a few webinar slide decks that bring new meaning to Death by PowerPoint, so wading through could be slow going.

Scribd

Originally a social reading site, Scribd has become a valuable information tool for publishing houses and news organizations. It houses many presentation files that are considered potentially useful for background information gathering and research. Practically anything can be uploaded, with the expectation that it is freely distributable.

You would not upload files to Scribd to gain visibility, stature, fame, or fortune. You would do it to contribute to a collective reservoir of knowledge that would be appreciated by others.

SlideBoom

Developed by iSpring Solutions, the leaders in PowerPoint-to-Flash conversion, SlideBoom is one of the most robust services of all. There is little that you could throw at SlideBoom that it couldn't catch—video, embedded audio, complex animation, precise slide timing.

SlideBoom is not as well known as SlideShare or SlideRocket, so it would not be the best choice if your primary aim is page views. But coupled with the iSpring add-in for on-the-fly conversion of PowerPoint to Flash, it is more accurate than most other services. If your needs are to have the most faithful reproduction possible of complex slides, SlideBoom is hard to beat.

As an aside, we're fans of iSpring, too, as we create many of our web promos with it. Figure 18.4 shows our easy effort in PowerPoint to create an image

Part Three: Design

Figure 18.4
Creating video from PowerPoint has never been easier, thanks in part to Flash export add-ins like iSpring.

Download 18-04.pptx and 18-04.swf

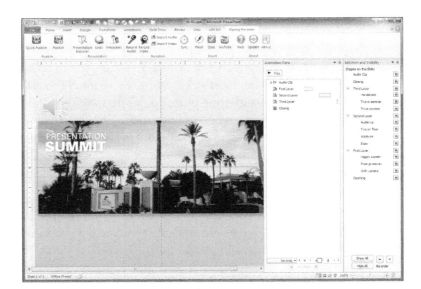

collage, complete with a snappy audio clip. With iSpring, we pump it out to Flash with a single click and create squeaky clean multimedia files.

SlideShare

The oldest and most heavily-trafficked of the group, SlideShare is essentially the YouTube of presentation files. With nearly 60 million unique visitors monthly, SlideShare is where people post work that they want to have noticed by peers, potential employers, and would-be clients. In addition, it's a hangout, with regular contests, blog postings, channels, webinars, discussions, and meetups. Figure 18.5 shows its rather extroverted personality.

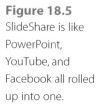

Figure 18.5
SlideShare is like PowerPoint, YouTube, and Facebook all rolled up into one.

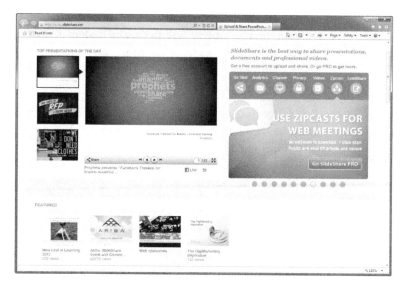

SlideRocket

All of the afore-mentioned services want you to upload your PowerPoint files to them. SlideRocket wants you to ditch PowerPoint altogether. Billing itself as an authoring platform, it offers multimedia integration, full hyperlinking, and synced narration. Yes, you could upload a PowerPoint slide deck as a starting point, but it's best for you to think of SlideRocket as its own beginning.

When you create a presentation for SlideRocket, it doesn't live there and here, only there. Sliderocket is entirely cloud-based—you are beholden to an Internet connection. This is a matter of perspective, of course, and company reps would argue that you are not shackled to a PC or a thumb drive—you could present from anywhere.

As this is a different paradigm altogether, SlideRocket needs to be a bit evangelist to get people over on the concept. Its website is full of content extolling its own virtues, and sometimes, it's difficult to separate wheat

Figure 18.6
SlideRocket offers one of the more robust authoring toolkits around. It's more work than just uploading slides to a site, but is worth the effort when you want to provide more than static slides.

whypptsucks.com/
18-06.htm

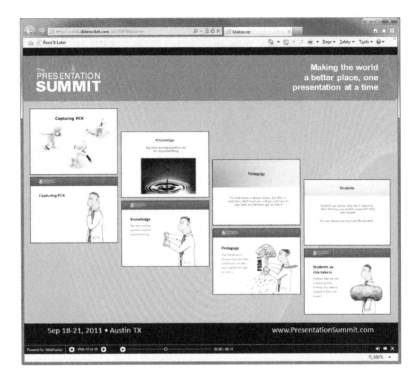

from chaff. That said, it is a powerful platform, which we used to promote last year's conference with a recreation of one of our makeover sessions, shown in Figure 18.6.

Zoho Show

Rounding out this list is a leaner alternative to SlideRocket's online authoring. Zoho Show offers simple tools and lots of ready-made templates and objects to jumpstart slide-building. Earnest PowerPoint users will likely find the interface tedious, and the social networking tools are deficient, but those too busy to make peace with PowerPoint would find safe haven here.

Insurance in the Cloud

Distinct from slide-sharing, there is a second niche of services that allows you to upload files to a connected server and then access them anywhere. It goes by many names—online backup, online sync, online collaboration—depending upon your own purpose.

Online file storage is less interactive than slide-sharing, as the files just sit there. But don't underestimate the value in files that just sit on a server that can be accessed anywhere, anytime, from any device. I find it enormously comforting to know that the presentation that I was up all night preparing lives on my hard drive and on my backup drive, as well as on a cloud server, making it accessible to me from any Internet-connected computer in the world, from my Android phone, and from my iPad.

In many cases, using the cloud is the easiest way to transfer a file. I don't like having to wrestle with iTunes to copy a file to my iPad, and I find it the height of kludge to have to email a file to myself just so I can access it from my phone. Online storage services all have simple interfaces and easy-to-install apps that simplify and "de-kludge" the process.

I have tested many of these services, all of which offer free accounts and paid upgrades that provide more storage, security, and/or features. All of these would suffice for typical purposes:

- DropBox

- iCloud

- SkyDrive

- SugarSync

I gravitated to DropBox and opened a free account, providing me with 2GB of storage. Were I seeking a service for online backup, 2GB would not be enough, and I would have to pay for more storage or choose a service whose free account offers more capacity. As it is, for sharing files, 2GB is ample.

So I have a file I want to share with you. It's a cool promo for the conference, extolling the virtues of our fabulous Help Center. I have blended some video interviews with some nice still footage, and synced it with the legendary and aptly-named Beatles song. I have cut the video, created it as an MP4 file, and I have placed it in the Public folder in my DropBox account. DropBox allows folders to be private, semi-private, password-protected, and in the case of the one called Public, completely open and unrestricted. The URL and QR to the video file is

▶ www.whypptsucks.com/helpcenter.htm

As long as that video file resides in the Public folder, you can access it from any device that supports DropBox (which is almost all of them) and play it. And then decide to attend the conference...!

Hosted Video

The previous scenario could have been used for any type of digital content; we chose video just as an example. We actually prefer to handle video a different way. We make a lot of videos over here—between tutorials, portfolios, and conference propaganda, we probably have close to 30 of them posted at BetterPresenting.com. I make them all myself, using PowerPoint, Adobe Premiere Elements, and/or Proshow Producer, and it used to be quite an ordeal to upload and manage them all (not to mention a healthy chunk of storage needed).

Now we send all of them out to be hosted elsewhere, just as millions of people do at YouTube. We prefer the Vimeo service for its ease of use and greater flexibility, but no matter which service you choose, you can count on the following:

- Support for high-definition
- Options for third-party sharing
- Full-screen and playback controls
- Custom URL
- Customizable embedding
- Compatibility across all popular devices

The other critical advantage that robust video hosting sites enjoy is better streaming. Videos that would otherwise take several minutes to buffer before playback will start in just a few seconds and rarely need buffering time.

When you host a video elsewhere, you can establish all of the parameters—name, size, resolution, embedding status, URL—and replace the actual video as often as you need. Here is how we placed the Help Center video into action with a video service:

1. Using Proshow Producer, we blended video snippets with still photos, interviews, and a soundtrack.

2. We exported from Proshow in one of several standard formats. We chose WMV, but could have chosen MOV, AVI, MPG, or others.

Part Three: Design

3. We uploaded the WMV file to Vimeo and proceeded to set several parameters, starting with simple stuff like Title, Description, and Thumbnails.

4. Then we answered several questions about if and how to embed the video, after which we were furnished with the necessary HTML to show and run the video from a web page.

5. The code to embed this video looks like this:

```
<iframe src="http://player.vimeo.com/video/33841766?
title=0&amp;byline=0&amp;portrait=0&amp;loop=1" width="960" height="720"
frameborder="0" webkitAllowFullScreen mozallowfullscreen
allowFullScreen></iframe>
```

You could take that code and place it on a webpage or a blog post and a little thumbnail would appear, and if a visitor clicked it, the video would play in a 960x720 window. Be our guests!

6. We dropped that code onto our Video Vault page, and the clickable thumbnail automatically appeared, with the description below it.

▶ View the video at Vimeo: www.vimeo.com/betterpresenting/help-center

See it at our website: www.presentationsummit.com/video

Part Three: Design

The Version 2010 factor

With its improved support for video, PowerPoint 2010 gets to play in this sandbox. Version 2010 offers video support in two critical areas: 1) Better handling of imported video; and 2) Export of slideshows to video format.

1 These two improvements have changed the way that we create many of our training videos, as we now use PowerPoint to create split-screen tutorials, in which I appear on the left half of the screen and my slide images appear on the right.

2 Once we import the video, we create bookmarks in it and trigger animations off of them. Interpreting the task pane shown here, the imported video is called final cut.wmv, and it contains eight bookmarks. Pictures 1-5 are each screen images, timed to appear when the playback of the video reaches each bookmark. Ending music (outro.mp3) is also timed to a bookmark, set on a five-second fade-in.

When all of the pieces are assembled, this is exported as a WMV file, using version 2010's Create a Video command. That video is then taken over to Vimeo for hosting.

Download 18-08.pptx to see how it was built. View the hosted video at vimeo.com/ betterpresenting/addicted

Socializing

Perhaps the most compelling reason for all this sharing is to leverage your social network. When you upload slides to sharing services and when you use video hosting services, you make it easy to showcase your efforts at Facebook, LinkedIn, and Twitter. Thanks to permanent and customizable URLs, it is trivial to share your work with the people in your networks. We have a few recommendations:

- While you could upload a video file to Facebook, it is better to create a link to the one you have hosted. Not only is it easier to manage just one video and refer to it from links (instead of uploading multiple copies of it), but the quality of the playback will be better.

- You can set up automatic updates through the cloud, so that new uploads to slide-sharing services or changes to existing content would automatically trigger a notice on your Facebook wall, LinkedIn status, or at Twitter. You can also create blog postings that get fed automatically to your social networks. Be careful, however, lest you end up in an infinite loop that could bother your friends and followers. For instance, if you choose to announce updates to your content, it might happen with the smallest change, which would be akin to your telling the world what you had for breakfast. And if your blog is set to update at Facebook, which in turn sends out a tweet, make sure that your tweets are not set to trigger blog postings. If so, you'd be on a never-ending treadmill.

Working Your Back Channel

It used to be that we would look with scorn at audience members who were playing with their mobile devices during a presentation. Those are the good old days—today, if audience members seem to be distracted, they might actually be busy disseminating the ideas they are hearing in real time.

Twitter has created the ultimate back channel for modern-day presentations, and instead of measuring the success of your talk by how attentive people look, you might have to count how many heads are pointing lapward at mobile devices. The more tweets a seminar gets, the wider its reach becomes.

Presenters can tune in to their own Twitter tags and get nearly-immediate feedback on their talk. In fact, some presenters actually take the pulse of the audience during their presentation.

I'll get back to you when I decide if my prevailing reaction to that idea is excitement or fear...

Part Three: Design

ran out of emphasis options (the bullets are already set bold), so he needed to resort to underlining. The swoosh has moved to the bottom, where it collides with the text, and the watermarked aircraft remains on these pages. I kept thinking about what a nice image it is...if only people could see it.

4 When untinted, the aircraft in the background creates a stunning image. It's clear and sharp, and is set against a beautiful sky-blue background. It was crying out to be used in a more prominent way.

5 Dropping the plane down a bit on the slide accomplishes two things: 1) It depicts a stronger sense of motion, as the plane is now flying up into the slide; and 2) It creates great usable white space (blue space?) along the top half of the slide.

6 With a more prominent logo, and sensibly-sized titles, this creates a much stronger identity for the curriculum. And with so many new hires coming through these courses, this becomes a first impression of the entire airline.

Trainers expressed concern over titles that would be too long to fit that space, and you can probably guess what my response was. Shorten them! Who needs titles that long?

As it turns out, they do, as much of the wording for this curriculum must follow FAA requirements. However, when we removed the upper-case lettering, every title fit. For any that require more words, the subtitle is set smaller and could accommodate that. Our technical editor Geetesh Bajaj insisted on his own commentary here: "These slides look happier!"

Part Three: Design

7 Interior slide designs were kept very clean and simple, because heaven knows there will be enough content asking to be used. The curvy line was replaced with two straight ones, using the US Airways colors, and the fading rule below the title matches the accent color below.

The title is formatted bottom-aligned and the main text top-aligned. That ensures that the space above and below the fading rule will always be the same.

8 This second layout represents only a subtle change, but it has proved crucial to the content creators, who kept getting into trouble with bullets of one, or with attempts to remove the bullet, causing funky indents. This master accommodates complete sentences (a fact of life, due to the FAA regulations) that should not be formatted as bullets.

9 The concept of a transition slide was foreign to the department—content creators simply reused the title layout. This design is similar to the title, but with the aircraft tinted deep into the background.

The more challenging part of my time spent with US Airways involved my admonitions about reducing the amount of verbiage on slides (see the facing page for a couple of doosies).

This involves much more effort and forethought than the creators probably anticipated. Many harbor the belief that they can bring in someone like me to make their lives easier and reduce their workload. In fact, many of my suggestions to them involved putting forth more effort, not less. Creating the appearance that your slides are not working so hard is only accomplished by your working hard.

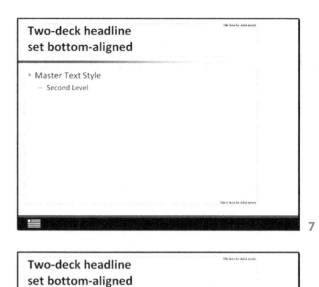

Before

After

Solavie: Giving a Facelift To a Face Product

Proof that Facebook can be good for business, I reconnected with Pam, a high school friend from about 175 years ago. As we wrote on each other's walls, she told me about Solavie, her line of skin and face care products that feature specific formulations based on the climate in which you live.

Most health and care products focus on your skin-type, not your environment, and that not only caught my interest, but also the interest of the QVC shopping network. QVC editors asked her to visit with them so they could determine whether to carry her product line.

The graphic work done to this point was elaborate—in fact, too elaborate for a presentation that needed to feature the woman as much as the product. Pam is an energetic and passionate advocate for her ideas, and I felt it critical that she shine during the QVC visit.

Therefore, a few things bothered me about the slides that Pam showed me. First, the watery background, while clever and on message, displayed as a drab gray and only served to reduce contrast and readability. Second, the first two content slides in the deck, **2 & 3**, would put Pam on defense. All of those data points and all of those paragraphs would derail even the most experienced presenter, which Pam was not. We had to find a way to brighten up the imagery and ensure that Pam could get out from under the slides.

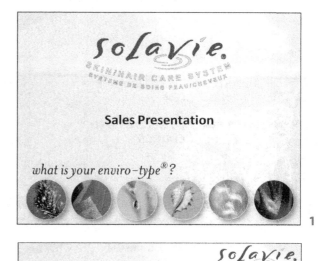

1

Beauty Industry Current Climate & Myths

- 1964 - Skin types
- 2008 - Enviro-types®

The Truth Behind Organic/Natural Skin Care

- Aqueous Solutions
- "Preservative Free"
- "Sulfate Free" - "Coconut Oil Derivative" is Sodium Laureth Sulfate.

Market Opportunity

- Industry Analysis quote 20% growth annually.
- Natural Skin Care has brand caché at premium price points just as Organic Foods.
- Demand for natural/organic skin care products of integrity, quality and authenticity
  has registered with the beauty industry from the top down.

2

Ingredients

Solavie Eco-Global Skin/hair Care System's ingredients are blended according to ancient tribal medicine rituals—the harnessing of a variety of native plants and phyto-nutrients in essential oils, plant extracts and anti-oxidants. We then concentrate according to predictable conditions within each enviro-type®: Mountains, Urban, Tropics, Shore, Plains or Desert.

Solavie is formulated to avoid wasting unnecessary ingredients.

All ingredients are vegetable-derived, non toxic, inert (non-reactive) substances beneficial in their applications of blending, absorption, or preservation of natural ingredients.

100% natural mineral-rich hot springs water boosts the effectiveness of anti-oxidants, and carries nutrients deep into skin/hair cells for optimal absorption. *Paraben-free. Sulfate-free. Toxin-free.*

3

On the positive, the logo is beautiful and the six enviroment icons are clean and descriptive. I wanted to create visual memory around them.

4 As far as I was concerned, if Pam just wanted to put up this one slide and talk, she'd likely succeed. The longer this title slide stays up, the more those six icons become ingrained and the more that Pam just talks, sharing her expertise and her passion for the product.

5 I normally resist such a strong and intrusive running footer, but not in this case. I loved the logo along the bottom left and wanted every opportunity to tie in those icons with the six enviro-types that represent Pam's innovation. (See Page 139 for a discussion on the animation technique we devised for introducing each of the six types.)

6 The icons also served as gateways to information on demand—content that would be too dense, unless specifically asked for by the QVC staff. For instance, clicking the Shore icon from any slide whisks you to this slide, after which you are returned to your previous location.

Pam had never heard of a wireless remote and I insisted that she purchase one. The last thing I wanted was to have her tethered to a notebook—we didn't know the type of room she would be in, but I wanted her free to roam it.

She suffered the type of withdrawal typical whenever I remove all of the text on slides, as her entire experience with giving presentations was limited to displaying documents on the screen and then repeating them. As always, though, when you find someone who has something compelling to say and you give her a chance to say it, good things happen. QVC liked what she had to say and carried the product for several seasons.

4

5

6

Before

After

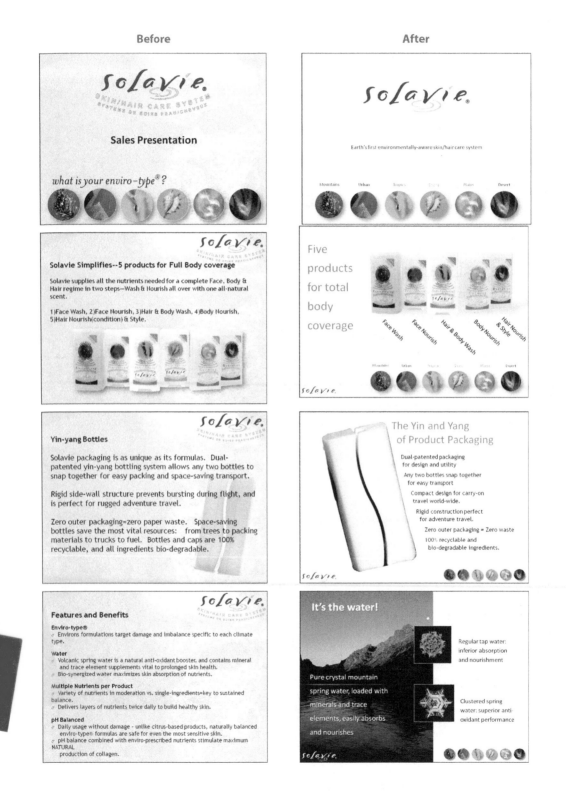

Hillary Clinton Commits Death by PowerPoint

As part of her narrative on being the more electable candidate for the hotly-contested 2008 Democratic nomination, the campaign for Senator Hillary Clinton distributed a PowerPoint slide deck to Democratic members of the House of Representatives on May 9, 2008. It was her hope that it would be viewed by many uncommitted superdelegates who might decide to commit support to her.

1 Not to suggest that she lost because of this, but the slides that the campaign sent up to Capitol Hill that night did nothing to help Clinton's chances. If the Clinton campaign had sought my advice, I would have pushed, at a minimum, for an entirely different approach to the design and execution of this self-running presentation. But if I'm being completely honest, I would have advised them against sending out a slide deck at all.

Those of us not in and around the Capitol did not get to see the actual slides, just low-resolution representations like the ones at right. But there were enough pixels for us to conclude that Clinton's staff did indeed succumb to Death by PowerPoint.

The slides contained a decent attempt at branding, via a slide header that contained the campaign logo. Beyond that, however, the slides exhibited a near-total lack of cohesion and design. Let us count the ways…

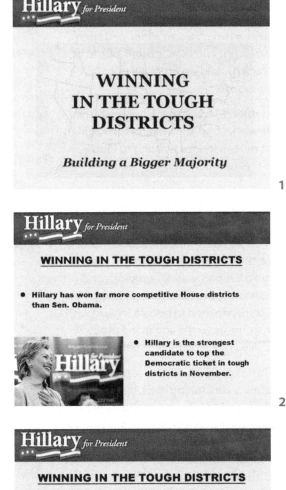

Headlines shout in all caps and all have underlines (**2** and **3**). I can only wonder how many congressional aides clicked on them, thinking they were hyperlinks.

The headline isn't even a headline—it's more like a running header. The slides do not actually contain true headlines.

Photo use is haphazard with one image of the senator stuffed into the lower-left corner on two different slides and then a non-descript and incongruous photo of the capitol building dropped onto another slide.

The table (**4**) is too much for any busy professional to deal with and the PacMan chart next to it does nothing to illuminate the message.

We're not sure where the bar graph (**5**) came from, or the pie chart (**6**), but they are clearly static images, not live charts. How do we know this? Because on both slides, the images were pasted on top of the text! It is particularly egregious and embarrassing on Slide 6, where it appears that someone tried to cover a legend with an opaque rectangle, and in the process, concealed much of the final paragraph.

The last slide (**7**) lacks any sort of punch befitting a concluding slide. It repeats the photo from Slide 2, repeats the running header, and offers a concluding sentence that appears to have been massacred by a committee on political correctness. This slide also displays the line "Paid for by Hillary Clinton for President." We hope they didn't pay much for it.

As I said, we did not see the actual slide deck, so we cannot say for sure whether the Clinton team attempted to create builds to sequence some of the chunkier data, like the charts and graphs. If we give her content creators the benefit of the doubt and assume that they did create builds for the more dense slides, then they are guilty of creating no navigational assistance whatsoever for the viewers working through the slides. In other words, if they did click through a build, they would have no way of knowing when that slide's sequenced information had concluded.

Hillary *for President*

WINNING IN THE TOUGH DISTRICTS

Of those 20 districts, Hillary has now won 16, most by large margins.

District	Member	District	Member
AZ-5	Mitchell	NH-1	Shea-Porter
AZ-8	Giffords	NY-19	Hall
CA-11	McNerney	NY-20	Gillibrand
FL-16	Mahoney	NY-24	Arcuri
IN-2	Donnelly	OH-18	Space
IN-8	Ellsworth	PA-10	Carney
IN-9	Hill	PA-4	Altmire
KS-2	Boyda	TX-22	Lampson
MN-1	Walz	TX-23	Rodriguez
NC-11	Shuler	WI-8	Kagen

'06 Pickups in Bush Districts

Clinton: 16   Obama: 4

4

Hillary *for President*

WINNING IN THE TOUGH DISTRICTS

- Hispanics make up more than 10% of the voters in 6 of the districts

- Nationally, Hillary has won Hispanic voters by 30 points (64-34).

- In Texas, she won by 34 points (66-32).

The Hispanic Vote in '08 Primaries

Clinton 64%   Obama 34%

5

Hillary *for President*

WINNING IN THE TOUGH DISTRICTS

Hillary has also won 10 of the 15 districts rated "toss up" for 2008 by the Cook Political Report. Sen. Obama has won only 4.

Of Cook's 80 "competitive" districts, Hillary has won 40 to Sen. Obama's 31.

Excluding caucus where turn out is lower than in prim general elections, has won only 23.

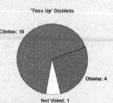

'Toss Up' Districts

Clinton: 10   Obama: 4   Not Voted: 1

6

The Makeover

This should not have been a slide deck in the first place; it should have been a document (elaboration coming).

Be that as it may, as we ponder how we would go about recreating these slides (pretending that we were actually hired to redesign them; we were not), we note that there is nothing in the original slide deck to move someone to take action. There is only an appeal to the intellectual component of the argument and that is rarely enough to compel someone to action.

8 The irony in all of this is that this visually unappealing and unemotional slide deck was put together by the same campaign that created a killer website, replete with thousands of excellent photos. In about 90 minutes, I was able to produce an entire makeover of the slides, relying just on low-res screen grabs of website photos.

9 I did not concern myself much with a slide master or a color scheme, as I knew the layout of each slide would be determined by the photo I chose for it. But I did set a standard for typeface (Verdana) and size (28 for titles, 20 for text).

10 The other common element I employed is a favorite technique for helping blend text with a photo—the gradually-changing transparent fill. Over areas that need less contrast and a darker background, I create a black rectangle and set its transparency to go from 0 (solid black) to 100% (completely transparent). I then set the text over the less transparent part.

11 The remake of the table slide was the most arduous, requiring first a photo with sufficient open space and then a trip into image-editing software to blur out the background. Perhaps I should have gone a different way with this slide, instead of trying to burn the table into a photo, but I only allowed myself 90 minutes. So this is as good as it got.

Again, it was remarkable how easy it was to get good imagery of Senator Clinton and equally unfathomable why the campaign itself ignored all of it.

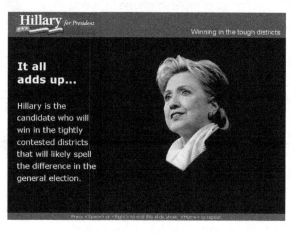

11

12

Still Not Good Enough

While I think that the makeover is much better than the original, there is still a fundamental disconnect that is taking place here with the campaign's appeal to superdelegates.

In short, this message should not have been created as slideware; it should have been a PDF document. Without a live person advocating these positions, the bulleted content is insufficient for fleshing out the argument, in the original slide deck or the improved one.

Clinton's arguments are too nuanced to be made by static bullet slides, especially poorly-crafted ones. They require deeper discussion and development, and if that is not going to be made by a live presenter, it needs to be made by printed words.

This deliverable should have been a completely-formatted document, created in InDesign or Xpress, or at a minimum, Publisher, with evocative photos, fully-formulated paragraphs, and integrated data charts. The whole thing should have been RIPed to a PDF file with relevant links to URLs for yet deeper analysis.

The data and the argument were potentially compelling, but I score this as a missed opportunity for the New York Senator…

Blame it on
The Handout

The No. 1 source of annoyance among business audiences today is the slide with too much text on it. And the No. 1 reason for that? Content creators asking for their slides to do double-duty. The 4Home team at Motorola is living proof.

1 If I had a nickel for every time a client explained slides like this as being necessary for the handout...I'd have a lot of nickels. This is classic Death by PowerPoint, brought on by a futile desire for this slide to function both as the visual component of the presentation and the printed handout. This slide met the typical fate: it failed at both tasks.

2 For the classic problem comes the classic response: shorten, shorten, shorten! With no small amount of elbow grease and cajoling, we ended up here.

3 We then found the perfect photo to help tell this story: a young couple in front of a modern television, controlling it with a tablet. It was everything that Motorola wanted to convey to potential customers.

But this failed as the handout. It didn't print well and the simplified text message did not provide enough context. To all of this I was tempted to say, "well duh." This slide was not designed to serve as a handout, and indeed, would perform poorly. So keep reading...

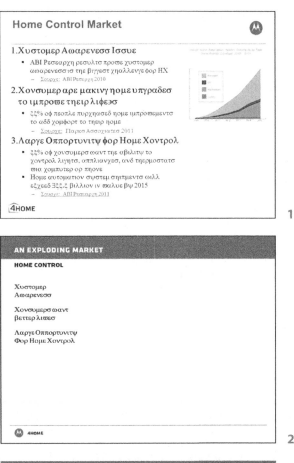

Part Three: Design

4 While most PowerPoint users know that you can place content on the Notes page other than just text and the slide thumbnail, very few know that there is a Notes master that governs its global design. Here are the elements that I placed on the Notes master, ensuring their appearance on every Notes page.

You can see where I'm going with this: the Notes page will house the handouts.

5 In less than 10 minutes, we were able to produce this page. All of the critical detail fits comfortably on this larger page size and it is much more readable. If nothing else, it is portrait, not landscape—most people prefer reading from pages that are taller than they are wide. Beyond that, the type is smaller, more legible, better laid out, and easier to follow. Everything about this page says to your audience members that you gave some thought to a better way to create a printed leave behind than the knee-jerk impulse to print the slide.

Now for the tradeoff: You lose your Notes page for the purposes of creating your own speaker notes. I would take the trade in a heartbeat; my speaker notes make up a mediocre commodity, easily created in Word or even Notepad.

I wish that Microsoft would give us a real Handout master. Until then, the Notes page fills the bill nicely.

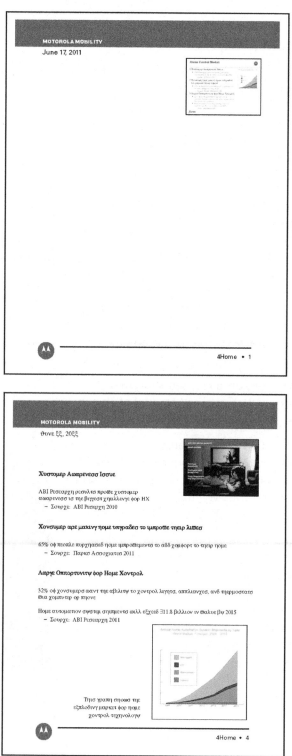

4

5

Death, Taxes, and Public Speaking

We would like to start by telling you what this part of the book will *not* do. These four chapters will not teach you the art of public speaking. I couldn't do that if we were in the same room together—to suggest that the pages of a book could do it would be mere pulp fiction. There are some who believe that outstanding public speakers were born with their talents and that all the training in the world couldn't equal that. We won't participate in that debate, because we're not interested in whether you were preordained to be a great speaker—we care only about making you better than you are right now. And on that score, there is only good news: there are real, tangible, physical behaviors that you can perform to make you a more effective presenter. And that is our focus here.

Better than Bullets

What if we told you about a visual aid that is more effective than PowerPoint, less abused than bullet points, and does not require the rental or purchase of a projector?

The lights can be completely up while you use this particular aid and a screen is not required. You do not need extensive training to use it, and you don't have to buy a book like this one. You do need to read a short chapter in said book, Chapter 20 to be precise, but that's all.

Best of all, you do not need to buy this visual aid. You already own it. In fact, you own two of them, and that's good, because they work best in pairs.

We refer, of course, to your hands—the best sidekick a good storyteller could possibly have. Your hands are how you direct attention, how you bring nuance to an idea, how you provide color commentary to complement your slides' play by play.

20

Communicating With Your Hands

Here is the most important piece of advice that we can give you about your hands:

Show them!

When you offer the palm of your hand to your audience members, you do the public equivalent of baring your soul. It is an important component of the trust-building process, and trust is the first ingredient of a good presenter-audience relationship. This doesn't change with the size of your audience: one or one hundred, your hands might say more about you than anything else.

You might be a natural at this and not need any direction. Most aren't. Most need to make conscious efforts to work their hands into a presentation in a way that feels natural and genuine. And I can write about this until my hands fall off from writer's cramp and it won't be as effective as your seeing it in action. All of the following photos are still images taken from low-resolution video, but they capture moments in time when various speakers have become one with their hands.

One of the most polished presenters in our community is Jim Endicott, who authored the foreword for this book. No stranger to anyone who has attended the Presentation Summit, Jim describes himself as introverted, almost shy, when he is not speaking; put him in front of an audience, though, and he comes alive.

Figure 20.1 has captured one of Jim's trademark gestures, as he asks his audience "who among us wants their presenters to be perfect?" He doesn't have to verbally ask for a show of hands; by raising his own hand, he invites audience members to raise theirs. And with the "who among us," phrase, he removes potential barriers between himself and his audience. In these five seconds, and with this one gesture, he creates a connection with the room that he will be able to cultivate over the next hour.

Even with an audience of presentation professionals, most in the room are unaware of this complex dynamic. They just know that they're interested and engaged in what their seminar leader has to say, and our evaluations confirm this.

Jim concluded the point by sharing a personal experience and Figure 20.2 shows a body in perfect sync with the words. If he were actress Sally Field, the caption might read "You like me!" Kidding aside, arms out and palms open says to the group "I'm hiding nothing...this is the real me...I'm willing to be vulnerable." These messages resonate loudly on many levels, most of them

Figure 20.1
This show of the hand is how Jim Endicott asks his audience members for a show of their own hands.

subconscious. You probably don't know Jim Endicott, but don't you feel as if you could place your trust in him from seeing this photo? His hands help to give you that impression. Download the video to watch for yourself.

▶ Jim is quite deft at making gestures while holding a wireless remote. Believe me when I say that this takes practice. The first time I tried to count to one in public, while my index finger was on the slide advance button, I used my second finger. That didn't look too good...

Figure 20.2
Jim invites trust with gestures that open him up.

whypptsucks.com/
20-02.mp4

Better gestures while seated: The instructor's challenge

Half of the work that I do with PowerPoint is instructional. Therefore, I often find myself seated at a table behind a computer, actively working with a software application. While the audience accepts this physical barrier between us, I must still work to overcome it.

Figure 20.3 shows two such moments. No subtle gesture at my sides or even in front of my chest will be absorbed by others in the room. All of my gestures must be wide and/or high. Most of the time, my audience members are not even looking at me—they're watching the screen. And when they watch the screen, I'm not just asking them to view a PowerPoint slide; I'm insisting that they follow my cursor as it drives software.

When I have a point to make, I have to bring their attention back to me, and I am not comfortable blanking the screen (my point might only take 10 seconds, yet many in the room will prefer to continue to study the screen). From that seated position, I am going to have to make an emphatic gesture, requiring good posture and good computer screen clearance.

I have a simple measure for a good day leading a seminar: if my shoulders are sore and my back hurts, it means I've done well...

Julie Terberg is a brilliant designer who has chosen PowerPoint as her medium. We hired her to speak at the conference without knowing her

Figure 20.3
Seated presenters must work their bodies and hands even more.

whypptsucks.com/
20-03.mp4

aptitude as a presenter. We frankly didn't care—she can design such incredible slides, we figured, we'd find a way to get the knowledge out of her, even if she didn't speak English.

Figure 20.4
For her design makeover clinic, Julie Terberg was in the zone.

Julie uses personal warmth and her design instincts to tell stories about her work. She looks back on her debut year at the Presentation Summit and describes herself as having been stiff. We're not sure that's true, but in any event, by her third year, she had come into her own. Figure 20.4 shows her describing a continuum from one idea to another: "With a good color scheme, all of your decisions become easier, from simple slides [left palm] all the way to complex charts, timelines, and infographics [right hand]."

She made several references to those complex elements made easier with a well-crafted color scheme, and she was able to do so merely by holding her right hand out to the side. She had already defined that space to be "all that complicated stuff," and a wave of the hand was all that was required to refer to it later.

I suspect that she did this without awareness. When you get on a roll, you experience the best kind of intelligence, where your body knows instinctually what to do without your brain having to get involved. We athletes call it being "in the zone"—that all-too-fleeting experience where everything is working right with minimal effort.

Let's not assume—let's ask her...

[sixty minutes later]

```
RE: Were you in the zone?? - Message (Rich Text)

File  Edit  View  Insert  Format  Tools  Actions  Help

Reply   Reply to All   Forward

From:     Julie Terberg
To:       'Rick Altman'
Subject:  RE: Were you in the zone??

I do remember trying to connect with members of the audience,
looking for understanding nods and grins from those who got the
point I was trying to make. I certainly didn't pay attention to
my hand gestures. Nor do I remember them! My attention was on the
group, and making sure they understood the information I was
trying to convey.

JT


-----Original Message-----
From: Rick Altman
To: Julie Terberg
Subject: Were you in the zone??

Hi Julie!

I'm having lots of fun with my PowerPoint book. In Chapter
13, I write about how you were practically unconscious in one of
your presentations. We athletes call it being "in the zone,"
where your body and your soul know what to do without your brain
having to tell them. Do you remember that? Were you in the zone??

RA
```

Active Hands, Quiet Body

Ask anyone who knows me—I'm a hand-talker. My hands are in constant motion while I speak. My clients, my audience members, my friends, and the high school girls on the softball team I coach—they will all readily attest to this.

While I was once concerned about my hands being too active, I have since come to realize the value of channeling that energy, and it has caused me to re-evaluate advice I used to give on this subject. In the first edition of this book, I wrote about the so-called neutral position, and its importance as a base from which to start gestures. "In order for a gesture to have impact," I wrote, "it must come from a position of rest. Just like bold type, it is the contrast that makes it work."

While audience members tell me that this neutral position looks natural, it feels anything but, and I grew self-conscious trying to make peace with it. Trying to quell the continual motion that my hands craved led to a litany of compensations:

Using a Lectern

While I normally choose not to, it's no crime to stand behind a lectern, and there are some occasions where the extra formality is appropriate. For situations where you are speaking from freshly-written notes and you need them, a lectern can be a convenience.

But you must understand that a large hollow box of usually-fake wood between you and your audience members can act as a barrier and will not help you in connecting with them. You will need to work harder to compensate:

- You should pause more often, making sure to look up from your notes for several seconds at a time. Ideally, you would begin your next thought while still looking out before having to refuel and take in more notes.

- Stand as upright as you can. In fact, lean over the lectern—audiences will feel it.

- Above all, make sure your gestures are up and out in front of the lectern.

Figure 20.7 depicts a typical challenge for not only using a lectern, and making sure that gestures are sufficiently emphatic, but also for managing furniture traffic. We'll return to that subject in Chapter 22.

Part Four: Public Speaking

Chapter 21

Fighting Nerves

I remember the first time I came face-to-face with paralyzing nervousness, and all I was doing was sitting on a couch. It was 1978 and I was 19 years old. Six years prior, I stood up in front of 200 people and chanted in Hebrew for my bar mitzvah. But that was nothing compared to this scene.

It was the ninth inning of Game Two of the 1978 World Series between the Dodgers and Yankees, and L.A. rookie Bob Welch struck out Reggie Jackson to win the game. I was sweating vicariously for Welch, who looked like he was about to walk into a gas chamber. He faced Mr. October, and he struck him out.

I've never seen anyone so nervous and I've never been so nervous for someone else. What I didn't consider, however, is whether Jackson was nervous. Years later, he told us. "If I'm not nervous," he said, "then there is something wrong. If I don't feel those butterflies, it means maybe I don't care as much as I should."

I always feel better about my own anxiety when I think of that quote, and so should you. It is neither realistic nor helpful to believe that you can quell your nerves; it would be better to learn to live with them. If the greatest World Series performer in history was nervous, it's okay for you to be, too. Here are a few strategies to help you become one with your nervous half.

21

The Lowdown on Laughing

This might be the oldest advice on record: start with a joke. Laughter relaxes you, it makes you feel more comfortable, and it allows you to loosen up. It is the classic icebreaker.

Well, what if you're not funny? What if your joke bombs? As Jerry Seinfeld said to George Castanza one afternoon, that's a pretty big matzah ball hanging out there.

Unless you have a joke that is guaranteed to be funny and is relevant to the topic of your presentation, the risk is too great. Besides, I have a better idea than trying to make your audience laugh...

Make yourself laugh.

I'm very serious about this, pun intended. If the audience laughs at your joke, it *might* make you feel better. If you laugh, it is virtually guaranteed to make you feel better. And the stakes are much lower.

This talk today on warehouse efficiency, it seems kind of funny that I should be the one leading it...[chuckle]...and if you ask my mother about this, she'll agree...[snicker]...because you've never seen a kid growing up with a messier room than mine. How I got to this point where I am expected to act as an authority on this subject is...[laugh]...well, that's just beyond me...

Audience members might laugh along with you or they might not, but it doesn't matter either way. You're not trying to be comically funny, and so this isn't a joke that can bomb. It's funny to you in a reminiscent way and therefore it is appropriate for you to see the humor in it.

You know that story about "If it's Tuesday, this must be Belgium?" I now know what they mean. This is my fourth city in four days, and yesterday I woke up and literally forgot where I was...I [laugh], I thought I was already here in Austin, about to speak to all of you. I left the hotel and immediately got lost, until I realized that I was still in San Antonio. So...[laugh] to say that it's good to be here takes on a whole new meaning.

This anecdote might not be funny to your audience but anyone can see why it might be funny to you, so again, it doesn't seem like forced humor. It almost doesn't matter what kind of story you share—*make it up if you have to.*

Laughing uses good muscles, not bad ones (more on this soon) and it's easier to make yourself laugh than it is to make a roomful of strangers laugh. So all around it's a better strategy to employ.

How Slow Can You Go?

It's been over 100 pages since we introduced one of our universal axioms, so here goes—Universal Axiom No. 4:

> **However quickly you think you're speaking, it will seem even quicker to your audience.**

And Universal Axiom No. 5:

> **However slowly you are speaking, you can always slow down even more.**

When you speak quickly, you do more than just make yourself nervous; you make your audience nervous. The quicker you go, the more fidgety you get. You don't give yourself any time to make large gestures, so all of your gestures are small ones involving small body parts. Small, fast, fidgety little gestures. And out comes the dreaded fig leaf once again.

The whole thing spirals, as your fidgety gestures make you speak even quicker, which in turn makes your body try to keep up, and so your gestures become even more halting and spastic, because that's all you have time for, and the quicker you speak, the higher your voice gets, and that raises the frequency of the entire room, and through it all, *you drive your audience nuts!*

But if you slow down your speech...

...you'll slow down your entire body...

...and that will calm everyone down.

So why do we do speak so quickly? It's not enough to just say we're nervous and that's why we speed up. What is making us speed up?

Much of the time, it's a fear of the unknown: you don't remember what's next or you're just not confident about your next transition. You have stopped living in the moment as you fret about what you are to say next. Very few people forget about what they are talking about now; it's always that they forget what comes next.

When you know what your next idea is, it's uncanny how much easier it is to discuss your current idea. Absent of panic or dread, you can practically luxuriate in your words. And then, you can indulge in the holiest of all moments before an audience:

You can pause.

No, I mean a long pause.

Longer.

Longer still, and look at people while you pause.

This is not an awkward pause; it's a commanding pause. You have complete control of the room and everyone knows it. And how have you won the room? Why have you become so confident? Because you know where you're going. You know what you want to say next, so you can live in the moment, without panic, fear, or fig leaves.

▶ See the discussion in Chapter 8 (Page 45) about displaying all bullets at once vs. having them appear one by one. We are staunch advocates of the all-at-once practice, precisely for the reasons discussed here: it gives you context, makes it easier to focus on the current topic, and reduces the risk of your forgetting what you are to say next.

This is one of the most wonderful feelings when speaking before an audience—when I know my material so well that I can completely control the pace. I can linger on points, make extended eye contact, take questions, invite debate. Once I have established this level of control, no reasonable pause feels uncomfortable. Even if I am 30 feet away from my notes and I completely forget what I want to say next. If I control the room, nobody will think it odd if I silently walk the 30 feet back to the lectern, spend five seconds looking at my notes, and then five more collecting my thoughts.

Anyone who has ever gone to Toastmasters or taken a course in public speaking has had to perform the exercise where you must make three seconds of eye contact with an audience member before shifting your gaze. I would argue that five seconds of silence is a better drill.

It's all made possible by knowing your transitions. Practicing them is more important than rehearsing the flow of a particular idea.

Air Under the Pits

The symbiosis between the voice, the body, and the nervous system makes for a fascinating study. Unless it's *your* body we're talking about, whose byproduct of this relationship is usually profuse perspiration. Then it's not fascinating; it's frustrating. Each one of these parts of the system is responsible for changes in the other:

- If you are nervous, it will show in how you move your body and how you speak.

- Changes to your vocal pattern create change in body motion, which affects pulse and heart rate.

Part Four: Public Speaking

- Command over your body can create command over your speech and your nerves.

We have already discussed the syndrome whereby a nervous speaker accelerates his or her speaking pattern, which in turn causes the entire body to speed up. Whether fidgets are the cause or the byproduct of your nerves, they are not your friend, as they perpetuate the cycle and they affect your audience.

So think big.

Think about making big gestures, not little ones. Create a reason to raise both arms above your head or out to the sides. Get some air under your armpits!

Working gross motor skills is equivalent to slowing down your vocal pattern. Your body responds more positively to a big action than to a little one. A big gesture can actually help relax you. At a minimum, it takes longer to make a big gesture than a fidget, and that creates a better, slower pace for you. Our advice about making yourself laugh has relevance here: laughing uses your diaphram, a big muscle.

I've found that raising both arms over my head, can be interpreted many ways and audience members are generally willing to view the gesture in context.

CONTEXT: Question from an audience member about a situation that troubles her.

ME: That frustrates me too [gesture]. It's like whatever you do, it comes back to bite you. Try doing this...

CONTEXT: We solved a problem or addressed a difficult issue.

ME: [gesture] Thank the heavens, you figured it out!

CONTEXT: I ask an intricate question and an audience member answers it correctly, showing that she understands its nuance.

ME: [gesture] (Nothing needs to be said—the gesture serves as a "Eureka!")

Now if you feel like an idiot doing this, don't do it. The gesture has to be a part of you, but it's worth the effort to find one you are comfortable with. One colleague likes to cup his hand to the side of his head and then move it away, as if he has just had an epiphany and all this amazing stuff is flowing out of his brain. He uses that to great effect in many scenarios.

I know a woman who likes to hold one finger up, but she really goes for it, raising it well above her head. She uses it to mean "Listen up," "wait a minute," or "here's the beef."

Another uses her hands very effectively to create relationships in time, distance, or some other set of variables (just as we saw Julie Terberg do in the previous chapter). "Over here, you have the question of cost," she might say with her left palm outstretched all the way out to one side, "and over here is the issue of resources," as she stretches out her right hand. Having created those two spaces, now anytime during that conversation, she can stretch out her left palm and the audience knows she is talking about the cost factors. She has created a terrific cerebral connection with her audience...and she gets to air out her pits.

Find your own big gestures and use them to engage your audience, to improve your pace and vocal pattern, and to help quiet your nerves.

◆

As I look back on this chapter, I have to laugh. It seems as if we are advising you to become a phony:

- Fabricate a story to laugh about.

- Conjure up situations in which you can make long pauses.

- Make up a gesture and fake your way into using it.

But let's face it, speaking in public might always feel like an artificial situation to you, so it makes sense that a few artificial devices can help you with it. Anything that helps get you to a place where you can speak naturally and share ideas freely is a good thing.

Natural speaking through fabrication...what a concept.

If, however, the lectern is to function more like a home base—the shallow end of the pool, if you will—then it would be better to move it to audience right. You might use it to: offer your initial greeting; refer to your notes; take questions; drink water. But you would want to swim out into the deep end for most of your talk and that would be done on the other side of the room.

As an alternative, you could position the lectern audience *way* left and only use it occasionally. One way or the other, however, you want it out of the way.

Positioning your computer

Does your presentation involve software demo or some other active use of a computer (as opposed to just using it to project slides)? This part of the discussion involves a bit of thought, and it is here where my advice has evolved across the life of the book. I used to advocate positioning the computer in that sweet spot of audience left; now I hold the opposite point of view.

If you are demo-ing software, your screen becomes the focal point and you become more of a narrator. You will likely be seated at a table or standing behind a lectern that houses your notebook. In this scenario, it is not as important where you are; you want your audience watching your screen. They are probably not reading left to right but following your mouse as you drive the interface.

You should do this from audience right. That way, should you want to emerge from behind the computer and shift the focus back on you, you can take up the preferred position audience left without the furniture getting in the way.

What about if you are not demo-ing software—where does your notebook computer belong then? Should it be in front of you so you can monitor what you are projecting? Should you activate PowerPoint's Presenter view, whereby your speaker notes are shown on your internal display while the main content is projected out?

These strategies are fine...as long as you can take your eyes off the damn thing. Remember Universal Axiom No. 1:

> **When stuff moves on screen, your audience has no choice but to watch it.**

With your notebook right in front of you, you become a member of the audience in this regard: every time there is an animation or a transition, your eyes are going to go to it, and that could become a distraction and a barrier between you and your audience. I would rather see you become more comfortable getting your computer out of the way altogether and you referring to the same screen that your audience is watching (more on this soon).

Simply put, anytime your notebook screen is in front of you, there is the risk of your becoming fixated on it and distracted by it. The best scenario is to have nothing between you and your audience.

> This discussion assumes your use of a wireless remote to advance your slides. You have one, right? And a backup? A presenter not owning a wireless remote is like a carpenter not having a hammer.

Notes and tables: a challenging combination

If you require speaker notes but were given only a table, not a lectern, you will have to work harder to maintain audience connection. At a lectern, you only need to look down a short distance to see your notes—you can probably do it just by moving your eyes. But if your notes are on a table, the geometry worsens. The angle and the distance from your head to your notes both increase. At a minimum, you'll wish you had printed them in a larger typesize. Here are some tips:

- Spread your notes across the table so every page is visible. Don't leave them in one stack.

- Make prominent marks at your transition points. You need to be able to see your transitions at a glance.

- Take questions often, and every time you do, walk to the table and use it as an opportunity to check your notes.

- Be mobile. It's a long way down to your notes from a standing position, and the more stationary you are, the more you call attention to that distance. But if you can sneak a peak while you are walking up to the table, walking away from it, or even just turning to one side of the room or the other, it is less conspicuous.

The head table dilemma is why many of my colleagues travel with folding lecterns that can be placed on that table. Raising your notes closer to eye level is always more comfortable.

The Presenter's Triangle

This discussion suggests an entire strategy for positioning the various elements in your ballroom. It goes something like this:

1. On the left side of the room (when facing the screen), draw an imaginary line from the left-most audience member to the far left edge of the screen.

Figure 22.1
The Presenter's Triangle provides a blueprint for positioning all front-of-the-room elements.

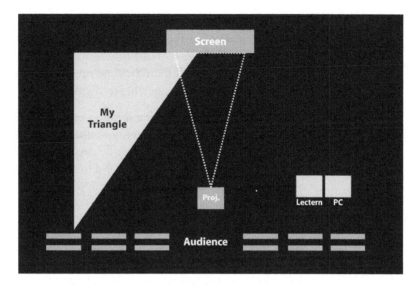

2. That line helps define a triangle, in which you can comfortably circulate, without fear of being in anyone's view of the screen. You'll see in Figure 22.1, we have cheated a bit toward the center with our triangle; that's okay.

3. When you want to speak to points on the screen, you would move to the back of the triangle, near the screen.

4. When you want to make a strong point, you would move to the front of the triangle.

5. When you want to just talk, you would find a point in the middle of the triangle.

6. The computer and lectern are placed audience right, their relative positions being determined by which would see more use. Unless you have an elaborate setup or are teaming up with another, you probably don't need a six-foot table for your computer; if you can get a square table or even a cocktail round for your computer, so much the better.

In my preferred room setup, I remove the podium altogether and keep my triangle completely clear. I expect to spend about 75% of the time on my feet so I only need a small table for my PC. I place it close to the audience so it is out of the way when I work the room and so I can more easily make eye contact from a seated position should I need to.

I don't use notes for the times that I am sharing ideas and discussing the key points of my topic, but I keep fastidious notes for when I have to show software. Those notes, of course, live at my small PC table.

Without a lectern, it means that I am out in the deep end all the time except when seated at the PC. This was a bit daunting at first—nowhere to hide, nowhere to retreat—but I find it much easier to engage the audience this way. It's almost as if I am showing my audience members my willingness to be exposed and vulnerable to them.

I like the analogy of swimming in the deep end. The shallow end of the pool is where the friendlier water is—your lectern, your notes, your bottle of water, your computer. But to really engage an audience, you need to swim out into the deep end and spend time in your audience-left triangle with no notes, no computer, no lectern. Just you, them, your voice, and your hands.

The key is to avoid drowning. That tends to happen when you run out of things to say and forget what you want to say next. It's okay if you don't remember every topic to discuss—that's what your notes are for—but you need to at least know when to consult them.

Look over your notes and identify the times when topics move from one to the other so naturally that you will never forget those transitions—when you know that you can stay out in the deep end for a while. Those are the times when you could be at the top of your game—when you are in command of your content and the pace with which you deliver it. Look for places in your notes where you know your content and your transitions well and get right out in front of your audience. In Figure 22.2, I have identified in my notes when I intend to swim in the deep end and when I need to return.

When to return to the shallow end

The simplest reason to return to your lectern or table is if you know there is a portion of your presentation that you will not be able to remember. We're not talking about remembering a passage word-for-word, which you should never try to do. We're referring to a passage that you forget to even bring up. The one where, 10 minutes later, you realize that you skipped entirely. Your best defense against forgetting these passages is to not even try to remember them—just know when it is time to refer to your notes.

Here are a few other times to return home:

- If you intend to quote somebody or read a short passage from another work. Don't try to do this by heart—it's fake. If you are reading a quote or passage that somebody else wrote, read it!

- If you want to relate an anecdote that has a fair level of detail. Trying to remember those details could sprain your brain.

- When it's time to change the pace of the presentation. Being in the deep end can be tiring for you. Returning home is like taking a moment to rest.

- When you get thirsty. I get such dry mouth that I need to bring my water with me to the deep end.

When to avoid the deep end

The smaller the room, the less opportunity there is to work it and trying to carve out a triangle or swim into the deep end might make you feel foolish. In a conference room, for instance, where a dozen or so people are watching you from around a table, you can make eye contact with everyone from your lectern or maybe even from your seat at the table. In a room of that

Johnny, it's Time to Come Home...

Your notes can tell you when it's time to head to the deep end, but they won't be as helpful in bringing you back. In Chapter 8, we discussed a strategy that you can implement to ensure you know when the last bullet on a slide has displayed (on Page 49, involving an inconspicuous rectangle or other object that automatically appears after the last bullet). You can use this same strategy to notify you when you should return home.

1. Identify the parts of your presentation that you know really well and the places where you would be more comfortable working from your notes.

2. Create a thin rectangle, fill it with a color close to your background, and place it on the edge of the slide or in some other place where it can be inconspicuous.

3. Animate it to Appear, After Previous.

4. In the Animation task pane, move it up or down until it is in the desired place in the sequence of animated events. If necessary, move it in between a set of bullets.

When the rectangle appears, it means it is time to return home to consult your notes.

1		Rectangle 3: Succeeding in business today
2		Multitasking is key
3		The new definition of team player
		Rectangle 5
4		Gadget central: how wired are you?
5		New marketing avenues are changing the rules

Figure 22.2
Take notes on your
notes to tell you
when to venture
out and when to
return

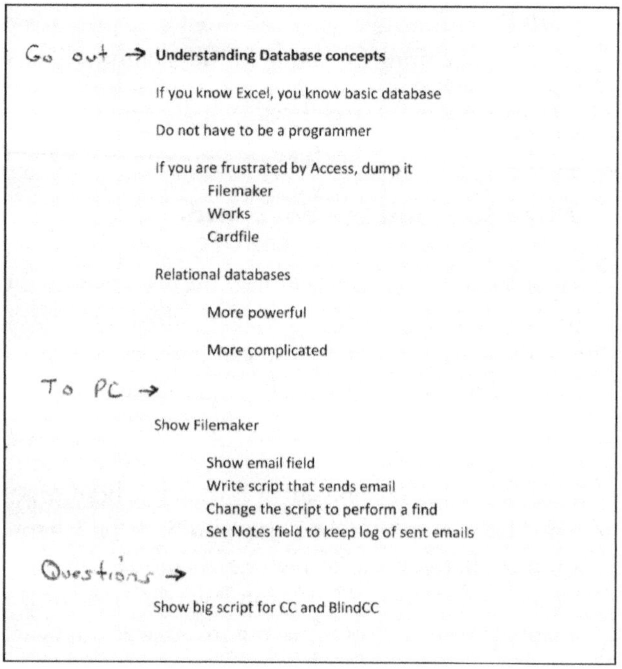

Go out → **Understanding Database concepts**

If you know Excel, you know basic database

Do not have to be a programmer

If you are frustrated by Access, dump it
Filemaker
Works
Cardfile

Relational databases

More powerful

More complicated

To PC →

Show Filemaker

Show email field
Write script that sends email
Change the script to perform a find
Set Notes field to keep log of sent emails

Questions →

Show big script for CC and BlindCC

size, the geometry changes and it would probably get awkward and uncomfortable if you journeyed too far from the table.

The Magical B Key

We've spent a fair amount of toner in this chapter discussing how you can create the best possible relationship with your projected content. We would be remiss if we didn't mention the best way of all to do this.

Turn off the projector

Axiom No. 1 is more powerful than you think. Stuff doesn't have to move on screen to compel an audience to look at it—it just has to project. If it's there, people are going to look at it. And if it's been there for awhile, and you're no longer speaking to it, it's now just digital flotsam.

There is no better way to refocus attention than to blank the screen. And you can do that with one click:

- Press B to turn the screen black.

- Press W to turn the screen white.

- Press the Blank button on your wireless remote.

If available, that third choice is the best, but even if you have to retreat home or head to wherever your notebook is to do it, it's worth doing when a slide has gone stale and/or you want all eyes on you. In all cases, the key or button is a toggle: press it again to redisplay the screen.

I wondered out loud in the first edition whether it is better to blank the screen with black or with white. In this decade, with projectors becoming so bright, it is common for us to present in rooms with the lights up. I wondered if a white screen might sink more smoothly into the background. Having become aware of this since, I have concluded that even with bright rooms, black screens are better than white.

White or black, the screen should only go blank when you want it to, so please turn off your screen saver...

Mythbusting

Let's end this chapter by challenging a few of the conventional points often made about presenting to an audience.

Myth No. 1: Don't cross in front of the screen

If you never cross in front of the screen, how do you get to the other side of the room? I've seen presenters go to inordinate lengths to avoid committing this unpardonable sin, including walking down the aisle to walk around the projector and (true story) walking behind the screen.

Please.

If you need to move to the other side of the room, please just walk in front of the screen! Don't look into the projector and don't stop or dilly-dally. If you can keep your train of thought and continue speaking, it will seem perfectly natural. Trying somehow to avoid the screen will appear contrived, unnatural, and ultimately far worse than whatever perceived transgression is associated with casting a shadow on the screen.

Myth No. 2: Never turn your back to your audience

I once saw somebody trip over a chair trying to walk backwards, so obsessed was he with heeding this advice. Once again, common sense must be allowed to prevail, otherwise you're going to do yourself far more harm than this supposedly bad thing could possibly do to you.

While it is generally sound advice to not speak with your back to the entire audience, I think it came about because of this next one...

Myth No. 3: Don't look at the screen

This is the more prevalent myth, and it's nonsense. How come everyone else gets to look at the screen and you don't? That's not fair!

Looking at the screen is more than perfectly appropriate; it's an essential device to direct attention. If you look at the screen, it is virtually guaranteed that every member of your audience will, too. You don't need to completely turn around—a simple rotation of the hips will get the job done. When I do this to look at the screen, I know that my entire audience is looking at it, too.

And really, what's the alternative? If you look at your notebook computer screen instead, it's a disconnect on several levels. Now you're looking down at something that they don't get to see.

Everyone is looking at the screen; it is completely natural for you to do so, also. Busting this myth became truly liberating for me as I now interact with the screen in a much more effective and natural way.

Myth No. 4: Laser pointers are rude

Now this one has some truth to it. Most people who use laser pointers haven't practiced enough, so the little dot jumps all over the place and drives people nuts. The worst is when a presenter is done pointing at something but forgets that he or she still has the laser on, sending the little dot careening all over the screen.

You really don't need a laser pointer to point at the second bullet of a four-bullet slide. If you want to talk about the second bullet, refer to it by name—the "second bullet" or "second idea." Better still, and this harkens back to the previous myth, walk over to the screen and touch it. There is nothing more direct and compelling than using your hand to direct traffic.

A laser pointer becomes effective when you have to call attention to an element on screen that is not so easily identified. The part of a photograph where the sun meets the horizon...the part of a clamp that failed on a forklift...the fifth icon from the left on the second toolbar down...these are all good opportunities to use a laser pointer.

To use a laser pointer correctly, tuck in your elbow to anchor your arm to your side; don't let it float in open space. Once it is anchored, then activate the laser. Try to hover it for about two seconds, then turn it off.

Myth No. 5: Silence is bad

_____.

Chapter 23

Thoughts From The Experts

As I look over the last three chapters, I am reminded of an episode of I Love Lucy from 1954. Ricky and Fred take up golf and turn Lucy and Ethel into golf widows. They decide to take up the game, too, and during a lesson, Lucy hears 15 individual pointers (knees bent, elbow straight, wrist firm, back slightly tilted...that kind of stuff) and attempts to incorporate all of them at the same time. The resultant swing that she perpetrates is physical comedy at its finest.

I wonder what would happen if you took all of the advice over the last three chapters and tried to incorporate them at once. Would you end up like Lucy? Maybe I have done nothing more than ensure paralysis by analysis. If I were you, I would get my money back for this shoddy excuse for journalism right now.

If I have turned you into knots trying to keep up with all of the points made here in Part Four, read this chapter instead. It takes a big step back and offers quotes from noted presenters and commentators on the presentation community. In the process, you just might find some common principles essential to being a good presenter.

23

Know Your Audience

When asked, dozens of public speakers waste not a moment to turn the equation 180 degrees. It has less to do with you, they say, and more to do with your audience, as we declare emphatically in Chapter 15 and several other places along the way. Stand on the left...stand on the right...turn here, don't turn there—none of that matters if you don't have a firm grasp of what your audience is looking for, why they chose to show up, and with what they hope to walk away.

Emma Crosby
Anchor for Sky News

"You have got to imagine that you are talking to just one person who is in their living room or in their office. You have to think about them constantly, inform them as much as you can, and more importantly ask the questions that they want the answers to."

Anthony Frangi
Author,

"What makes a good presenter? Someone who can stand up and gain the respect of an audience, no matter what size.

"Good presenters know their subject matter inside out and it shows. When a person is passionate about the topic, their eyes light up, body language is positive and their voice excitable.

"Becoming a good speaker means you must learn to work or connect with your audience. A presentation is for the benefit of an audience. Effective communication skills are essential for anyone in business. Standing up to make a presentation is not just about opening your mouth."

Be Yourself

Experienced presenters learn something that inexperienced presenters do not, simply because it takes years upon years to learn this: audiences do not want perfect presenters. They want presenters who are more or less like them. They want to be able to relate to them, and nobody can relate to perfection.

Jim Endicott
Presentations Coach
President of Distinction Communication

"Several years ago I found myself watching a television show called the Actor's Guild. Every week they bring in Hollywood stars who are interviewed about

Julie Terberg

"A good presenter pulls you in, makes you want to stand up and say 'Aha! I understand.' and 'Yes, I agree!' A good presenter tells a great story, making connections from personal experience. A good presenter is well-rehearsed, rarely referring to notes or script. A good presenter makes a speech seem effortless and conversational. A good presenter is compelling, thought-provoking, and articulate.

"A good presenter uses many memorable visuals to help you grasp ideas and concepts. Later on, those images are easy to recall as you replay the presentation highlights in your mind.

"A good presenter leaves a lasting impression."

And Finally...

"All the great speakers were bad speakers at first."

Ralph Waldo Emerson

"If you have an important point to make, don't try to be subtle or clever. Use a pile driver. Hit the point once. Then come back and hit it again. Then hit it the third time—a tremendous whack."

Winston Churchill

"Make sure you have finished speaking before your audience has finished listening."

Dorothy Sarnoff, Broadway singer and author

"If you want me to speak for an hour, I'm ready now. If you want me to speak for 10 minutes, I'll need two weeks to prepare."

Mark Twain

"Today's public figures can no longer write their own speeches or books, and there is some evidence that they can't read them either."

Gore Vidal, 1952

"According to most studies, people's number one fear is public speaking. Number two is death. This means to the average person, if you go to a funeral, you're better off in the casket than doing the eulogy."

Jerry Seinfeld

"Is sloppiness in speech caused by ignorance or apathy? I don't know and I don't care."

William Safire

"There are always three speeches, for every one you actually give. The one you practice, the one you give, and the one you wish you gave."

Dale Carnegie

"I might not remember what you said, but I'll always remember how you made me feel."

Maya Angelou

Working Smarter, Presenting Better

"I'd like to cover a few advanced topics, too," I wrote to one of several interested publishers of this book. "If there's time," came the response, "and if the page count allows it."

Reason No. 34B to publish this book myself: there is never enough time and the page count never allows it. Yet as we enter the home stretch, we suspect that a great many of our readers will see this set of chapters as the most useful of all.

If you've made it this far, you deserve to sink your teeth into some truly advanced material, which the next few chapters seek to offer. Then we'll degenerate into an anarchy of tips and tricks in our final chapter, Junk and Miscellany, without which few books bearing my name are ever published.

Chapter 24

Creating a Smarter Interface

When we first began to get to know version 2007 several years ago, we were disappointed in the program's apparent lack of support for customization. Using version 2003, we learned some amazing techniques for fine-tuning menus and toolbars, only to discover that almost all of it was removed from the then-new interface of version 2007.

We advanced users were initially dismayed with the bone that it seemed Microsoft was throwing us with the so-called Quick Access Toolbar. And there are still times when we long for the methods by which we could completely rearrange the version 2003 tools. That said, we have discovered just enough cool things with the modern interface to assuage our pain somewhat. This chapter shares those discoveries.

24

The Version 2007 Downgrade

While PowerPoint 2007 reflected improvements in many areas over older versions, interface customization was not one of them. Program developers were so enthused about the Ribbon and the way it was designed, they did not want us tinkering with it. The list was depressingly long of what we could not do:

- Add to or rearrange the commands on the Ribbon.
- Change or remove a command or group on the Ribbon.
- Add tabs to the Ribbon without programming code.
- Use toolbars and menus from earlier versions of PowerPoint.
- Change the font or font size used on the Ribbon.
- Replace seldom-used commands with ones used more often.
- Save, swap, and migrate your customized interface to other places and to other people.

Version 2007 debuted a much-improved look and accessibility for all of the settings within the PowerPoint Options dialog, including the Advanced tab shown in Figure 24.1—sort of a one-stop shop for all geeky stuff across the application. You access these options from the Office Button, the round icon at the top-left of the PowerPoint 2007 screen, or from File | Options in 2010.

The other significant interface change introduced with 2007 was the Quick Access Toolbar (QAT), a row of icons across the top of the interface. You can place any command you want there and it will hold many. But you cannot change them from icon to text and the QAT can only live in one of two locations: above the Ribbon or below it.

This seemed meager compared to the extraordinary customization capabilities in version 2003, but again, a few factoids mitigate this.

If You Know It, Type It!

If you're like me, one of the more frustrating aspects of modern versions of PowerPoint is the where-did-they-put-it syndrome that has us searching every ribbon for a function that we used to access in our sleep. For instance, in V03, I would type Alt+D | S to reach the Set Up Show dialog box in about less than one second. I could pull down the Slide Show menu and then click Set Up Show, but the keystrokes are faster and seem easier to me.

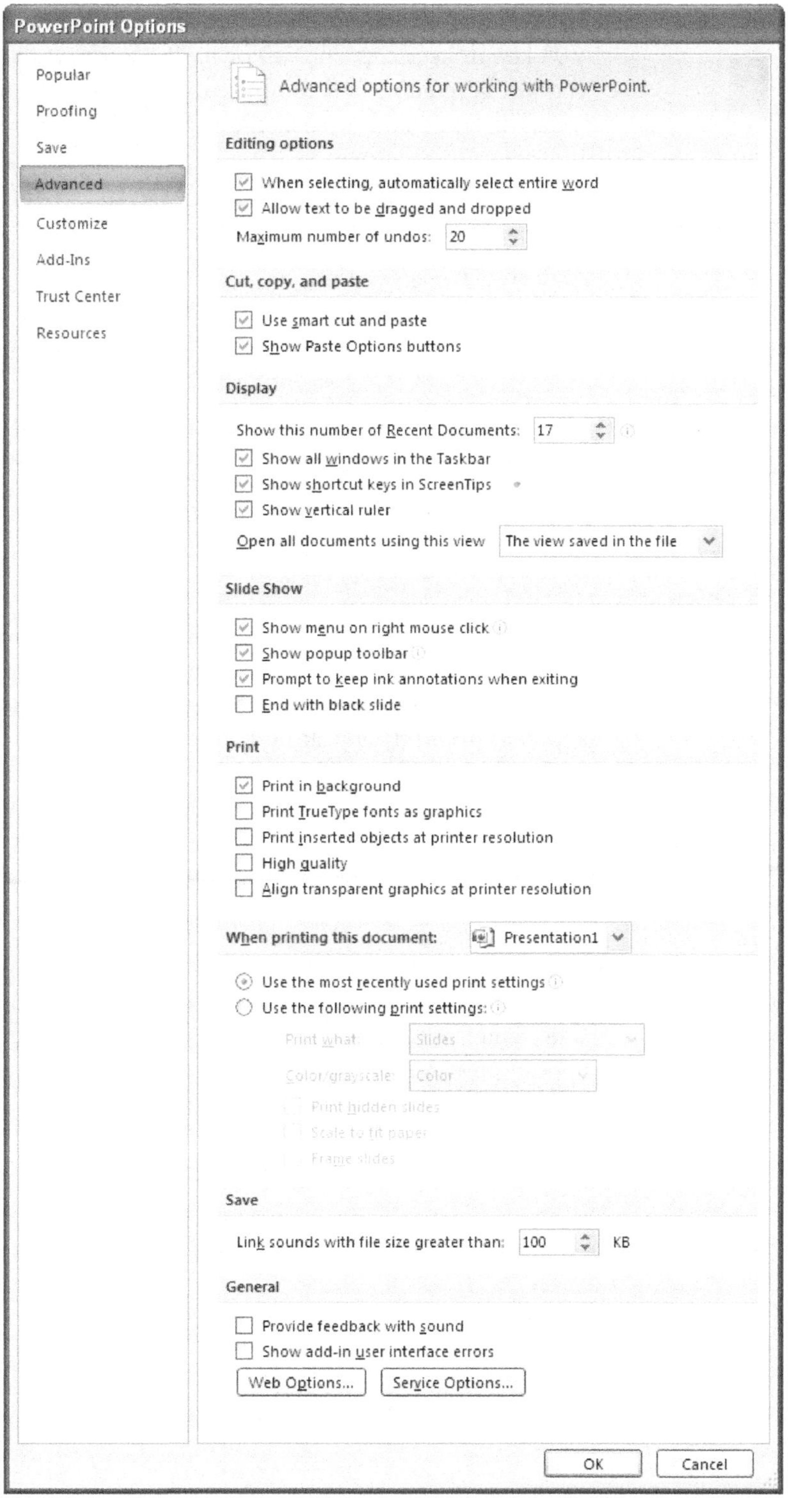

Figure 24.1
Version 2007 enjoys a redesigned and much more accessible set of options.

So imagine my pleasant surprise to discover that modern versions honor V03 keystroke access. Alt + D by itself doesn't mean anything to V07, but if you just keep going and complete the sequence, the software figures out what you mean and executes the command for you. So...

In order to	I press
Invoke Paste Special	Alt + E | S
Switch to the Notes page	Alt + V | P
Insert a photo	Alt + I | P | F
Open Replace Fonts	Alt + O | R

All of these keystrokes work in modern versions. There are no cues on the interface—you just type them blind, as if you were in V03.

When in Doubt, Press Alt

While learning your way around might be a chore for months to come, there is an easy way to embark on that journey, and once you find what you're looking for, an easy way to access it. Just press Alt once and note the keys that promptly appear under the main menu:

From here, press the corresponding letter to activate the desired ribbon. Once you learn the key designations, you won't have to wait for them to appear: press Alt+N to go immediately to the Insert menu. And once there, note all of the keystrokes that appear:

This becomes a handy cheat sheet as well as the door to fast access.

Figure 24.4
Adding commands to the QAT is powerful and easy.

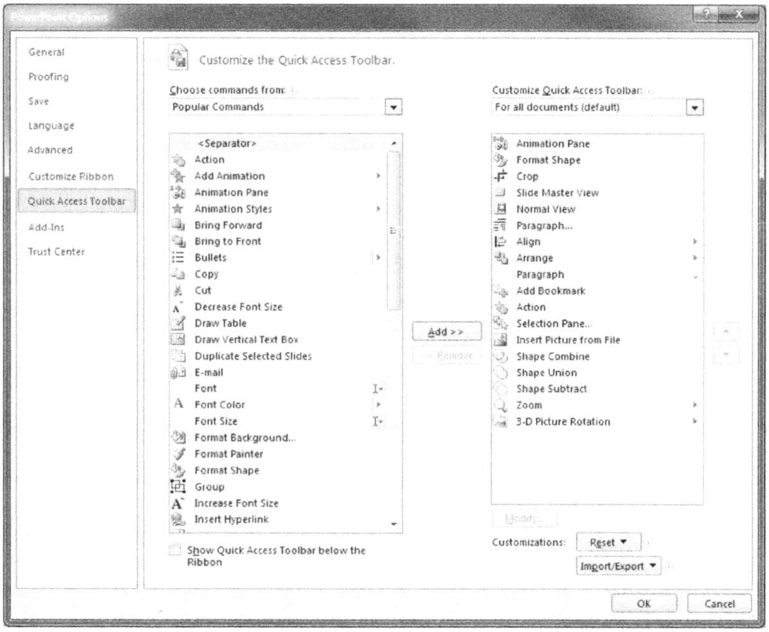

The QAT: Blunt but Effective

Because I'm a keyboard-aholic, these two techniques were tremendously gratifying for me to discover. Mouse-centric users might not have as much cause for celebration, but still the QAT is an important resource to leverage for economy of motion.

The QAT's qualities begin with the ease with which you can place onto it any command you can find. And as you can see in Figure 24.4, it's simple to do: browse the commands on the left and add any you want to the list on the right. The Choose Commands From dropdown includes sets of commands

Figure 24.5
The author's QAT

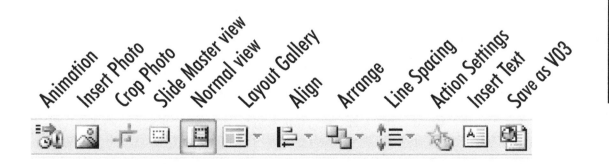

based on category as well as a vast master list of every command that exists within the application, including a few dozen that do not live on any ribbon and would therefore never be found except via a trip to this dialog.

Figure 24.5 shows the 12 commands that I have placed on my QAT. I will no doubt continue to grow this list as I discover more and more commands that I would prefer to access with one click instead of a hunt across the menus and then a dive into a particular ribbon. But the first nine are essential and I chose them carefully. This is because the Alt key works on the QAT, also. Press it and you'll see this:

This brings an unprecedented level of access to my most-used commands, well beyond what I had with version 2003:

In order to	I press
Invoke the Animation task pane	Alt+1
Crop a photo	Alt+3
Switch to Slide Master view	Alt+4
Change a Layout	Alt+6
Adjust Line Spacing	Alt+9

As you can see from the image above, once you get past nine, you need to press two keys along with Alt. As the list grows, it will reach 01 and then begin counting up from 0A through 0Z. We haven't gotten past 0Z to see what happens next—our video card runs out of resolution...

Thanks to the QAT and these Alt-key tricks, my creative workflow is exceptionally high when working with my bread-and-butter commands, and then it falls off markedly when I have to hunt through the Ribbon tabs to find an uncommon command. Many years after the debut of Office 2007, I know that this remains true for many of you, as well.

Customizing the Ribbon

Version 2010 users can go one step further: you can add your own tabs to the ribbon and your own groups of commands to tabs. This helps those of

Chapter 25

Creating Intelligent Presentations

I have written a significant chunk of this book while seated in the same chair. I have begun with Chapter 1 and have written most of the book in order. I am a creature of habit and I am most comfortable when there is order to the things I do. I don't view this as unusual—most people display this same tendency in one or more areas of their lives.

We're a race of linear thinkers and most of our presentations reflect that. We start at the first slide, end with the last slide, and expect to advance in order. This is not broken and I'm not here to try to fix it. However, leaving that mindset, even temporarily, stands as one of the most important improvements you can make as a presentation professional.

This chapter is all about how you can breathe life, flexibility, and creativity into your presentations by thinking in a nonlinear way. This is an impossibly vast topic, about which entire books have been written. Like the chapters before, we'll get to fifth gear in a hurry and will be speaking to you as if you are an advanced user who knows his or her way around the program. Seat belts optional but recommended...

25

Click Here, Go There

The irony is not lost on me that we will work through these non-linear topics in a very linear way. The path to excellence might be circular, but the path to learning it goes in a straight line. Here are the topics we'll be discussing:

- Moving at will to a specific slide

- Jumping to a different presentation

- Opening a non-PowerPoint document

- Creating a menu-driven interface within PowerPoint

The classic example to illustrate this idea is the presentation that runs long. I'm sure this has *never* happened to you, but you've no doubt been in the audience when a presenter, we'll call her Kathleen, allows a midway Q&A session to run long and now finds herself with five minutes left and three complete ideas yet to explore. So what does she do? She flies through her slides so she can get to her final idea, which promises to crystallize everything she has tried to say over the last 45 minutes.

Will you remember Kathleen's dramatic and powerful close when you drive home that afternoon? Not likely—instead, you'll remember all the content she dismissed as so much slide junk as she whizzed through it. You might even wonder about a slide that looked pretty good as it flashed before your eyes, because that's the way we humans are: we're more interested in what we can't have than what we can.

Your first impression is likely to be of a person who did not completely have her act together. She became imprisoned by her own linear thinking and she paid for it.

At the core of the solution is your understanding of the basics of hyperlinking. As with a web page that offers you a way to jump somewhere else, a presentation can be programmed with this same intelligence. It's done through the Action Settings dialog, a powerful set of controls that has earned a spot on my QAT.

Any element that can sit on a slide can be programmed as a hyperlink, and Figure 25.1 shows the list of choices for standard hyperlinking. When running a presentation (i.e., when in Show mode), clicking an object programmed with a hyperlink will cause you to promptly move to the location you have set.

If Kathleen had programmed a hyperlink to her concluding slides, her audience might have never noticed that she was running long.

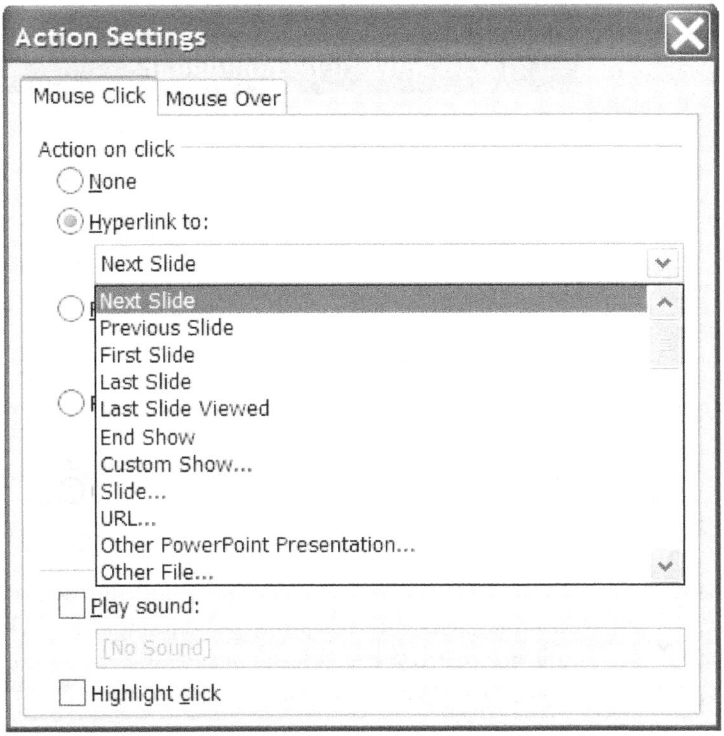

Figure 25.1
The hyperlink is the cornerstone of non-linear thinking.

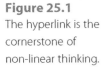

Hidden vs. Visible Hyperlinks

There are two basic methods of implementation and the one you choose is a matter of situation, preference, and even philosophy.

Roadmaps

We know many accomplished presenters who place their hyperlinks directly on the slide, in plain view of the audience, where they will never forget about them. For times when you want your audience members to see that you are making a turn onto a different street, a visible hyperlink is perfect. When I presented on this topic last year, one of my main slides looked like Figure 25.2 on the following page. Using those example buttons accomplished three important objectives:

■ It helped keep me in the flow by reminding me what to do next as I worked through a complicated set of tutorials. I was seated at the computer, in full-scale building mode, and I appreciated not having to retreat to my notes. I knew exactly what to click next to take me to the next point I wanted to make.

■ My audience could create a visual of my progression of topics, helping them understand the concepts better.

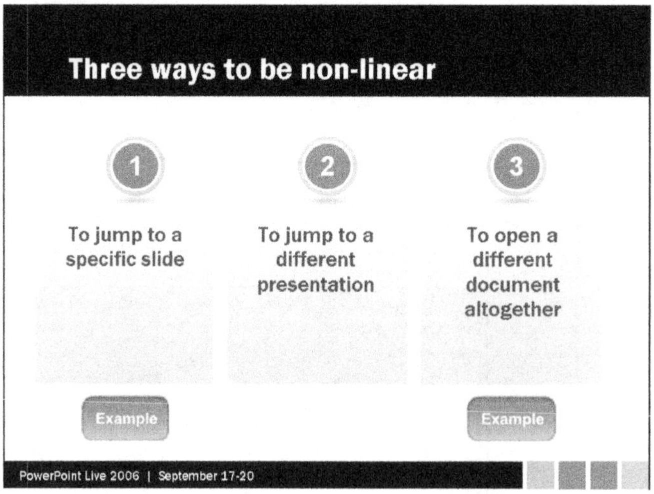

Figure 25.2
Visible hyperlinks
are invaluable for
working through
complicated tasks.

Three ways to be non-linear

1 — To jump to a specific slide

2 — To jump to a different presentation

3 — To open a different document altogether

Example   Example

PowerPoint Live 2006 | September 17-20

- ■ They could see examples of the very techniques I was teaching.

To see these
hyperlinks in action,
download 25-
02.pptx from the
whypptsucks.com
web site.

Many presenters have no reticence about showing their inner workings to their audiences, and I count myself among them. This just says to your audience that you have given considerable thought to how you want to approach a topic. It says that you are organized.

Secret passages

Invisible hyperlinks are equally handy for those times when it is not essential that your audience members follow how you get to a certain place. This is how Kathleen would have used the technology to jump to her conclusion without anyone noticing how far behind she got.

A hidden hyperlink can take one of two forms: 1) an object that is almost literally invisible, devoid of fill or outline; or 2) an object that is part of the slide design. We favor the second approach, as it is all too easy to forget the location or even the existence of invisible objects. In Figure 25.2, the small square at the extreme bottom-right of the slide has been programmed with a hyperlink that jumps to my last topic. If I run out of time, I can just click that rectangle and begin my conclusion. Nobody has to know about the dozen slides that I skipped over.

Flexible Intelligence

In Kathleen's case, she would have been grateful enough for a one-way ticket to her concluding slides. You, however, can build further intelligence into your slides by creating a way to return to whichever slide you were on before making the jump. Your web browser has a Back button and PowerPoint offers the Last Slide Viewed hyperlink choice.

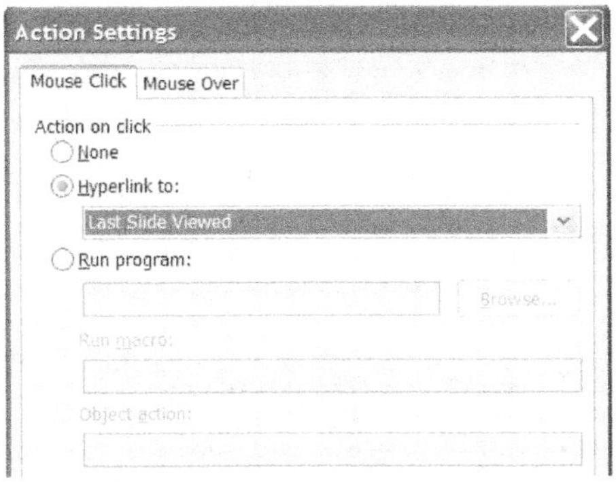

Program this hyperlink into a permanent object and you know you can always return to whichever slide you were on before the jump.

This argues for a more global view of your hyperlinking scheme, so ask yourself the following questions:

Hyperlinks Never Get Lost

Hyperlinks jump to specific slides in a presentation and it is important to note how PowerPoint identifies the slide. When you create a hyperlink, you identify the destination by its content, not by its position in the slide deck.

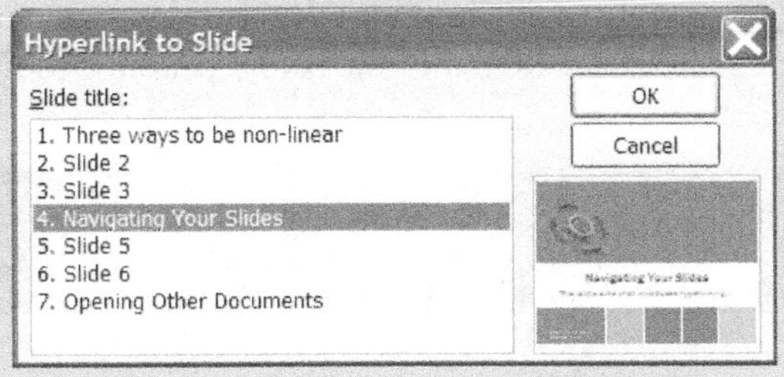

You are not creating a hyperlink to whatever slide happens to be the fourth in the deck; you identify a specific slide. If you were to move the Navigating Your Slides slide to a different place in the presentation, the hyperlink would find it just fine.

And while you identify a slide by its content, PowerPoint understands that you might change the slide's content. You can rewrite the title, change out all of the text, convert it to a chart layout, or remove all content entirely—PowerPoint will still keep the hyperlink in place.

- What are the specific slides that I might need to visit at any given time during the presentation?

- Do I want to show my links or not bother my audience with them?

- If the latter, are there slide elements that I could use for them?

It is unlikely that you would know the precise slide that you would be on when you wanted to employ a hyperlink, so they are best created on the slide master or on a layout.

Figure 25.5 shows an introductory slide for a presentation on creating graphics for PowerPoint, a topic that I cover regularly. There are four main subject areas that I know I will cover, and then there are a couple of additional subjects that might come up during Q&A, represented by hidden slides within the slide deck. Let's focus first on creating access to the two topics not on the agenda; here is how you would do it:

1. Go to the slide master.

2. Select the first small square in the lower-right corner and create a hyperlink to the hidden slide that represents one of the topics.

3. Select the second small square and create a hyperlink to the second topic.

4. Select the third small square and create a hyperlink to Last Slide Viewed, ensuring that you can return to whichever slide you were on before you made the jump.

Now let's talk about the four main topics. The most common way to work with an agenda slide like this one is to repeat it throughout the slide deck,

Figure 25.5
The three small squares on this slide would be perfect for creating hyperlink access to and from hidden slides that you might decide to show, or might not.

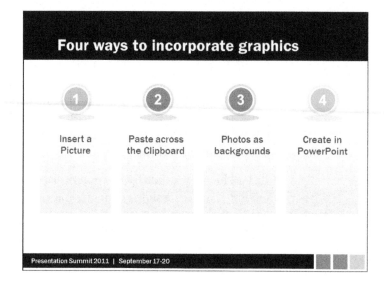

right before each of the topics. This is clumsy, requiring that you manage changes made to the slide across all of the copies. The better approach is to have this slide function, not just as an agenda slide, but as a menu:

1. On the slide (not on the master), select one of the numbers that corresponds to one of the topics.

2. Create a hyperlink to the slide that begins that topic.

3. Repeat those two steps for the other numbers on the slide.

This slide deck will serve you, its presenter, much more ably. No matter where you are in the presentation you know that you are one click away from any of your four main topics. However, as you begin to refine your thinking about menu-driven slides, you will likely find shortcomings with the techniques shown so far:

- You would need to find a way to get back to the menu and this particular slide design does not have an obvious global element for that. Perhaps the long black bar along the bottom would suffice, but it's not intuitive and wouldn't be readily remembered.

- And when would you click it? You would also have to remember when one topic is over. Or you would need to place a hyperlink on the last slide of the topic to return to the menu. Not impossible to do, just not convenient.

- There would probably be some concluding slides after all four topics. How would you get to them?

These criticisms are not show-stoppers, and you would do perfectly fine implementing these strategies to provide more flexible navigation through your topics. But you can do better, and it involves creative use of a PowerPoint function that goes underutilized. So keep reading.

Linking to Custom Shows

One of the most powerful combinations available to the non-linear thinker is the marriage between hyperlinks and custom shows (a group of slides defined as a subset within a slide deck—see Chapter 11). With these two features working together, you can create a menu-driven slide deck that provides you with excellent navigation and ease of operation. Let's return to the photo-cropping tutorial discussed in Chapter 17, where we showed three different ways to provide training on the best ways to crop photos. Here is how you would create it:

1. The menu slide for the tutorial has three main topics, each one designed to introduce a set of slides in the deck. Whether you are the presenter driving the slides or the viewer working a self-running presentation, you would click on any one of the three title blocks to automatically jump to that topic.

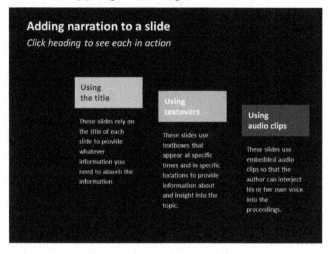

2. Note the structure of the slide deck: With the exception of the menu and the conclusion, all of the slides are hidden, as indicated by the cross-out over the slide number. Each of the three topics begins with an all-black intro slide (Slides 2, 9, and 16).

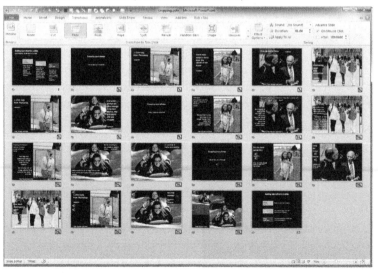

3. Using the instructions discussed in Chapter 11, create three custom shows, one for each of the three topics to be covered.

4. To assign a hyperlink to a custom show, you simply designate it from the Action Settings dialog. The key requirement is to check Show and Return, which ensures that when the custom show is finished, you are returned to the primary show that is running.

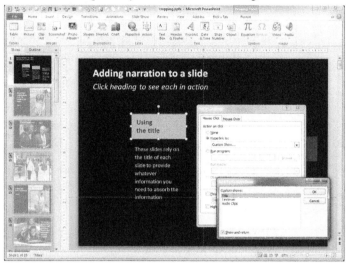

▼ Download cropping.pptx to take apart this slide deck and inspect the hyperlinking.

The only slides that would be visible if you advanced normally through the deck would be the first and last ones. The meat of this deck is stored in the hidden slides that are called as custom shows. Thanks to the Show and Return option, when you run through all of the slides of a given topic, you are automatically taken back to the menu. You don't need to remember to click on a link or anything—you just advance until you're back.

Here is a popular variation of this strategy: 1) make the concluding slide hidden and create access to it via a hyperlink; and 2) Set the slide show to repeat on a loop. This way, any inadvertent clicks of the mouse would be ignored (or more accurately, would take you to the end which would automatically loop back to the beginning). When it is time to end, you click the hyperlink to the concluding slide. You can experiment with that using the cropping.pptx file.

Nay-saying

There are three typical criticisms against the use of hyperlinks, none of which we accept:

You might accidentally click a hyperlink Well, yes, I suppose, but so what? If you accidentally clicked anywhere on a slide, you would advance without wanting to. With your Last Slide Viewed button, you can always return with just one click.

Part Five: Working Smarter

You might forget that they're there And you might not. What does it hurt to have them there?

You can just use the built-in navigation It's true that you can advance to any slide by simply typing its number and pressing Enter, pressing End to reach the last slide and Home to go to the first. But this is not nearly as good as building in your own navigation. Using the built-in navigation assumes three things that you can't really assume:

- You remember the exact number of the slide you want. I never do.

- The last slide of your deck is the one that you would want to jump to. Rarely is that the case with my presentations—I usually design a summary slide before my conclusion slide.

- Ditto for returning to the beginning of the presentation. Usually, menu-type slides that you would want to return to are not the first slide of a presentation.

If you have never tried creating your own navigation to make a presentation more flexible, you owe it to yourself to experiment with it.

Navigating Outside a Presentation

With the basic hyperlinking engine, you can seamlessly integrate content from outside of the current PowerPoint file. You can create the following types of links:

- **To other presentation files** Link to another presentation and it begins playing without delay or prompting. When that show ends, you are returned back to the show you were originally in and the slide you were originally on.

- **To a web page** Click on a URL link and that page opens in the default browser, as defined by your system. The presentation remains running underneath and you can Alt+Tab to it anytime.

- **To any document** Any file that you can double-click on in a My Computer window can be linked to from within PowerPoint.

- **To an application** With one backdoor maneuver, you can call up any Windows application without actually opening a document.

Are you pro-choice or pro-freedom?

There are two factors that take the discussion deeper, and the first one is how you activate a hyperlink. Few things in the presentation business are more satisfying than watching an accomplished presenter who is adept with

If you did not check Display as Icon, PowerPoint would create a thumbnail of the first slide in the file and show that on the slide. There are plenty of times when that would be useful, and you can decide that for yourself. In this scenario, we are not interested in providing a visual cue for the hyperlink.

5. Click OK and note the icon appearing in the middle of your slide.

6. Move the icon off the slide. In the image below, the gray area to the right of the slide is not the slide background; it is actually outside the slide boundary.

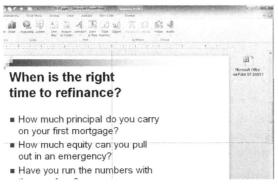

7. From the Animation ribbon, click Add Animation, and note a new option at the bottom of the list: OLE Action Verbs. This awkwardly-named choice refers to ways in which you can place an inserted object into the animation stream. Choose it to reach this dialog box:

The purpose of this animation is not to determine how the object makes its appearance on the slide—it's not even on the slide. This animation determines what the object does when its turn comes around.

8. Click Show.

9. Verify that the animation will start On Click.

10. Move it in between the bullets so that it is fourth in line.

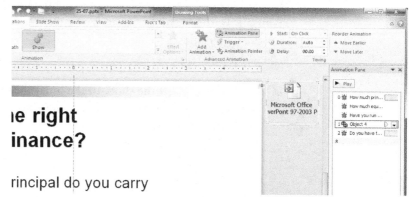

Here is a play-by-play of this slide in action: 1) The title and first three bullets appear; 2) You advance once and the payments.pptx slide show promptly appears; 3) You advance through it, and when it ends, you find yourself right back where you were. Your next click makes the fourth bullet appear.

Audience members have no idea that you ran a secondary presentation file. They just know that a relevant set of data appeared on screen to help them understand the question of interest for a refinance.

▶ The critical requirement to this method is that the payments.pptx file must continue to reside where PowerPoint originally found it. Each time you open for editing the file that contains the link, you'll be asked whether you want to update the presentation with current data. If you made changes to it recently, click Update.

Microsoft Office PowerPoint

This presentation contains links to other files.

• If you update the links, PowerPoint will attempt to retrieve the latest information.
• If you don't update the links, PowerPoint will use the previous information.

Note that file links can be used to access and share confidential information without your permission and possibly perform other harmful actions. Do not update the links if you do not trust the source of this presentation.

[Update Links]   [Cancel]   [Help]

The safest course of action is to place all linked files in the same folder as the .pptx file that contains the links. PowerPoint will always look there before pronouncing a link dead.

Thanks to the ability to place the linked object in the animation sequence, this is by far the most elegant technique for running a secondary presentation within a primary presentation. If you know when and where you want it to run, you can reduce the task down to a single click of a wireless remote or mouse. No other technique approaches this level of simplicity:

- If you created a standard hyperlink to the presentation, you would have to use your mouse to click on the hyperlinked object, requiring you or someone to be at the computer.

- If you chose to embed the presentation instead of keeping it externally linked, you would have to re-insert the file as an object anytime changes were made to it.

- By dragging the icon off the slide, you make the transition completely seamless to your audience members. If instead you wanted to create a visual cue for the jump to a secondary presentation, you could choose to show a thumbnail of the slide. And if you did that, you might want to add a conventional animation to it, so that it would fade onto the slide at the right time.

▶ If you use a wireless remote that includes cursor motion and click capability, you might be able to have it both ways: work the room and move your cursor to a hyperlink and click it. Our observation, however, is that few presenters are deft enough to perform this action elegantly while commanding a room full of people. At a minimum, you will want lots of practice if you want to have your cake and eat it, too.

Using PowerPoint to Teach PowerPoint

At the Presentation Summit, we find ourselves in an interesting conundrum: how best to use PowerPoint to show how to teach PowerPoint, all the while aware that everyone is watching how we use PowerPoint and how we behave as presenters. *Paralysis of analysis* comes to mind as the operative phrase for the risk we undertake of calling so much attention to the process of presenting.

One particular challenge: how to transition from showing a presentation, which we would normally do to frame the topic and introduce the technique to be discussed, to editing a presentation, which we would need to do in order to teach the technique.

continued...

Opening non-PowerPoint content

Using inserted objects is useful for just about any secondary data or application you want to show, whether it is a PowerPoint file or some other document. I regularly call upon PowerPoint to open Photoshop files, databases, fully-designed illustrations, even applications that take control of digital cameras when tethered by a data cable. It bears repeating and emphasizing:

> **Anything that can be launched from My Computer can be launched from within PowerPoint.**

You would use the same procedure detailed earlier:

1. Use Insert Object and Create From File.

2. Browse to the file and create a link.

3. Add an OLE Action animation to it, choosing Edit as the action.

Using PowerPoint to Teach PowerPoint

(from previous page)

Inserted objects can help smooth and integrate this transition, because you can call for a secondary presentation to be opened for editing, instead of opened as a show. In Step 8 on Page 269, choose Edit instead of Show—that will cause the PowerPoint file to be opened for editing, not shown as a slideshow.

You can no longer navigate with your wireless remote—the only way to return to your primary presentation is by Alt+Tabbing back to it, by closing down the secondary presentation file, or (the best choice) by clicking the Resume Slide Show button that appears on the toolbar. But that's okay, because the whole idea here is that you are about to actively use PowerPoint to teach an aspect of it, so you inevitably have your hand on the mouse, ready to drive.

We've found a caveat to this that is worth noting: PowerPoint normally tunes the external display correctly when you are displaying through a projector, so your audience usually sees everything correctly. But sometimes your own internal display can go bonkers when you switch back and forth between showing a presentation and editing one. To prevent this problem, make sure that your internal display is running at the same resolution as your external one.

You can't go wrong if you set everything up for good old XGA, 1024 x 768. All components will behave well at that resolution, and even though today's equipment can run at higher resolution, your audience members and their aging eyesight might not appreciate how small all those little parts of the interface become at higher resolutions.

PowerPoint as operating system

If you regularly use PowerPoint to demonstrate or to teach, you'll find that it can function quite ably as a main platform, almost like an operating system. You could build slide masters with inserted objects and hyperlinks and create templates tuned for teaching specific skills. Coupled with navigation buttons and prompts for choosing one path or another, you can create a completely interactive, self-paced set of tutorials or demonstrations on just about any topic.

I'm not at all certain how many different types of elements can be inserted into PowerPoint and I learn about new ones almost on a daily basis. Just the other day, I discovered that the digital slide shows I create in ProShow Producer can be run as objects within PowerPoint by finding and inserting a behind-the-scenes file. Once you understand the plumbing, you will make similar discoveries on the road toward using PowerPoint as the means by which you can open anything.

Creating Killer PowerPoint Menus

Here's the scene: you are speaking to a room of—whom would you like to be speaking to?—let's say, a group of A List Hollywood celebrities, and you are offering them advice on—what would you like to be an expert on?—let's say, you're advising them on how to better interact with the public.

Brad Pitt asks you the following question:

Brad: There's public and there's private-public. If I'm at a ballgame, I expect that I'm going to be asked to sign a few autographs. But when I'm in a small restaurant, in a corner booth, with Angelina—that's the time that I really need for my privacy to be respected.

You: That's a really good issue you raise. It's not on our agenda, but it's worth taking a few minutes to explore.

You walk to your computer and click once. Up pops a row of topics on the top of the slide, one of which is entitled Privacy. You click it to retrieve a rich presentation of photos, quotes, and advice to celebrities who feel stalked in public.

Brad gives you a seated ovation (he stands for nobody), and other audience members are so impressed with your ability to provide this level of detail on the fly that they all text their agents and tweet their followers to recommend you being hired as special advisor.

All this because you clicked once on a slide.

To see a video on this topic, visit http://vimeo.com/ betterpresenting/ intelligent

This fantasy was brought to you by one of the most powerful techniques that we know for infusing a presentation with flexibility and intelligence: a customizable menu that you can make appear at any time. If you can anticipate the kinds of questions that might arise during a presentation, few things are more impressive than being ready to address them.

You already know part of this solution: hyperlinks to other presentations or to custom shows within your presentation. When done properly, the objects containing the hyperlinks are never more than one click away, and upon that click, they appear on screen, not unlike the Windows Start menu, ready to take you somewhere.

Triggering the menu

The key ingredient to this capability is the trigger: a technique whereby clicking on one object triggers the animation of another object. Figure 25.9 shows the basic mechanics of this technique. The oval has been given a fade, set to appear On Click. The question is what click? The answer comes from the Timing dialog of the rectangle's animation, where we have instructed the animation to take place when we click the rectangle.

Click the rectangle to see the oval.

Those are the basics of a trigger. As with a standard hyperlink, the idea is to find a design element on the slide and make it be the trigger for the menu. Once the menu appears, standard hyperlinks take over. Here is how we would build one for our Hollywood audience.

Figure 25.9
The idea of clicking one object to make another appear is central to a good menu.

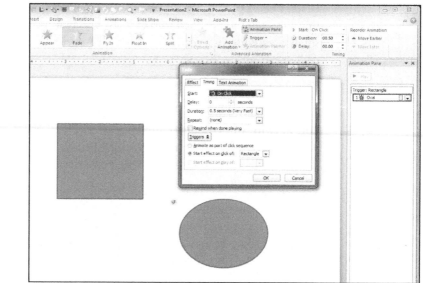

Figure 25.10
The stage is set for this menu: room for it top-right, and rectangles to act as triggers lower-right.

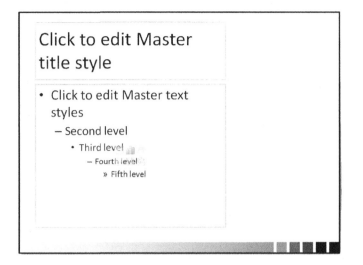

First off, the whole idea of this menu is that it be just a click away, anytime, anywhere. That means that it must be built on the slide master or onto a layout, and Figure 25.10 shows the one that we built for it. The rectangular quadrants along the bottom provide a good opportunity to create triggers, and we have shortened the size of the title and content placeholders to accommodate the menu's appearance at the slide's top-right corner.

I do not like the look of hyperlinks applied to text (they get underlined and they change color, just like the old-style web-page hyperlinks in the 1990s). Therefore, I take on a bit of extra work when I create hyperlinks for text strings: I either apply the link to the entire text string, or when I must hyperlink text that is part of a larger string of text, I create nearly invisible rectangles over the text and apply the hyperlinks to them.

Creating the text is easy—in this case, just five short items. Notice that I am zoomed way in, as is my standard practice for performing precision placement on a slide.

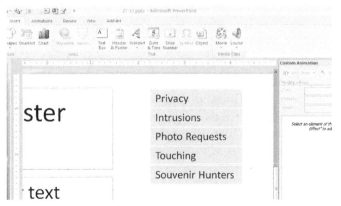

Once the text is in the correct position, I use the Action Settings dialog to create the hyperlink, in this case to a separate file called privacy.pptx. Each of these five text strings will be given a hyperlink to a file. In the alternative, I could create custom shows made up of hidden slides and hyperlink to them.

Once I have drawn and positioned the text strings and created the hyperlinks, it's time to animate them. So I drag a marquee around all of the text and group it (this is not essential, just recommended for keeping the animation sequence easier to deal with). I apply a fade to the group and set it to appear On Click, Fast. In modern versions, you can use the Selection and Visibility pane to name your group something better than Group 19.

With the animation in the task pane selected, it's time to create the trigger, using the Timing dialog. But first I must know the name of the object that's going to act as the trigger, and so I have selected it, and using Selection and Visibility, I have named the rectangle Menu Trigger.

I select the group, right-click, choose Timing, click Triggers, and then choose the rectangle as the object that will start the animation.

To make the effect a bit more refined, I also create an exit fade for the menu, triggered to the same rectangle. Now my little rectangle acts like a toggle to my hidden menu.

Letting go of our Brad Pitt fantasy, however reluctantly, you can use this technique successfully if you have any inkling at all about related topics that might be raised in a presentation. These would be questions not quite germane enough to be part of your main talk, but worthy of discussion should your audience ask.

Design your main slide master so it can accommodate a block of text and then think of five or six topics that you might be asked about during the presentation. Prepare short slide decks for each one (or hidden slides on the main deck) and hyperlink to them. Your audience will be impressed beyond belief—chiefly with your ability to anticipate their questions, but also with a technique within PowerPoint that they probably have never seen before.

Trainer Heaven

The techniques uncovered in this chapter can be put to great effect in countless situations. Of all the strategies discussed throughout this book, the ones in this chapter carry the greatest potential of taking you to an altogether different level of proficiency as a presenter and as a content creator.

And if I had to identify one group in particular that would benefit the most, it would be those who use PowerPoint as a training tool. The demands put upon students learning from a PowerPoint presentation are different than with an audience listening to a sales pitch or a keynote

Part Five: Working Smarter

address. In short, the demands are much higher. They need to pay closer attention to details, they usually take many more notes, they are often following along with their own notebooks, and if they are learning a software program, they are likely watching smaller elements on screen, like icons, tools, and menus.

As the trainer, this increases your burden, also. You have to minimize extraneous screen activity, avoid being herky-jerky with the mouse, and eliminate unnecessary dialog boxes and windows that are not relevant to the task.

You can achieve all of that with effective use of hyperlinks, linked objects that automatically open data files, visual cues, and interactive menus. These are the ingredients to a cleaner and more enjoyable experience, both for you and for your students.

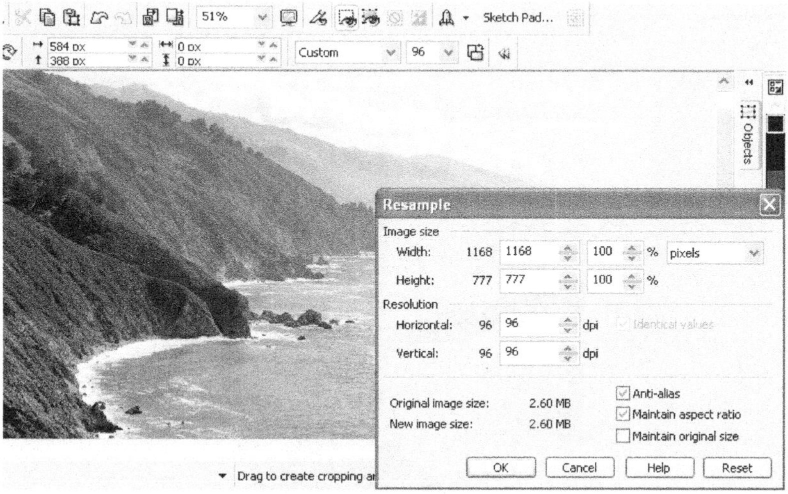

Figure 26.1
Measuring the dpi value of a photo being saved in pixels is meaningless and confusing.

This application here is just one of many programs that commits this error. If you were to adjust the dpi value in this dialog box, the software would compensate by changing the image size. This might lead you to believe in the relationship between dpi and screen resolution, but it is really tantamount to two wrongs making a right. So just remember this:

> **When sizing a photo for PowerPoint, the only thing that matters is its size in pixels.**

If the image were destined for a magazine and were being measured in inches, that would be different. But it's not, so please stop thinking about dots and inches. Instead...

Think pixels

Let's start by making this really simple, so if you get fed up with this chapter right now, you'll already have the important part:

> **Try to use photos that have at least 1024 pixels of width or 768 pixels of height.**

Over 90% of all presentations delivered today are projected at XGA resolution—1024 pixels across by 768 pixels deep. Even with the trend toward widescreen projection, these numbers will serve you well. If your landscape photo is sized at 1024 pixels wide or your portrait photo at 768 pixels high, you guarantee its fidelity when projected full screen. You'll be exercising overkill for photos less than full screen, but the increase in the file's size is utterly insignificant (read on for our feelings about overkill). If you deliberately decrease the size of your photo because you don't intend to use it full-screen,

Figure 26.2
PowerPoint suffers
from inchitis, just
like other
programs.

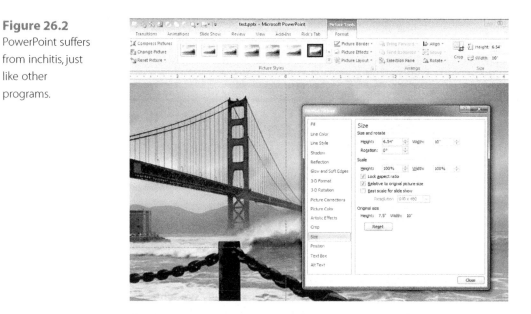

Murphy's Law will immediately prevail, your design will change, and you'll need it full screen. Just keep it at that size, even if you're using it smaller.

This discussion assumes that you have control over the size of the photo, but many times you don't. Like when you get sent a 150-pixel wide thumbnail and you're expected to do something with it. As soon as you take the dpi nonsense out of the equation, you can think rationally about this situation and reach an intuitive solution:

You must display it in PowerPoint at a small size!

And how do you know what size to make it? How can you size it to 150 pixels? You can't, because PowerPoint is brain-dead this way, also! Look at Figure 26.2 and you'll see that PowerPoint insists on measuring this photo in inches.

For more detail on the resolution misconception, visit the PPTFaq site and read pptfaq.com/faq00075.htm.

Fortunately, you are operating in a very forgiving medium. It really doesn't take a lot to make a photo look good on a computer display or out of a projector. You don't have to worry about color-matching, trapping, registration errors, CMYK conversions, or any of the issues that send those in the print business to early retirement. If it looks good on your screen, there's a good chance it will look good when projected or shown. If you can test it out on the ultimate output device, so much the better.

Just use common sense here: a low-resolution photo (i.e. one that has a small size, like 150pixels wide), will not look good if sized to full screen. Plan on using it as a small image in your slides.

The BetterPresenting Photo Lab

In order to make these points real and practical, we need to use real photos, talk about real numbers, and see real results inside slides.

Figure 26.3 is a photo of my two daughters outside on a sunny fall day in San Francisco. It's several years old and they would kill me if they knew that I was using a photo that featured glasses and braces, so please don't tell them. It was taken with a Canon Rebel, on its medium resolution setting:

Resolution:	8.1 megapixels
Dimension	3456 pixels wide
	2304 pixels high
Filesize	3.3MB

This photo is considered low resolution by SLR standards but high resolution by camera phone standards. Given that most of us project our slides at 1024 pixels wide, you can see how much extra resolution we have to work with. It also gives you an idea of how large your PowerPoint files might grow; we'll discuss that in detail soon.

When imported into PowerPoint, it is such a large photo that my older daughter's head barely fits on the slide. In Figure 26.4, we have superimposed the size of the actual slide so you can get a sense of how large the photo is. The slide thumbnail on the left of the figure will give you the same indication.

Figure 26.3
This photo was taken by a Canon digital SLR camera set on medium resolution, 8.1 megapixel.

Figure 26.4
When imported to
PowerPoint, this
photo is many
times larger than
the slide itself.

With just this photo, the PowerPoint file is 3.5MB, but before you go on
auto-pilot and conclude that it needs to be shrunk down, consider

▪ You could zoom and pan this photo and maintain high fidelity.

▪ You could confidently use this photo as an extreme close-up:

Above all, you want to be free to make these kinds of decisions later in the
project, which is why we advise keeping your photos at full resolution. Let's
continue the experiment and you'll see for yourself...

At 1024 pixels wide...
We have taken the photo into an image editor (Photoshop, PhotoPaint,
Paint Shop Pro, ACDSee, et al) and reduced it to 1024 x 682 (we told it to
size the width to 1024 and allow the height to adjust in proportion).

▼ Download photo_lab.pptx for a complete analysis and recap of the experiments discussed in this chapter.

The result is a photo that looks fine when displayed at full-width and is a fraction of the size of the original: 254KB, down from 3.3MB.

For most people and most situations, this photo will fill your needs, from full-slide down to thumbnail. But if you get ambitious and strive for the extreme close-up shown earlier, you will be disappointed with the results if you have already downsized your photos. Even on the black and white pages of this book, I'll bet you can see the difference between the 1024-wide image below and the full-resolution one on the opposite page.

Look at her hair, the texture of her skin, and the eyelashes. Whatever differences you see here, shown three inches wide and in grayscale, multiply many-fold for color output on a high-resolution display.

Once you size the photo down to 1024 pixels of width, you close the door on close-ups like this one. There are no longer enough pixels in the photo to provide the detail needed.

At 800 pixels wide...

When downsized to 800 pixels wide and then shown at full-slide, we did not see much difference in image quality compared to 1024 pixels. That suggests to us that most of the damage was already done by taking the photo down to 1024. We also didn't save very much file space: from 254KB to 185K.

At 640 pixels wide...

When displayed at full-slide width, you can clearly see that this photo does not have as much detail. The file was about 40K smaller than the 800px-wide photo.

Figure 26.8 shows the four resolutions that we worked with in this little experiment, and displayed at this small size, I'll defy you to see a difference. On my 24-inch display, I have to practically touch my nose to the screen to discern the subtle differences in Erica's lashes.

But in Figure 26.9, it's a different story altogether, as once again, the demands of such a tight zoom are too much for the versions of this photo that have been reduced in size. The other scenario in which lack of resolution shows up is with a sweeping pan across a photo, available for you to see if you download photo_lab.pptx. An effective pan requires that the photo start out significantly larger than the slide itself, and that spells trouble for photos that have been sized down to fit the slide.

Keep those pixels!

This is one of two reasons why I recommend that you *not* downsize your photos before importing them to PowerPoint.

When I have a rich presentation to prepare that will be run on my own computer, I really don't care how large my PowerPoint file becomes. I just want every possible creative option available to me. Pans and zooms are standard operating procedure when I'm hoping to evoke emotion with a photo montage and for those two maneuvers, I need every last pixel.

You might be concerned about a drop in performance with photos this large—don't be. On any desktops or notebook that I have purchased since 2003, I have noticed none whatsoever. Ditto for my iPad.

I would be more nervous on your behalf if you were aggressively reducing the resolution of your JPGs before using them in slide decks. Have you carefully tucked away the original file, in case you want to make a print? It's

Figure 26.8
These four photos range in resolution from full fidelity down to 640px, but when shown at these sizes, you wouldn't be able to determine which is which.

Figure 26.9
Close-ups like these, however, expose the photos that have given away too many of their pixels.

just too easy to forget to do that and I argue that it is unnecessary to have to burden yourself with that responsibility.

If you have a slide deck you have to send to someone else or make available as a download, you might need to take measures to keep the file size down. (Although even then, with broadband Internet widely available and cloud-based storage, do we really care so much about that?) In any event, I still do not recommend you downsize your photos before import; there are better ways to address this situation.

Managing the Move

Should you choose to get aggressive with the size of your rich presentation files, there are three courses of action available to you:

- Resize your photos before importing them to PowerPoint.

- Let PowerPoint do it for you, with the Compress Pictures command.

- Use third-party software that compresses the entire PowerPoint file.

If you have a preferred image-editing application, you not only know how to size a photo, you've probably done it countless times already. For those with less experience, I recommend picking up a copy of ACDSee Photo Manager, the versatile image viewing, organizing, and editing tool from www.acdsystems.com. With a buy-in starting at $70, you get a handy array of tools and a friendly interface, as shown in Figure 26.10. I own Photoshop, PaintShop Pro, and PhotoPaint, and yet I often reach for ACDSee for quick crops, format conversion, and changes in size, thanks to the program's quickness and accuracy.

PowerPoint has its own built-in compression function, available for any selected photo in a file (via the Compress Pictures command on the Picture Tools Format tab of the Ribbon).

This procedure works according to algorithms that nobody has satisfactorily explained to me. Sometimes it reduces the size of a file by many factors and other times it does nothing. At least as of version 2010, PowerPoint uses correct terminology, ppi instead of dpi.

As for after-market tools for file compression, we like NXPowerLite from the London-based Neuxpower company. For under $50, you get an easy-to-use utility that takes care of business with no backtalk. And wow, does it

Figure 26.10
ACDSee proves to be a handy investment for anyone who works ambitiously with photos.

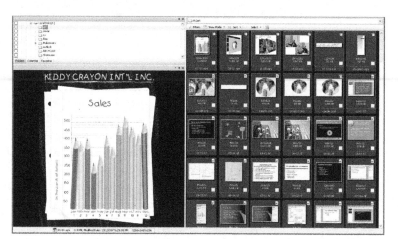

work—our photo_lab file went from 4.3MB to 900K with no discernible picture loss. www.neuxpower.com.

Microsoft MVP Steve Rindsberg and his PPTools suite of programs offer an optimizer, among many other useful PowerPoint utilities, and you can find out about them at www.pptools.com.

The most important part of this whole process is insuring against downsizing your photos without having originals tucked safely away. If you are in Photoshop about to downsize an image, take a moment and save the file in native .psd format. Ditto for PhotoPaint and a .cpt file.

Once again, because we know how easy it is to forget to save photos in native formats, we like the post-production compression tools such as NXPowerLite. Reducing images once they are already in PowerPoint removes all risk to the original photos.

A Modern Treasure Trove

There is an awful lot to like about the handling of imported photos by modern versions of PowerPoint—enough to make you think twice spending anything, let alone $1,700, on image-editing software.

The Format ribbon positively comes alive when you double-click an imported photo. Most of the offerings are one-click operations, making the following variations of a photo all trivial:

In clockwise order after the original photo (left) are brighten, darken, increase contrast, place inside shape and apply shadow (technically two separate operations), double-frame style, and monochrome recolor.

Yes, one-click operations are impressive—even more important is the type of control you can wield over a photo if you actually spend a few minutes with it. The gateway to quality time with a photo is the inconspicuous and easily-missed arrow pointing down from the Picture Styles group on the Format ribbon, shown below:

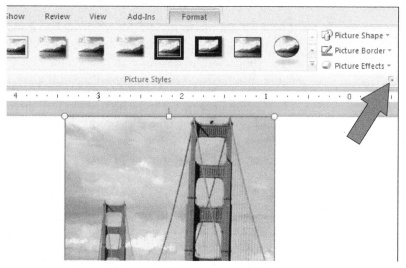

That is your gateway to the Format Picture dialog, an evolved and interactive dialog that combines many of the most powerful functions available for photo editing: shadowing, three-dimensional formatting, rotation, and recoloring. This dialog does not require that you close it in order to see the effect you have requested; it occurs in real time, inviting experimentation. The effect below would require a significant effort in an image-editing program like Photoshop. In fact, if I'm being honest, I would have to say that I wouldn't know how to accomplish it.

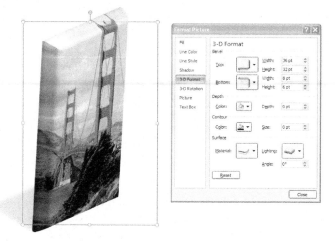

Depth of Field

Even today's point-and-shoot cameras are capable of manipulating light to affect how a camera focuses. On a bright day, you can really learn a lot about this dynamic, because you have a lot of room to adjust. These two photos were taken just 10 seconds apart:

The one on the left was taken with a slow shutter speed, and to compensate, the camera closed ("stopped down") the lens by a considerable amount. This results in a greater focal length ("depth of field"). The photo on the right underwent the reverse: very fast shutter speed which caused the lens to open much wider. That results in a much shorter focal length. You can see all the way across the street in the left photo but you can barely see five inches past the flowers on the right photo.

If you need a photo to be descriptive, the greater depth of field would serve you well. If you want it to be dramatic, the shorter depth of field is what you want.

If you didn't do this out in the field, the digital darkroom can help you in one direction. While making a blurry photo sharp is next to impossible, going from sharp to blurry is quite possible. It requires proficiency with your image editor's selection tools. With them, you can isolate the background and make it blurry. That helps bring focus and drama to the foreground.

Figure 26.17 shows a photo undergoing such a transformation. The softball coach has been "masked" (appearing in these pages with a white glow around his periphery). Masking allows us to work on just him or just the background. In this case, the coach was unaltered and the background behind him underwent a "Gaussian Blur," so named for the mathematician who developed the algorithm two centuries ago.

Zoom

There is nothing like a good telephoto lens to allow you to sneak up on people and get good candid shots. A good zoom feature on your camera also lets you alter reality. Witness these two photos, both taken from the exact same position.

With a normal 35mm lens (left), you get a good sense of the distance between the foreground tree and the background tree. A telephoto lens shrinks the observable distance between foreground and background and the 300mm lens used on the right gives the impression that you can practically touch the tree in the back.

As with a short focal length, zoom can add energy and emotion to a photo, but it does so at the expense of realism. Use zoom for drama, but if you need your photo to be accurate, use a normal lens.

The most important thing to know about zoom is to avoid "digital zoom" at all costs. Scroll the menus until you find out how to disable it. Resist using it with your smartphone (very few smartphones offer true zoom—all iPhones and Android phones provide only digital zoom). If a camera you are considering for purchase makes a big deal about it—if that's the best feature they have to advertise—run away fast! To reiterate:

Avoid using your camera's digital zoom!

Optical zoom uses the lens itself to bring the subject closer—the physical elements of the lens move in order to change the field of vision. Digital zoom does nothing more than enlarge a portion of the image using an interpolation that has nothing to do with making the image better. Only bigger.

This treatment is similar to what you could do using the crop tool of your image editor, with one important difference: your software is much better at it than the camera is.

Figure 26.19 is a photo taken at the maximum level of optical zoom. It is a sharp, focused image taken with a Samsung Galaxy Nexus and its 5MP built-in cameraphone.

Figure 26.19
If you wanted to get a closer look at these oranges, there is a right way and a wrong way to do it. Digital zoom would be in that second category.

In order to zoom in even more on the oranges, you have two choices: 1) use your camera's digital zoom; or 2) crop this photo and then enlarge the remaining area. While it's easier to push a button on your camera than work the photo with software, the results aren't even close.

The photo on the left is a product of 30 seconds spent in PowerPoint cropping and then enlarging the photo. The one on the right is my camera's pathetic attempt to do the same thing. Turn off digital zoom and pretend you never heard of it.

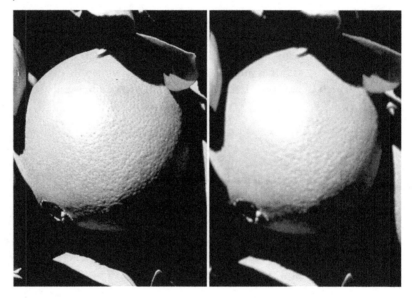

Flash and exposure

This one's easy, right? You use it when you are indoors and you turn it off when you are outdoors.

What if I told you that you might have better results if you were to do the exact opposite? Using a flash indoors tends to overpower the existing light, creating bright and often harsh images. If you can shoot without flash, the natural light of a room tends to be warmer. Here is a simple example:

On the left, the candle is overwhelmed by the flash and the granite counter looks cold and harsh. But on the right, the scene is captured more realistically—the candle was the only illumination, it's supposed to be dark. The shot on the left is plenty bright and descriptive, and it's easy to take. The one on the right requires a steady hand (much slower shutter speed), but if you seek realism of a scene, the effort is worth it.

Meanwhile, a nice bright summer day, with the sun directly overhead, could spell death for your ability to capture facial features. Witness these photos of a nice Yosemite hike at Vernal Fall:

All of that rushing white water in the background captured the lens's attention (left), and everything else was underexposed. But the addition of flash (right) provides enough light to cut through all of that glare.

Outdoor flash is much more subtle—you rarely have to worry about it looking artificial, as you do indoors. It just provides a bit of illumination to fight backlighting and dark shadows from midday sun. The auto-husband removal is an optional feature, usually costing extra.

The risk of shooting indoors without a flash is that your images will be blurry. As the camera struggles to get enough light, it slows down the shutter considerably, amplifying any bit of shake you might introduce. You can help by telling the camera that it doesn't have to try so hard to get sufficient light. Find your camera's exposure setting and reduce it, effectively telling it that it is okay if the image is a bit dark. With that requirement eased, your camera will use a faster shutter speed, allowing you to take sharper photos.

And what about those dark photos? While it is very difficult to save a photo that has been overexposed, you would be amazed at how much information can be squeezed out of an underexposed shot. Absolutely no doctoring was done to these photos other than what we're about to describe. The photo on the left is exactly how my daughter took it, from inside a museum where flash photography was prohibited. The version of it on the right is the result of increasing the image's midtones. It took about 15 seconds in ACDSee.

The moral of the story: Don't be afraid to underexpose your shots, and don't give up on dark photos.

A load of crop

The single most important difference you can make with your photos is to remove parts of them. You play an important editorial role when you make decisions that help focus attention and bring more energy to a scene. We have so many examples of this, we have prepared a download for you, but we'll share one of them here in these pages.

Figure 26.24 is a typical example of a tourist or vacation photo, with the subjects placed right in the center of the shot and a bunch of noise in the background. Like we really need an ugly picnic table and iron barbecue back there?

▼ Download cropping.pptx for an interactive tour of photos made better with the right crop.

Most amateur photographers place their subjects in the center and probably will until the day they die. Fortunately, the digital age allows you to make your creative decisions after the fact, and Figure 26.25 shows the result of a simple crop. With the unattractive part of the background out of the picture, the truly beautiful part that is the Santa Barbara coastline becomes more prominent. And just by putting the two people a bit off to one side, the photo becomes vital and more interesting. This is not difficult at all to do in PowerPoint, especially if you create better access to the Crop tool. The hardest part is remembering to think about it, instead of just accepting a photo's default placement. It's a matter of thinking asymmetrically: *If I moved this person out of the center of the photo, would it look better? If I moved part of her off the slide, what would that do?*

Figure 26.24
This photo suffers from unimaginative composition and too many visual distractions.

Figure 26.25
Twenty seconds with a crop tool and now this photo is ready for a frame.

Figure 26.26
This photo is fine, and the headline is fine, but it will never be better than fine.

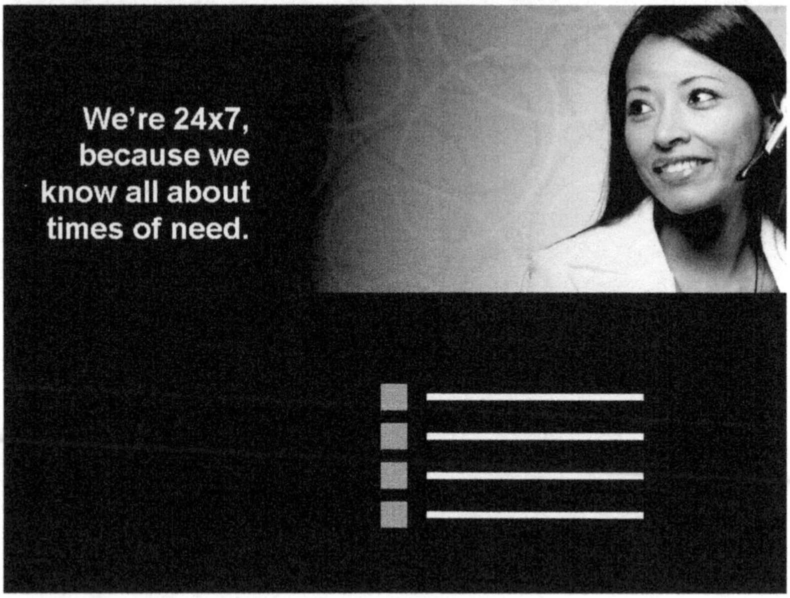

Figure 26.27
With one crop and three minutes with a transparent rectangle, this slide gets an infusion of energy.

The before and after examples on these pages are telling. Otherwise plain layouts give off completely different feelings with the help of simple crops. I also like that the subjects in the photo end up being bigger.

I use the Crop tool in PowerPoint often, and wasted not a moment adding it to my QAT. I have cut way down on mousing by being able to move the cursor to the photo, press Alt+3 to activate Crop, and begin cropping right away.

As you can tell, I love my digital cameras...all six of them. I still have my first one, a 1MP shoebox that Kodak introduced in 1995 for $800. As far as I know, it was the first digital camera made available in this country. When we used it at the 1996 CorelWorld User Conference to take photos and then, 10 minutes later, projected them in the main ballroom, it was nothing short of a miracle.

Figure 26.28
Cute girl...nice message...

Figure 26.29
Cute girl...nice message...powerful visual!

Figure 27.1
Thanks to clean PDF and technologies like SlideShark, PowerPoint slides can display accurately on an iPad. Too bad that presenters can't use it the way they would want to.

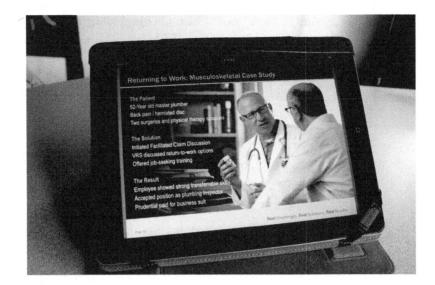

Keynote does not translate motion paths or simultaneous animations well, and my embedded objects that require the Windows OLE engine were obviously rendered inert. More troubling was the limited and non-expandable set of typefaces—only a handful of basic faces are available. Still, in relatively short order, I was displaying slides that were close enough to the originals to pass muster.

That was two years ago—today, I head straight to SlideShark to display my slides on an iPad. I wrote about this back on Page 183 and Figure 27.1 shows how clean the conversion is—much better than Keynote.

Back to my iPad journey of 2010. Next task: connect it to the projector. How? Where? A device that offers no USB connection is surely to be devoid of VGA connectors. The main power and docking port is the sole conduit to the outside world (except for WiFi) and Apple wants $29 for a VGA adapter. I didn't mind paying the $500 for the unit itself, but this $29 purchase continues to rankle me.

Still, the connector did its job and before long, Keynote was merrily sharing slides with my projector. The first-generation iPad only pumps video to the projector when actually running a slide show. If you drop out of show mode, the external display goes blank. This means that I cannot conduct software demos and tutorials and at first that disappointed me. But I have come to terms with the fact that the iPad is not intended to replace a computer. The question is whether it can handle the basic tasks within our profession. For instance, I will not try to create a presentation on the iPad; it is enough that I be able to show one. That seems like the appropriate litmus test.

Part Five: Working Smarter

And so far so good. I had moved my slides over to it and successfully connected it to the projector. Now how about the actual delivery? I whipped out my trusty wireless remote…you know, the simple $45 gadget whose receiver connects to the USB port…shoot, no USB port. How about my Bluetooth remote…damn, no BT support on the iPad.

Long story short (I know, too late): the iPad does not offer native support for the remote advancement of slides. The first one did not, the second one did not, and the third-generation iPad—beautiful, sleek, shiny, fast, and amazing—still does not. There are convoluted workarounds involving Apple TV or an iPhone running remote control software, but they fail my simple litmus test: Can I plug in or turn on my wireless remote and use it?

When I first discovered this hole in the iPad's capability, I was sure it was I missing something, until I turned to the online community of experts that hang out at apple.com:

"I want to advance slides on my iPad."

"Just touch the screen once."

"I need to be able to do it remotely."

"You're asking for too much. It's not a computer."

"That is not asking for too much."

"Apple had to draw the line somewhere."

"How do I work the slides if I can't advance them."

"Just place the iPad on the lectern."

I got so close — I transferred all of my slides, converted them successfully, and got all the way to the actual projection of my slides through the projector, which you would have thought to be the biggest obstacle of all. And now when it comes time to actually deliver the presentation, I am required to stand behind a lectern? I have spent the last five years advocating against the use of lecterns. This little gadget was about to turn me into a hypocrite.

Here is where the irony becomes almost too much to bear. Can you imagine if Steve Jobs were tasked with presenting from his iPad? The master of modern-day presentation, having to stand behind a lectern?

Apple's decision to not include a USB port with any of its iPads has effectively prevented me from using it in my profession. That saddens me, because I had high hopes for it. And of all people, you would have thought that one of the most celebrated public speakers of our era would have made sure that this would have supported his craft.

My iPad 2 is a much better device than the original and I have enjoyed using it. I am confident that I got a job last summer because I showed my portfolio on it—I looked cool doing it. I love leading small meetings with it, where we can all gather around it. It is that environment in which the iPad shines: where others can sit close enough to see it, I can sit close enough to touch it, and it can visually guide a small group through my story or message. I love that.

Having heard the rumors for months of Microsoft's imminent support for Office on the iPad, having seen a round of third-party services step in to fill that gap (see Chapter 18), and coupled with the announcement of the product's third iteration, I was hopeful that this most significant of omissions would be addressed.

Instead, the iPad 3 has given us a nicer-looking screen, a faster processor, and a better camera. I'm still trying to find a single user who thought that the screen resolution was deficient, the processor slow, or the camera weak. Apple improved three areas that nobody felt were lacking in the first place.

And still no USB port.

To the legions of presentation professionals, who watch technology with rapt interest, I have no choice but to regard the iPad as a curiosity and a toy. To writers like me who offer comment on the state of our art, the iPad remains on our can't-recommend list. That's a shame, because it could be so much more.

Never Paste Again!

Do you actually know what goes on when you use the Clipboard to transfer text or a graphic from another application? Do you know what you are really asking for when you press Ctrl+V or click the Paste icon?

Most don't. If they did, they might never do it again.

The Windows Clipboard is a more sophisticated tool than most know, able to carry many formats of an element at once. In fact, when you copy something to the Clipboard, you are usually placing the object there in many different formats. Furthermore, the default choice—the one you get when you ask for Paste—is often problematic:

- With a graphic, the default choice is an OLE-linked graphic that will attempt to open the native application if you double-click the graphic. If you share this with others, who do not own that application, fireworks could result.

- With text from a word processor, it is HTML-formatted rich text in the size and typeface of the original. If you are pasting text into a list of bullets, that might be the last thing you want.

- Even with text from another location within PowerPoint (from title to bullet, text box to title, etc.), PowerPoint will keep the original formatting intact, even though the destination location will have formatting established of its own.

Sometimes the default choice is correct. And sometimes PowerPoint is able to figure out what you want, via its Smart Cut and Paste feature, on by default in Options. But we don't want you playing roulette with your slides. We want you to make informed choices when you transfer information onto a slide.

We want you to use Paste Special.

The Paste Special dialog box shows all of the flavors available to you, enabling you to choose the right one. It's not always obvious which is the right one, but with experience you'll get better. Take the case of this CorelDraw graphic:

The default choice embeds the entire graphic, editable from a double-click. This sounds attractive, but since OLE was first introduced in 1992, it has never lived up to its promise, remaining fraught with stability problems.

If the graphic you created is made up of vector objects, you would want to choose one of the Picture options, Windows or Enhanced Metafile. The EMF format can hold 32-bit graphics, but that distinction is rarely relevant within PowerPoint, making these two flavors essentially similar. If the graphic is mostly bitmap data, you would want to choose Device Independent Bitmap.

In the case of text, if you are pasting lines of text into a series of bullets, you would most likely want the text to conform to the format you have established for those bullets. That means choosing Unformatted Text from Paste Special.

Practice and experience make perfect here, so start invoking Paste Special instead of just pressing Ctrl+V.

The alternative is to use PowerPoint's Paste Options button, which appears (sometimes inconspicuously) whenever you issue the Paste command:

This text came from Word and it had very specific formatting. What happens to that formatting when it arrives in PowerPoint? You decide, with the Paste Options button...

(Ctrl) ▾

Paste Options:

Keep Source Formatting (K)

I prefer using Paste Special, as it informs me of all the choices and makes me more capable when it comes to sharing content within applications. And with the ability to add Paste Special to the QAT, it becomes the fastest way to perform safe and reliable data migration from other programs into PowerPoint. On my system, it's a quick Alt+9 and I'm there.

Start Me Up...

I expect that most of you know that F5 starts a presentation. If you didn't know that, now you do: pressing F5 from anywhere while in Edit mode automatically switches you into Slide Show mode (i.e. your presentation will run). That beats the heck out of mousing up to the View menu or Ribbon and then clicking Slide Show.

With Version 2003, PowerPoint inherited an even better keystroke: Shift+F5. When you're building a presentation, you probably spend a great deal of time checking out how particular slides look and perform. If you're working on Slide 70, you're not terribly interested in starting your slide show from the beginning, and you might have grown to loathe that tiny icon in the lower-right corner called Slide Show from Current Slide. Loathe no more—just press Shift+F5, and you will be whisked into Slide Show mode starting at whatever slide you're on.

But not too many of you know what happens if you press and hold Ctrl while clicking that tiny Show from Current Slide icon. Do you know? The slide show plays in a small window at the top-left corner of your screen:

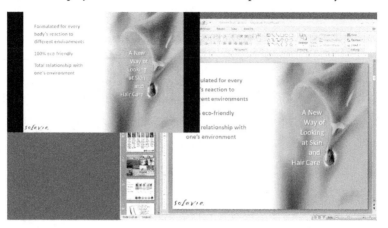

That's a way-cool trick for times when you want to see how a slide behaves and be able to work on that slide at the same time (changes made in Edit mode are dynamic and immediately show up in the Slide Show window).

So that got me thinking: maybe there are other buried treasures around this part of the interface. So I started poking around, and this is what I found:

Keystroke	Icon	Result
Shift	Normal View	Enter Slide Master view
Shift	Slide Sorter	Enter Handout Master view
Shift	Start Slide Show	Set Up Show dialog
Ctrl	Start Slide Show	Run slide show in small window

Also, don't forget that there is a Play button in the Animation task pane to help you with timing and sequencing.

Disappearing Slide Masters

There is one more point of possible angst concerning templates: those with multiple sets of slide masters might be at risk of losing those masters that are not in use. In another example of creating trouble through simplification, PowerPoint will (sometimes) remove slide masters that are not in use.

To be precise, PowerPoint's slide masters (sometimes) default to not being "preserved"—that's the term that Microsoft uses for a slide master that should remain in the file even if it is not being used by any slides. This can be (sometimes) maddening and so you should be (sometimes) vigilant.

It's easy to be (sometimes) glib and (often) sarcastic in the last chapter of your book—why the *sometimes*? Because this doesn't always happen. About half the time, PowerPoint automatically preserves the masters. But when it doesn't, you're hosed. So get in the habit of always looking for the little push pin next to the slide master's thumbnail:

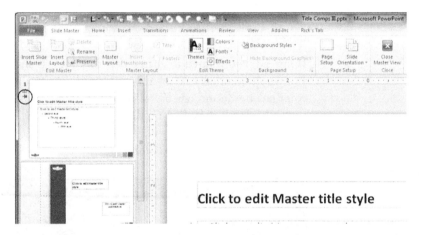

Click to edit Master title style

And if you don't see it, right-click the thumbnail and choose Preserve Master. Why didn't Microsoft just make Preserve a permanent setting? There are times when I wish the company had, but there are also times when I am grateful for the choice. When I am cleaning up old slides and performing makeovers and redesigns, I will typically create my "After" slide master in the original deck and begin the process of transferring slides from the original masters to the After one. It is here where I will set the old masters to be unpreserved, as I methodically assign the new design to original slides. When one of the old masters no longer is controlling any of the slides in the deck, it just goes away.

Making Peace with Color Schemes

If I had the sense that PowerPoint users might wake up one day and become enamored and riveted by PowerPoint's engine for controlling color, this would become its own chapter.

I have no such impression. Some very talented presentation designers completely ignore color schemes and others use them but don't understand their basic premise. So here is a brief tutorial on the function that you probably do not use and if you do you probably don't understand very well.

When you apply a color from the color scheme to an object on your slide, you are not just instructing the object to display a particular color. In the case of Figure 27.5, you are telling this circle, "you are to be filled with the color that is assigned to Position No. 5."

Position 5 happens to be a shade of blue right now, but it could be something different if you changed the definition for Position 5, if you used a different color scheme, or if you imported this slide into a different presentation file.

If instead, you wanted to ensure that this circle is always a specific color, you would manually define that color, either with the standard or custom color palettes found when you choose More Fill Colors. Once you choose a manual color, it shows up on the Recent Color row, visible below. Recent colors have a shorter shelf-life; they don't stay on the Fill dropdown for very long after you close PowerPoint.

Figure 27.5
Think of a color scheme as a set of ten color definitions.

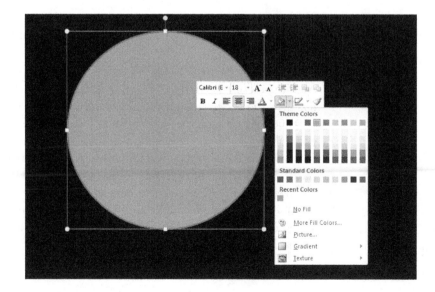

You can now copy this circle to a different presentation file, move the whole slide there, swap in a different color scheme, or change out the entire template—this circle will remain the shade of blue that it is right now. You can use this knowledge to great effect if you plan for it:

- If the Coca Cola Company hired you to create slides, you surely would not make Coca Cola Red one of the colors of the color scheme, where the possibility existed that a different presentation could change it to Pepsi Coca Blue. You would create a custom color, so it would never change.

- If you have designed some nice accent lines between the title and subtitle, you would want their colors to match the rest of the slide and change if you changed the color scheme. For that, you would pick one of the ten scheme colors.

▼ Download color_schemes.pptx for a demonstration of how color schemes operate.

Colors from the scheme can be chosen any time there is a question of fill or outline. I regularly create a gradient fill using two complementary colors so that if the scheme changes, the gradient will still look good. There is plenty more to know about color schemes, but the distinction between the ten colors of the scheme and manually-assigned colors is the part that any user can put into use right away.

The Trouble with Tables

Like many people who use it, I enjoy/suffer a love/hate relationship with PowerPoint's Table function. It's great to have a mechanism that allows for quick creation of grid-based information—doing it with tabs or separate text boxes would be painful.

However, once you are done creating it, the Table function dumps you right at the point where you would need it most—creating a build with animation. Table animation is limited to applying an entrance or an exit to the entire table, but that is not how columnar data needs to be presented. It needs (often desperately) to be sequenced row by row or column by column.

It boggles the mind how PowerPoint can animate a complicated chart by series or category but cannot animate a simple chart by rows or columns. The only plausible solutions are both terrible: 1) to break the table apart and then put it back together again in logical groupings so that it can be animated; or 2) place rectangles over the tables and set them to fade away.

This is painful enough, but wait there's more. Were you to try the break-the-table-apart strategy, PowerPoint won't actually allow you to ungroup a table. In one of the more glaring downgrades in the software's history (version 2003 allowed you to use the Ungroup command on tables), modern versions require you to cut the table to the Clipboard, and then, using the information on Page 307, paste it back as a metafile. Only then can you ungroup it, which you will have to do twice, and access the individual parts.

Can this possibly be worth all this trouble? Unfortunately yes, as sequencing tables of data is critical to effective delivery of the data's message. If Microsoft engineers address no other shortcoming in the upcoming version, we hope they work on this one.

Kool Keystrokes

Please note that this is not intended to be an exhaustive list of all of the keystrokes that exist across the application. Instead, this is my list of little-known and/or seldom-used shortcut keys, presented here in no special order. You probably know most of them...but who knows, maybe not all of them. Perhaps you'll find one that might prompt you to raise one of your eyebrows. That would be good enough for us...one eyebrow, up just a touch, as in "Hmm, I'll have to try that one..."

Keystroke	What it Does
Ctrl+F1	Toggles Ribbon on and off
Ctrl+click	Selects noncontiguous words of text, even in separate text blocks
Ctrl+[Ctrl+Shift+<	Size text down by 4pt increments
Ctrl+] Ctrl+Shift+>	Size text up by 4pt increment
Shift+F3	Toggles through application of lower case, upper case, sentence case for selected text
Shift+F9	Toggles view of grid
Alt+F9	Toggles view of guides
Alt+F10	Invoke Selection and Visibility Pane
Shift+F10	Invoke Context menu
Ctrl+Shift+Z	Removes all formatting from selected text
Up, Down, Left, Right	"Nudges" selected objects by small amount
Ctrl+nudge	Nudges selected objects in even smaller amounts

The makeover

I identified three basic types of slides—normal, before/after, and gotchas—and created layouts for each. I did nothing fancy; in fact just the opposite: these slides were crying out for a bit of conservatism. Navy blue backgrounds, white text for the regular slides, and black backgrounds for the before/afters and gotchas.

Just about anything would have been an improvement with the title slide. I was horrified to learn that it usually displayed for almost 10 minutes as audience members entered the ballroom. That's a long time for any static image, let alone a terrible one. Instead, I decided to go with a group of photos that would fade one atop the other.

The tricky part was creating the loop, so here's a challenge for you:

> **How do you make one slide loop indefinitely onto itself, and then when you are ready to begin your presentation, proceed to the second slide?**

Doing this without overtly running two slide shows is very difficult. I'd love to hear from readers who have conjured up other solutions, but here is the one that I came up with:

1. Create two custom shows—one called Intro, containing just the first slide, and one called Main, containing every other slide in the deck, starting with the second one.

2. Go to Slide Show | Set Up Slide Show and tell PowerPoint to run the Intro custom show. Also tell it to loop continuously.

3. From the Transition task pane, choose a Fade transition and set Advance Slide to Automatic After. For the After value, pick a duration

that makes sense. For instance, my photo fades are six seconds apart, so I told the slide to wait for six seconds before "advancing," which would simply send it back to the beginning.

4. Draw a rectangle over the entire slide.

5. From Slide Show | Action Settings, set the click action to be a hyperlink to the custom show called Main.

6. Set the transparency of the rectangle's fill to 99%, effectively making it invisible.

Now the first slide will loop until the presenter clicks on it once, at which point it will promptly advance to the second slide and proceed from there.

As satisfying as this was to figure out, this challenge was nothing compared to the task of cleaning up the text. I only showed you two of those ill-crafted text slides back on Page 316; there were actually over 30 of them.

Let's take a moment to frame the problem. Having created a layout for text slides, now I had to make all of the text slides conform to it. But none of the bullet slides was created using the standard content placeholders; the creator drew text boxes on blank slides and formatted them. As a result, reapplying the layout would have no effect except to create empty title and text placeholders.

It would seem that my options were to retype the bullets into the proper placeholders (out of the question!) or try some cut-and-paste maneuver, which, even with a script to automate it, was also unacceptable.

As with the loop, I'm not sure that there isn't a better way to solve this, and I hope to hear from others who have their own ideas. Here was mine, requiring an installed copy of Adobe Acrobat:

1. Send the entire presentation to a PDF file, using File | Save and Send | Create PDF Document.

2. Open the PDF file in Adobe Acrobat and immediately perform a Save As to plain text. Call it anything, like makeover.txt.

3. Open makeover.txt in Notepad and find your titles and bullets. Enter tabs to identify bullets.

```
makeover.txt - Notepad
File  Edit  Format  View  Help
Goal of Session
        To create an awareness and understanding of why it is import
        To give practical examples of how you can create that appea.
        To inspire you to action.
What exactly is curb appeal?
        Protect and enhance the asset
        Average $20,000 per unit in value between the curb and the :
        Sends the message "The owners who live here care about thei:
        Attracts people to your community who are also concerned wit
What exactly is curb appeal
        Makes the Community a "desired" place to live
        Safety Considerations
        Breaks downward cycle of deferred maintenance
        Creates emotional involvement by owners (engagement vs. dia.
        Creates a sense of neighborhood
```

This presentation does not have any second-level bullets, but if it did, you would have entered a second tab for each of them.

4. Save and close the text file and return to PowerPoint.

5. Open the presentation file that has the redesigned slide masters and place your cursor where you want to insert the bullet slides.

6. From the Home tab of the Ribbon, click New Slide | Slides from Outlines and find makeover.txt. Voilà...

Part Five: Working Smarter

The top row of thumbnails are new slides; the bottom row are old ones. What I particularly like about this conversion technique is that it makes no distinction between types of text. Like the funky GOAL OF SESSION title that is stuffed into a filled rectangle—it all comes out as text, at which point I can delete unwanted text quickly and format bulleted text many, many times faster than I could have had I performed a cut and paste.

▼ Download before.pptx and after.pptx to experience the agony and the ecstasy for yourself.

I converted 33 brain-damaged bullet slides and made them all conform to a redesigned slide masteer in less than 10 minutes. I don't even want to think about how long it would have taken to have fixed them the conventional way. The only caveat is to watch for double-spaces and weird line breaks that Acrobat inserts. You'll want to go on a search-and-destroy mission for them.

There are other ways to extract all of the text from PowerPoint, including special print drivers that create text files and OCR-type screen capture programs. However you do it, the key is to get all of the text into a text file, where then you can create a simple tab-based hierarchy to identify titles, bullets, and sub-bullets.

If you prefer, you could extract the text into Word or another word processor and format it with heading levels. PowerPoint will recognize that as an outline also. And remember, you need to use the Slides from Outline choice on the New Slide dropdown.

And In the End...

In order to create Chapter 23, I asked several people open-ended questions about the ingredients that make up a successful presenter or presentation. My good friend Korie Pelka, who crafts them for a living, had the shortest and perhaps the most apt response.

"Knowledge and passion."

How perfect is that? Without them, not much else matters. With them, not much else is needed! To circle all the way back to where we started, this book cannot help you with that first ingredient: you have to know your stuff before you can put to use a single paragraph that we have written here.

Passion, on the other hand, can be found in many forms and the best presenters ensure that audiences feel their passion. It is the key to all that is good about designing and delivering presentations, and 321 pages later, it is our hope that we have fueled your passion for creating your next one.

Index

Made in the USA
Middletown, DE
24 January 2019